AWAKENING
THE
NEW HUMAN

AWAKENING
THE
NEW HUMAN

THE EVOLUTION OF POWER, LOVE, AND HEROISM IN A TIME BETWEEN WORLDS

BECOMING THE POST-TRAGIC HERO
IN THE MIDST OF THE META-CRISIS

. . .

One Mountain, Many Paths: Oral Essays
Volume Thirty-Five

DR. MARC GAFNI

Author: Marc Gafni
Title: Awakening the New Human

Identifiers: ISBN 979-8-88834-090-5 (electronic)
ISBN 979-8–88834–089–9 (paperback)
Library of Congress Cataloging-in-Publication Data available

Edited by Elena Maslova-Levin, Paul Bennett, Talya Bloom, and David Cicerchi

World Philosophy and Religion Press,
St. Johnsbury, VT

in conjunction with

IP Integral Publishers

https://worldphilosophyandreligion.org

JOIN THE REVOLUTION!

CONTENTS

EDITORIAL NOTE ABOUT AUTHORSHIP, EDITING, AND THE RADICAL CONTEXT FOR THIS SERIES   XIII

LOVE OR DIE: LOCATING OURSELVES   XXIII

ABOUT THIS VOLUME   XLII

CHAPTER 1   **FROM THE MURDER OF EROS TO _HOMO AMOR_: LOVEPOWER IS THE WORD, AND THE WORD IS GOOD**

Power History and Love History: Recognizing the Murder of Eros   1

Understanding the Murder of Eros   2

Eros History and Power History   3

LovePower: Cosmos Is a Field of Allurement and We Are Each Its Unique Expressions   4

We've Been Together Before, and Our Intention Is to Go the Whole Way in This Lifetime   5

The Evolutionary Impulse Where Love and Power Come Together   7

The Many Distressing Disguises of the Murder of Eros   9

The Failure of Aliveness Turns Into Evil   12

Claiming My Unique Lovepower Is Not a Psychological Move   13

We Are Going to Stop Murdering Eros, and We're Going to Celebrate Each Other   15

CHAPTER 2   **THE ALCHEMY OF *HOMO AMOR*:**
                                      TRANSCENDING OUR PERSONAL PAST

Welcome to the Revolution in Love, for the Sake of Love,
and for the Sake of the Future   17

We Need to Re-Narrate the Story of Who Am I and Where
Am I   19

I Am Moving From *Homo Sapiens* to *Homo Amor*   20

I Am a Creator in the Interconnected Intimate Field
of Reality   22

In Prayer I Clarify and Recognize the Dignity of My Desire
and My Need   24

Your Unique Self Is the Unique Feature of the Seamless Coat
of the Universe   28

True Self, Unique Self, and Evolutionary Unique Self   30

The Whole Universe Gives Rise to an Atom   31

All of Reality Exists in Intimacy, All the Way Up and All the
Way Down   33

I Am a Free, Generative Node in the Field of Intimacy   34

CHAPTER 3   **BECOMING THE NEW HUMAN, *HOMO
AMOR*: STRATEGIES OF SEDUCTION
AND UNFURNISHING THE EYES OF
CONSCIOUSNESS**

Reality Is a Love Story, and We Are That Story: Between
Utopia and Dystopia   39

The Animating Energy of Reality Today Is the Algorithm
of a Success Story   41

We Are Here to Enact a New Reality   43

Unbearable Tragedy and Unbearable Joy   44

Becoming Lineage Holders in the Great Tradition   46

We Are a Band of Outrageous Lovers 48

Reality Needs You to Seduce Yourself to Your Own Greatness 50

Seduction to Invoke the New Human and the New Humanity 52

Music Is Made of Atoms of Time 54

Cleansing the Doors of Perception: Unfurnish Your Eyes 55

The Eye of the Flesh, the Eye of the Senses 56

The Eye of the Mind, the Eye of Reason 57

The Eye of Consciousness 58

Reality All the Way Up and All the Way Down Is Pan-Interiority 60

A New Paradigm in Science Doesn't Give You This Knowing 63

The Player of Music Becomes the Music 65

CHAPTER 4 **ATTACHMENT THEORY AND BEYOND: *HOMO AMOR* EVOLVES THE BLESSING OF THE FATHER**

The Blessing of the Father: Reality Is Proud of Us 71

We Need to Be Fathers and Mothers to Each Other 73

Beyond the Root of All Human Suffering 74

People of the Lie 75

We Must Be Beloveds to Each Other 77

You Are Welcome in the Universe! 79

The Welcome Home Sign in Cosmos Is the Field of Value Itself 82

We Have to Liberate Ourselves From the Idolatry of Mother
and Father 85

We Need to Up-level the Blessing of the Mother, and We Need
to Up-level the Blessing of the Father 87

Outrageous Love Festival Is a Laboratory for the Dharma 89

CHAPTER 5 THE NINE GREAT STATIONS ON THE
JOURNEY OF TRANSFORMATION

In the Human Journey, There Are Nine Stations of
Transformation 91

Station One: Pre-Personal 93

Station Two: Separate Self 95

Station Three: Social Self 97

Station Four: False Self 100

Puzzle Pieces Without Original Puzzle 103

Station Five: True Self 104

Station Six: Unique Self 107

Station Seven: Unique Shadow 110

Why Should You Integrate Your Shadow? 112

Station Eight: Evolutionary Unique Self 115

Station Nine: Unique Self Symphony 118

CHAPTER 6 FEEL YOU FEELING ME: THE NEW
HUMAN AND THE NEW NAME OF GOD

The Most Effective Altruism Is Telling a New Story of Value 123

The New Story of Value Lives in Us 126

Anthro-Ontology: How Do You Know What You Know? 127

The Core of *Homo Amor* Is My Capacity to Feel You 130

Evolving Love Is Ever Deeper Loops in the Mutuality of Feeling 133

The Divine Is the Infinite Intimate 135

CHAPTER 7 FROM *HOMO ARMOR* TO *HOMO AMOR*:
HEARTBREAK IS A STRUCTURE OF THE
INTIMATE UNIVERSE

Part One: We Need to Evolve the Source Code in Which We Live 139

We Live in an Evolving and Participatory Cosmos 142

Intimacy Is Always Broken and Then Recovered 144

Heartbreak Is the Natural State of an Alive Human Being 146

Prayer Affirms the Dignity of Personal Need 148

We Must Feel the Depth of Our Need 150

No Two Heartbreaks Are the Same 151

The Evolution of Tears Is the Expansion of Our Circle
of Intimacy 153

Evolving Tears From *Homo Sapiens* to *Homo Amor* 156

Outrageous Love Moves Us From *Homo Armor* to *Homo Amor* 158

The Evolution of Heartbreak Is the Evolution of Desire 160

I Am Willing to Feel Even What I Cannot Entirely Heal 162

Part Two: From Heartbreak to Desire to Need to Value 165

By Embracing the Heartbreak, I Find My Aliveness 168

Clarified Desire Equals Dignified Need Equals Value 169

Part Three: Heartbreak Is a Structure of the Intimate Universe 172

There Is Eros to the Broken Heart 174

CHAPTER 8   WHAT WE NEED FOR THE ATTENTION REBELLION TO SUCCEED

A New Story Generates New Reality 177

The Internet Is Designed to Scatter Attention 180

A Brief History of Attention 183

When There Is Nothing to Pay Attention To 185

To Be in Love Is to Place Attention 187

Seeing With New Eyes Is the Essential Quality of
the Erotic Universe 189

The Attention of the Infinite Differentiates Uniquely
Through Me 191

We Need to Reclaim Attention as a Value 193

CHAPTER 9   ALEXEI NAVALNY: TO LIVE IS TO
                  RISK IT ALL, THE UNIQUE RISK
                  OF THE HERO

The Eulogy of a Hero   195
The Response to Corruption Is Laughter   197
Navalny Lived and Died for Value   199
A Life Aligned With Value Is a Life of Joy   201
We Have to Take a Stand for Each Other   205
Value Is More Powerful Than Any Other Force   208
We Stand for the Democratization of the Hero   210
We All Have a Unique Risk to Take   213

CHAPTER 10   TOWARDS THE POST-TRAGIC HERO

I Cannot Be Welcome in the Universe Unless I Am a Hero   215
Hero Is a Fundamental Category of Reality   217
The Crossing: to Experience Myself as a Hero   218
Baraye: for the Sake of the Whole   221
When I Am Aroused, I Am the Hero: Reality Is Making Love 222
You Know and I Know That You Are a Hero   225

CHAPTER 11   MAD LOVE: WHEN MADNESS
                   BECOMES SANITY

To Love Madly Is to Be in the Field of Outrageous Love   229
Reality Is Constituted by Mad Love   232
Our Love Lists Are Too Short   235
The Mitochondrial Dance of Eros in Our Cells   237
My Mad Love Participates in the Whole   241
My Mad Love Is Wildly Powerful   243

My Madness Is My Protest 245

Clarifying the Split Between Sane and Insane 247

True Sanity Is Mad Love 249

Let's Reach for a World Beyond Betrayal 251

CHAPTER 12   THE UNIQUE OBLIGATION TO TAKE YOUR UNIQUE RISK

We're in a Time Between Worlds, a Time Between Stories 255

Modernity Got the Plotlines Half Right and Half Wrong 256

Value Got Exiled to Doing Evaluation 258

Existential Risk Demands a New Story of Value 261

Postmodernity Took Out a Loan From Premodernity 264

The Unique Risk of Taking Responsibility for the Whole 268

Uniqueness Is a Value of Cosmos 271

Unique Self Is Individuation Beyond Ego 273

To Actualize a Unique Self Symphony, We Each Need to
Take Our Unique Risk 276

To Take Our Unique Risk Means to Love Or Die 277

CHAPTER 13   THE VOID IS REAL, AND THERE IS A WAY HOME

We Are Facing Darkness 285

A Time Between Emptiness and Fullness 287

The Postmodern Zeitgeist and the Path of the Void 289

The Personal Experience of Void Begins With Betrayal 293

Everything Emerges From the Encounter With the Void 296

Tzimtzum: The Space of the Void That Is Sacred
Conversation 299

Postmodernity Is the Experience of the Void   302

An Entire Generation Is Thrust Into the Void   304

Taking the Void Seriously   307

How Do You Walk Through the Void?   310

Love Is Not Hard to Find—Love Is Impossible to Avoid   313

It's a Love Story, and It's Filled With Mystery   315

INDEX   **319**

EDITORIAL NOTE ABOUT AUTHORSHIP, EDITING, AND THE RADICAL CONTEXT FOR THIS SERIES

ORAL ESSAYS FROM THE ONE MOUNTAIN, MANY PATHS WEEKLY BROADCAST

This volume is part of the Oral Essays library, a series of lightly edited, compiled transcripts of oral teachings given by Dr. Marc Gafni and the late Barbara Marx Hubbard in their weekly online broadcast, *One Mountain, Many Paths,* which they co-founded in 2017. Originally called an "Evolutionary Church," *One Mountain, Many Paths* became a key venue for the articulation of an inspired and deeply grounded new Story of Value in response to the meta-crisis. Marc and Barbara—together with Zak Stein,[1] Kristina Kincaid, Ken Wilber, Sally Kempton, Lori Galperin, Aubrey Marcus and dozens of other thought-leaders over the years—began to articulate what they call a World Philosophy and World Religion[2] as a context for our diversity.

---

1 Zak, together with Ken Wilber, has been Marc's primary intellectual partner and an initiate lineage holder in CosmoErotic Humanism.

2 This project is grounded in four core organizational frameworks: 1) The Center for World Philosophy and Religion, co-founded by Marc Gafni, Zachary Stein, Sally Kempton, and Ken Wilber, and chaired over the years by John P. Mackey, Barbara Marx Hubbard, Aubrey Marcus, Gabrielle Anwar and Shareef Malnik, Carrie Kish and Adam Bellow, and Kathleen J. Brownback. 2) The Office for the Future, chaired by Stephanie Valcke and Ivan Bossyut. 3) The World Philosophy and Religion Press, founded and chaired by Aubrey Marcus, together with Marc Gafni and Zachary Stein. 4) The Foundation for Conscious Evolution, founded by Barbara Marx Hubbard and currently chaired by Peter Fiekowsky. For a complete list of key leadership, see the Office for the Future website, www.officeforthefuture.com.

Until Barbara's passing in 2019, she and Marc transmitted teachings together as evolutionary partners and "whole mates," weaving together insights and transmissions from their decades of practice, study, teaching, and activism into a synergy of wisdom, a grounded vision for future policy across all sectors of society.

Much of the *dharma* material below comes directly from Marc, so it was originally all in quotation marks—but that looked a little odd. So per his suggestion we removed them, and the reader should consider the paragraphs on the next several pages as one extended quote from him. We are joyfully grateful to Marc for the clarity of his *dharma*, the elegance and "second simplicity" of this language, and the mad, Outrageous Love with which he transmits his teachings.

Barbara and Marc called the mission of *One Mountain* "a Planetary Awakening in Evolutionary Love Through Unique Self Symphonies." We are an evolutionary community with a deeply grounded, radically alive, and "post-tragic" revolutionary spirit. We are activating a new humanity and awakening as a new species: *Homo amor*, the fulfillment of *Homo sapiens*.

One Mountain is committed to articulating a Story of Value that can become the ground for the new society that must be birthed in response to the meta-crisis. We recognize that we are living at a pivotal moment in history. In this "time between stories," the great moral imperative is to tell the new Story of Value. It is ours to do, personally and collectively, with great trembling and ecstatic joy.

FROM DOGMA TO *DHARMA*: ETERNAL AND EVOLVING FIRST PRINCIPLES AND FIRST VALUES

The teachings are grounded in decades of deep study across many wisdom traditions. Over the years, week by week, these teachings were incrementally developed within the framework of the *One Mountain, Many Paths* broadcast. We often refer to these teachings as *dharma*.

This word was originally used in lineage traditions to refer to something like universal law. This is a crucial realization: just as there is universal law in mathematical value, there is also a sense of universal law in ethics and value.

Historically, *dharma* often devolved into unchanging dogma. Evolution was ignored, and the natural process of *dharma* evolution became disconnected from its deep, eternal context. The weakness of the word *dharma* is that too often it did not include the evolving insights of the sciences, it confused local cultural truths with universal truths, and it used words like "eternal," as in "eternal Tao," as opposed to words like "evolution."

Eternal came to mean unchanging, and that kind of thinking often led to overly ethnocentric readings of *dharma*. Local systems would claim their religious and cultural insights as immutable, which stood in the way of the emergence of a genuine world Story of Value that is real, inherent to Cosmos, and backed by the Universe—even as it is also always evolving.

Or, as we often say, "eternal value is evolving value. The eternal Tao is the evolving Tao."

We have shown that, emergent from profound insights in the "interior sciences," eternal does not mean unchanging in time; it means what we call the deeper Field of ErosValue that is beneath culture, geography, and history, which lives beneath all individual and collective values, and beneath time and space itself.

As such, we have gradually transitioned from the term *dharma* to the term *Value*, in the sense of the Field of Value that lives beneath all values. This Field of Value discloses as First Principles and First Values embedded in a Story of Value.

Indeed, as the interior sciences knew and the exterior sciences imply, Reality arises in a Field of ErosValue in which an entire set of mathematical, musical, molecular, moral, and mystical values are the very ground of all being. That Field of Value is eternal—the true ground of the Good, True and Beautiful—even as it is evolving.

But of course, it is equally critical not just to talk about evolving value, but to ground the evolving value in its true nature, the eternal Field of First Principles and First Values, always reaching for ever-more life, ever-more love, ever-more care, ever-more depth, ever-more uniqueness, ever-more intimate communion, and ever-more transformation.

As such, when we refer to the word *dharma*, which still appears in these texts together with the word value, we refer to an evolving *dharma* grounded in an *eternal and evolving* Field of Value. Indeed, eternity and evolution are two faces of the whole, opposites joined at the hip, that characterize the nature of our Cosmos in virtually all of its expressions.

It's in these terms that we ground a robust world philosophy that integrates the validated, leading-edge insights of premodern traditional wisdom, modern wisdom, and more recent postmodern insights, weaving them together into a new whole greater than the sum of its parts.

This new whole is a shared Story of Value rooted in First Principles and First Values that are both eternal and evolving.

These First Principles and First Values of Cosmos are woven together into a new Story of Value as a context for our diversity, a new Universe Story. This new story gives us the best possible responses we have to the mystery, and to the great questions:

+ Who am I? Who are we?
+ Where am I? Where are we?
+ What should I do? What should we do?

It is only through such a shared Universe Story—a narrative of identity and ethos as a context for our blessed diversity—that we can realize how what unites is so much greater than what divides us.

Only a new Story of Value will allow us to both respond to the meta-crisis and participate together in birthing the most true, good, and beautiful world that we already know is possible.

THIS ORAL ESSAYS SERIES IS AN ENTRYWAY TO THE GREAT LIBRARY OF COSMOEROTIC HUMANISM

This Oral Essays series is part of the overarching project of the Great Library at the Center for World Philosophy and Religion, led by Dr. Marc Gafni, together with Dr. Zak Stein. The aim of the Great Library project is to articulate a robust and comprehensive new Story of Value, CosmoErotic Humanism, in the form of dozens of well-researched and extensively footnoted academic works.

Our vision is to provide the philosophical framework that will be vital for navigating humanity through this time of immense crisis and transformation.

To begin your journey into CosmoErotic Humanism, we tenderly refer you to the book *First Principles and First Values*, co-authored by Marc Gafni, Zak Stein, and Ken Wilber, under the name David J. Temple. David J. Temple is a pseudonym created for enabling ongoing collaborative authorship at the Center for World Philosophy and Religion. The two primary authors behind David J. Temple are Marc Gafni and Zak Stein, and for different projects, specific writers will be named as part of the collaboration, such as Ken Wilber and others.

Three other volumes complete this introduction: *A Return to Eros*, by Marc Gafni and Kristina Kincaid; *Your Unique Self*, by Marc Gafni; and *Education in a Time between Worlds*, by Zak Stein.

We hope that the Oral Essays in the present volume, with their informal style of transmission, will serve as an allurement and entryway for you into the more formal books of the Great Library that provide the robust intellectual underpinnings of the new Story of Value.

A NOTE ABOUT THE EDITORS

This Oral Essays collection has been edited by students of the new Story of CosmoErotic Humanism. Each of us has actively participated in *One Mountain, Many Paths*, and most of us have been in deep "Holy of Holies" study with Dr. Marc Gafni for many years.

We have been privileged to find ourselves well-versed in the teachings, and even emerging as lineage-holders of CosmoErotic Humanism.[3]

We view this editing project as a privilege and a deep practice of study and clarification. We experience ourselves as a *mystical editing society*, frequently meeting and conversing together about the content—the depth of knowledge and wisdom offered here—as well as the technical intricacies involved with publishing a beautiful and coherent series of books. In so doing, we function as a "Unique Self Symphony," which itself is a Dharmic

---

3 CosmoErotic Humanism is a world philosophical movement aimed at reconstructing the collapse of value at the core of global culture. Much like Romanticism or Existentialism, CosmoErotic Humanism is not merely a theory but a movement that changes the very mood of Reality. It is an invitation to participate in evolving the source code of consciousness and culture towards a cosmocentric *ethos* for a planetary civilization.

The term CosmoErotic Humanism, initially coined by Dr. Gafni and colleagues, points to a complex, multi-faceted, layered, and nuanced evolutionary set of insights that has evolved over decades of intensive research, teaching, and spiritual practice from deep within a wide range of wisdom traditions (including the Wisdom of Solomon lineage tradition, Bodhisattva Buddhism, and Kashmir Shaivism), as well as multiple disciplines including complexity theory, chaos theory, emergence theory, molecular biology, and the more classical disciplines of the humanities.

The seeds of CosmoErotic Humanism were planted with Dr. Marc Gafni's work on a two-volume, 1,000-page opus called *Radical Kabbalah* (Integral Publishers, 2012). This scholarly work, sourced from deep study within the esoteric lineage texts of the Wisdom of Solomon, points to a non-dual, or acosmic, realization which—unlike the prevailing conceptualization of non-duality—does not efface the human being; rather, it is highly humanistic in its nature. The next step in the evolution of CosmoErotic Humanism was the insight that all of Reality is evolving Eros, which lives in, as, and through the human being. A failure of Eros leads inexorably to the creation of narratives of "pseudo-eros." CosmoErotic Humanism is a response to the modern mental and social breakdown sourced in the proliferation of multiple forms of pseudo-eros and its broken narratives, such as rivalrous conflict governed by win/lose metrics and the dogmatic denial of intrinsic value in Cosmos, which together generate our current "global intimacy disorder."

term that connotes an omni-considerate collaboration between realized Unique Selves synergizing our unique gifts into a new emergence greater than the sum of the parts. Even as we worked diligently to standardize our editing styles, meeting on a weekly basis to debate the nuances of phrasing, we also operated from within a deep appreciation of the unique style that each editor brought to his or her work. As such, the reader might notice some variation in editing style among the books.

Please note that Dr. Marc Gafni has not reviewed these edited Oral Essays, as he is deeply engaged in writing the formal books of the Great Library. But he has been generous in responding to questions and providing overall guidance in the project. Overall, as Marc's students and students of the *dharma*, we have made it a key project at the Center to publish these pieces of work relatively independently.

OUR UNIQUE ORAL-ESSAY EDITING STYLE PRESERVES THE ENERGY OF THE ORIGINAL TRANSMISSION

Dr. Marc Gafni is a uniquely gifted teacher whose oral transmission is imbued with a quality that has proven transformative for his students. Many of us feel mystically transformed by both the content and the underlying energy of the transmission style. Therefore, as we like to say, *trust the magic ways the dharma comes through your unique understanding!*

As Marc's empowered students, colleagues, and beloved friends, we have a deep knowing that these teachings are vital for the survival and thriving of humanity as we know it, and we recognize the importance of publishing his teachings in a written format that will be accessible by future generations. At the same time, we sought to preserve the Eros of the original oral transmission with all of its nuance, power, and depth. Our intention in the editing process, to the greatest extent possible, has been to keep these spoken artifacts intact in order to maintain the flow of the original transmission. We have therefore chosen not to engage in intensive formal editing, as we found that doing so resulted in the loss of the energetic transmission that is so key to fully receiving the *dharma*.

After experimenting with many ways to present these texts, we developed a specific way of laying out the text on the page. Marc, in collaboration with Zak Stein and Russian intellectual/artist Elena Maslova-Levin—and ultimately all of the editors, through many conversations—developed a unique, artistic presentation of the text, using bolding, italics, bullet points, and other stylistic features which together serve to accentuate the immediacy of the oral transmission.

As part of this editing style, intended to preserve the integrity of the original transmission, we have refrained from removing the frequent recapitulations of key themes. We found that each recapitulation contributes something vital to the rhythm and music beneath the words, like the beating drum of our hearts. These recapitulations not only review previous material but also add important new emphases, perspectives, and elements of the new Story of Value. We ask for your patience as a reader to trust the rhythm of these texts, and we trust you as a reader to have the depth and steadiness to find your way through.

KEY COMPONENTS: LINK TO THE ORIGINAL BROADCAST, EVOLUTIONARY LOVE CODES AND PRAYER

To supplement the written word, each episode includes a QR code linking to the original broadcast on YouTube, as well as occasional links to featured songs and video clips.

Each episode also centers around an "Evolutionary Love Code," formulated by Marc. These codes are part of the ongoing articulation and distillation of the *dharma* as it unfolds and emerges, week by week, over the course of many years, through the mystical process we call Outrageous Love or Evolutionary Love.

Another core component of the *One Mountain, Many Paths* episodes is what Marc and Barbara called "Evolutionary Prayer." Prayer is experienced in *One Mountain* not in the old fundamentalist sense of a "cosmic vending-machine god" who is alienated from Cosmos. Marc refers to this as the "god you do not and should not believe in"—and he often adds, "the god you don't believe in does not exist."

GOD IS THE INFINITE INTIMATE

In fact, in the *dharma* of CosmoErotic Humanism, a new name for God has emerged: the "Infinite Intimate," who appears in first-, second-, and third-person expressions. Marc first shared this name as he heard it whispered in 2023, although earlier intimations and formulations of the name appeared as early as 2010.

In first person, God is infinitely alive and as intimate as our own first-person experience.

In second person, God is the infinitely intimate Personhood of Cosmos that knows our name and holds us—the God about whom we say, *whenever we fall, we fall into Her hands.* This is the God who is our Beloved, Father, Mother, Lover, and Evolutionary Partner.

Finally, in third person, God inheres in all of the First Principles and First Values of Cosmos, and in the laws of science (both interior and exterior) that govern manifest Reality.

Therefore, we have a realization of God as not only the Infinity of Power but also the Infinity of Intimacy.

In *One Mountain, Many Paths*, we are reclaiming prayer at a higher level of consciousness. And we are reclaiming prayer as deep, alive, loving, and intimate conversations with God as the Infinite Intimate who knows our name.

THE INVITATION

We invite you to find your way into this revolution. Each one of our Unique Selves and unique gifts are desperately needed as we co-create this new Story of Value together, as part of the covenant between generations, for the sake of the whole.

Let's *play a larger game* and evolve the very source code of consciousness and culture together.

With mad love,

The Editors

LOVE OR DIE

LOCATING OURSELVES: ARTICULATING THE ESSENTIAL CONTEXT FOR THE ONE MOUNTAIN, MANY PATHS ORAL ESSAYS

SETTING OUR INTENTION

Intention setting is everything.

We're here—as da Vinci was with his cohort in the Renaissance—**to play a larger game, to participate in the evolution of love, which is to tell the new Story of Value rooted in First Principles and First Values.**

- Our intention is to recognize the critical historical juncture in which we find ourselves.
- Our intention is to take our seat at the table of history and to say, *we take responsibility for this.*
- Our intention is to participate as revolutionaries for the sake of the whole.

What we're here to do is revolution; revolution for the sake of the evolution of love.

It's a revolution for the sake of the trillions of unborn lives that will not manifest:

- The unborn loves
- The unborn creativity
- The unborn goodness
- The unborn truth
- The unborn beauty

All of it looks to us.

Not because we're engaged in grandiosity. Not at all!

- We're trembling before She.
- We're trembling with joy at the privilege.
- We're trembling with joy at the responsibility.
- We're trembling with joy at the Possibility of Possibility.
- We have to enact a new story in this moment of time. Because it is only a new story that can change the vector of history.

The most revolutionary act that we can do—the greatest moral imperative of this time—**is to articulate a new story at this time between worlds and this time between stories.**

Story is not made up, as postmodernity suggests. **We all live in inescapable frameworks; our framework is the story we live in.** Right now, Reality lives according to win/lose metrics, a story that is generating existential risk. **We need to change that story.**

When we change that story, when we tell a new story—not a made-up story, but a new Story of Value, rooted in First Principles and First Values—**then it all changes.**

We need to participate in the evolution of the source code of consciousness and culture, which is the evolution of love.

It's the most important, exciting, evolutionary, revolutionary act that we can do to alleviate suffering: to be lovers.

Like Rumi, the great poet of Sufism, we have to be "mad lovers," because it's the only sanity.

To be mad lovers is to see around the corner, to not be so obsessed with the details of the contractions of my life.

Let me see bigger.

Let me take complete care of myself in every possible way, let me completely attend to those in my circle of intimacy and influence, and then—*let me expand my circle.*

That's what we're here for.

- Our intention is to participate in the *LoveForce*, the *LoveIntelligence*, the *LoveBeauty*, the *LoveDesire* that literally animates Cosmos all the way up and all the way down.
- Our intention is to participate in the evolution of love.

  [In the next few pages we will cover some key concepts which are essential to locating ourselves and setting the context for all the One Mountain, Many Paths Oral Essays. —Eds.]

OVERVIEW: EROS IS NO LONGER A LUXURY—IT'S LOVE OR DIE

Eros is life.

The failure of Eros destroys life.

Our lack of Eros is poised to destroy the world.

All civilizations have fallen because the stories that they lived in were, in some sense, stories based on rivalrous conflict governed by win/lose metrics. Every civilization was weakened by interior polarization caused by the lack of a shared Story of Value.

We now have a global civilization, but we haven't created a shared Story of Value.

We haven't solved the generator functions that caused all civilizations to fall. Our global civilization has exponential technologies and extraction models depleting the Earth of resources that took billions of years to create, which is going to lead to a civilizational collapse.

Existential risk is risk to our very existence.

The choice is clear: love or die.

It's that simple.

Eros is no longer a luxury. It is an absolute necessity for the survival of the individual and the planet.

In the last half a century, modern psychology has documented an age-old truth: a fully nourished baby who is not held in loving arms will die.

So too, our world, both personal and global—even with all the resources of intelligence and technology at our disposal—will die without being held in love, in the embrace of Eros.

We must embrace a personal path of love and a global politics of love.

Not ordinary love. Not love which is "mere human sentiment," but Eros, or what we sometimes call Outrageous Love, which is the heart of existence itself.

We live in a world of outrageous pain.

The only response is Outrageous Love.

WHAT IS EROS?

Eros is the experience of radical aliveness, moving towards, seeking, desiring ever deeper contact and ever greater wholeness.[4] Eros is the core fabric of Reality's being and the motivational architecture of Reality's becoming.

Eros is what animates the evolutionary impulse itself, from the very inception of Cosmos all the way to our very selves, who awaken to the realization that the evolutionary impulse throbs uniquely in each of us.

The realization of human awakening and transformation that lies at the core of the interior sciences is the invitation—or even the urgent and desperate demand—of a madly loving Cosmos animated by infinities of power and infinities of intimacy.

The demand—the desperate invitation, the plea, the tender and fierce command of Cosmos that lives inside every human being—is to awaken: to awaken to our true nature as unique incarnations of Eros and Ethos that are needed and desperately desired by All-That-Is. Said slightly differently: Reality is Eros. Or: God is Eros.

The failure of Eros destroys life. The collapse of Eros is always the hidden (or not so hidden) root cause for the collapse of ethics.

This is true both personally and collectively. We live in a moment of a world-wide and personal collapse of Eros. Our lack of Eros is poised to destroy

---

4 We define Eros through what we refer to as the Eros equation (one of a series of what we call interior science equations):

> Eros = Radical Aliveness x Desiring (Growing + Seeking) x Deeper Contact x Greater Wholeness x Self Actualization/Self Transcendence (Creation [Destruction])

There are good reasons for the formal language of the interior science equations in these writings, and the reader is invited to explore them on their own, in particular, in our work, David J. Temple, *First Principles and First Values: Forty-Two Propositions on CosmoErotic Humanism, the Meta-Crisis, and the World to Come* (World Philosophy and Religion, 2024).

the world. Humanity is currently experiencing what has come to be known as existential risk, a risk to our very existence, or what I will refer to as the Second Shock of Existence.

EXISTENTIAL RISK: THE SECOND SHOCK OF EXISTENCE

The first shock of existence is the death of the human being—the realization that we will die, which dawns in human consciousness at the beginning of history. We are not talking about the biological fact of death but the *existential* realization of death. Although the interior sciences disclose that death is a portal between two days (there is vast empirical,[5] philosophical,[6] and anthro-ontological evidence[7] for the continuity of consciousness[8]), death is also, in our own direct surface experience, a stark end. And that is obviously not a bug, but a feature in the system.

---

5 We refer to evidence gathered by the most serious of researchers, beginning with Henry and Edith Sedgwick at Cambridge University and William James at Harvard University, and continuing in highly rigorous form for the last 150 years, as recapitulated by Whiteheadian scholar David Ray Griffin in multiple volumes. See also, for example, Dean Radin, *Real Magic: Unlocking Your Natural Psychic Abilities to Create Everyday Miracles* (Potter/TenSpeed/Harmony, 2018), *The Conscious Universe: The Scientific Truth of Psychic Phenomena* (HarperCollins, 2010), and other books. Or see the earlier classic by Frederic William Henry Myers, *Human Personality and Its Survival of Bodily Death* (Longmans, Green, 1907).

6 This requires a cogent analysis of materialism and dualism, and the introduction of the far more cogent third possibility, which we have called "pan-interiority."

7 We discuss Anthro-Ontology in some depth in *First Principles and First Values*, and see also the fuller conversation in David J. Temple, *First Principles and First Values: Towards an Evolving Perennialism: Introducing the Anthro-Ontological Method*—both published by World Philosophy and Religion Press, in conjunction with Integral Publishers. For now, we will simply define it as an "innate and clear interior gnosis directly available to the human being."

8 See Dr. Marc Gafni and Dr. Zachary Stein's essay in preparation, "Beyond Death: Anthro-Ontology, Philosophy, and Empiricism." This essay is slated to appear in the book *Towards a World Religion: Homo Amor Essays*. The essay is also the ground for a larger book by the same authors, *Twelve Portals to Life Beyond Death: Responding to the Second Shock of Existence*, in which we discuss three forms of material: the empirical, the philosophical, and the anthro-ontological, and show how each form discredits the notion of death as the end.

Our first-person experience is that death ends this life. It is not the *totality* of our experience if we go deeper inside, but it is obviously intended to be the central, potent, and painful dimension of every human life. Indeed, as Ernest Becker potently reminded us, the denial of death is at our peril.

All the stories and all the plotlines and all the threads of living end at that moment. Whatever happens beyond, we have an actual experience of ending. **Paradoxically, that ending, the experience of the finality of mortality, is what presses us into life.** From the implicit demand of the first shock of existence, human beings were activated and pressed into creative emergence, and what emerged was all of human culture, both interior and exterior.

The second shock of existence is the realization of the potential death of all humanity. After all the stages of human history—matter, life, and mind in all of their stages of evolutionary unfolding—we have come to this place in the evolution of humanity, in which the gap between our exponentially expanding exterior technologies and our stalled (or even regressing) interior technologies of value has created dire catastrophic and existential risks.

This gap generates extraction models and exponential growth curves, rivalrous conflicts based on win/lose metrics, tragedies of the commons, and multipolar traps, in which everyone has to keep producing to the nth degree, including weaponized exponential threats to our very existence because we are afraid that the other parties are going to do it and not be transparent—hide it from us and then dominate us.

GENERATOR FUNCTIONS FOR EXISTENTIAL RISK

Let's outline clearly the main *generator functions for existential risk*.

Rivalrous conflicts governed by zero-sum, win/lose metrics. Rivalrous conflicts generate extraction models at the core of the economic system and exponential growth curves. Both of these drive and are driven by a contrived system of artificially manufactured desires and needs, delivered into culture by ever more precise forms of micro-targeting to individuals and groups through the ever more immersive environment of the internet.

Next, rivalrous conflicts and exponential growth curves animated by win/lose metrics generate **complicated, fragile world systems** highly vulnerable to myriad forms of collapse. Fragile local systems are made exponentially more fragile on a global level by our inability to meet global challenges with social, legal, political, economic, and ethical infrastructures that remain largely local.

All of this is a direct result of the failure to develop more adequate interior technologies that would be sufficiently compelling to displace "rivalrous conflict governed by win/lose metrics" as the motivational architecture for the human life world.

This failure has led to the conditions that will cause the implosion of systems that are already and quite literally on the brink of collapsing themselves. That's what we mean by the *second shock of existence*.

To recapitulate: the second shock of existence is not the death of the human being, but the potential death of humanity.

It is the *Death Star* moment of our species.

THE DECONSTRUCTION OF INTRINSIC VALUE

We stand in this moment poised between utopia and dystopia, at a time between worlds and a time between stories. We need a new Story of Value, eternal yet evolving, rooted in First Principles and First Values, which would become a universal grammar of value and a context for our diversity.

This is exactly what the Renaissance was. It was a time between worlds and a time between stories. In the Renaissance, we had been recently challenged by the Black Death, a pandemic that swept across Europe. The Black Death destroyed between a third to half of Europe and a huge part of

Asia. People died horrifically, brutally, in the streets. They had no idea how to meet this challenge, and so, in response to the Black Death, da Vinci and Ficino and their cohorts understood that they had to tell a new Story of Value.

That story was the story of modernity. Did they get it right?

- They got part of it right, which birthed, to use Jürgen Habermas' phrase, "the dignities of modernity," such as new ways of gathering information and universal human rights.
- But they also deconstructed the source of Value. They lost the basis for the Good, the True, and the Beautiful.

The basis used to be divine revelation: *God told us.* But this claim was owned by religion, and every religion began to overreach and over-claim. The revelation was thus often mediated through cultural categories and wasn't fully accurate.

Modernity threw out revelation, but was unable to establish a new basis for value.

Value was just assumed to be real. As it says in the founding document of the American Revolution: *We hold these truths to be self-evident*—that is, *we don't really have a basis for value; we just take it as a given.*

In other words, modernity took out a loan of social capital from the traditional world. The source of value was never worked out.

And then, gradually, value began to collapse.

- The Universe Story began to collapse.
- The belief that the Good, the True, and the Beautiful are real began to collapse.
- The belief that Love is real began to collapse.

As Bertrand Russell is reported to have said, "I cannot see how to refute the arguments for the subjectivity of ethical values, but I find myself incapable of believing that all that is wrong with wanton cruelty is that I do not like it."

What do you do if you grew up in a world in which value is not real? A world without a source of value, without a Universe Story, without a story of human identity, without a story of desire, without a narrative of power?

In the words of W.B. Yeats, *the center does not hold.*

- You have a collapse at the very center of society, because you no longer have Eros.
- You no longer have a Reality in which value is real, and so you have this lingering sense of emptiness.
- You have a complete collapse at the very center.
- We become *the hollow men and the stuffed men*, gesture without form.

And that's the source of our current existential risk.

THE DEEPER ROOT CAUSE OF THE META-CRISIS: A GLOBAL INTIMACY DISORDER

Above, I have outlined the major generator functions of existential risk. But there is a deeper cause for the existential risk that lurks underneath the rivalrous conflict governed by win/lose metrics and the fragile systems they engender.

And we cannot take the Death Star down without discerning and addressing this. We have already alluded to this root cause above, but at this point we need to make it more explicit so that, from this context, the adequate root response will become clear.

Modernity threw out the revelation, but was unable to establish a new basis for value.

This ostensibly surprising statement can be understood in a few simple steps:

1. All of the catastrophic and existential risk challenges we face are global: from climate change to artificial intelligence, pandemics, systems collapse, and exponential arms races.
2. Every global challenge self-evidently requires a global solution.
3. Global solutions can only be implemented with global co-ordination.
4. Global co-ordination is impossible without global coherence.
5. Global coherence is only possible if there is a global resonance between the parts.
6. Global resonance is only possible if we have global intimacy.

ONLY A SHARED STORY OF VALUE CAN GENERATE GLOBAL INTIMACY

Global intimacy—just like intimacy in a couple—is only possible when there is a shared story.

Not just a shared history, but a shared Story of Value.

- It is only a shared global story that can generate a new emergent quality of intimacy: global intimacy.
- A shared Story of Value must be rooted in shared ordinating values, or what we have called evolving First Values and First Principles.
- Intimacy requires a shared grammar of value as a matrix for a shared Story of Value.

The global intimacy disorder is the root cause for existential risk. The global intimacy disorder underlies the core generator functions for existential risk.

The global intimacy disorder is rooted in the failure to experience ourselves in a field of shared intrinsic value. This failure derives from the deconstruction of value.

Indeed, it is wholly accurate to say that **the root cause of the two generator functions of existential risk is the failed story of intrinsic value, or what we might also call the breakdown of Eros.**

1. The first generator function is **the success story.** Our modern success story is rivalrous conflict governed by win/lose metrics, which violates all the terms of the Intimacy Equation: there is no shared identity and no mutuality of recognition, feeling, value or purpose, and instead of *relative* otherness, there is *alienated* otherness. Such a story generates complicated fragile systems with no allurement or intimacy between the parts, systems which optimize for efficiency (as an expression of win/lose metrics) and not for resiliency and life.

2. The second generator function is **the deconstruction of intrinsic value** itself. The deconstruction of value is the sense that human value does not participate in the intrinsic value of the Real, for the Real is dogmatically declared to have no intrinsic value. Thus, there is no shared identity between the interior of the human being and Reality. There is no common participation in a field of shared intrinsic value. Instead of being intimate with value, we are alienated from value. And only intrinsic value can arouse will: political, moral, and social will.

To sum up, without a shared grammar of value there is no global intimacy, and therefore no global coherence, and no global coordination in response to catastrophic and existential risk, which means, put simply, there will be, quite literally, no future.

HEALING THE GLOBAL INTIMACY DISORDER REQUIRES THE EVOLUTION OF INTIMACY

But we are not hopeless. On the contrary, we are filled with great hope. Hope is a memory of the future. That memory of the future *is* the direct hit that takes down the Death Star, the culture of death. **The direct hit must be**—as it has always been in history—**the emergence of a new stage of evolution**.

Crisis is an evolutionary driver, and every crisis is, at its core, a crisis of intimacy: from the oxygen crisis of the single cells dying which generated multicellular life at the dawn of existence, to the existential risk in this very moment.[9]

> *The direct hit is therefore structurally self-evident: the evolution of intimacy itself.*

What is intimacy, as a structure of Cosmos all the way down and all the way up the evolutionary chain? We engage this inquiry in depth in other writings, but for now we will simply adduce what we have called the "Intimacy Equation":

> *Intimacy = shared identity in the context of [relative] otherness* x *mutuality of recognition* x *mutuality of pathos* x *mutuality of value* x *mutuality of purpose*

Intimacy is about the capacity of parts to generate a *shared identity* while retaining their otherness, or distinct identity. This requires multiple mutualities, including recognition, pathos (or feeling), value, and purpose. The parts must recognize and feel each other, even as they share value and purpose. But all of this must lead to intimate union—and not pathological

---

9 We demonstrate this principle in some depth in the multi-volume series, *The Universe: A Love Story* (forthcoming) (https://worldphilosophyandreligion.org/early-ontologies), *The Intimate Universe: Global Intimacy Disorder as Cause for Global Action Paralysis* (forthcoming), and in other writings of CosmoErotic Humanism.

fusion, where the distinct identity of the parts disappears—like subatomic particles that successfully become an atom, or two people who successfully become a couple.

THE DECONSTRUCTION OF VALUE IS THE DECONSTRUCTION OF INTIMACY

We have identified the global intimacy disorder as the root cause of the existential risk. But the underlying ultimate failure of intimacy is the deconstruction of value itself.

The deconstruction of value means that human value does not participate in any sense of intrinsic value of the Real. This is not about individual *values,* but about *the Field of Value* that underlies all of them. **When the human being**—moved, often sincerely or even nobly, by myriad cultural, historical, and psychological confusions—**claims to have stepped out of the Field of Value, then intimacy itself is deconstructed.**

The deconstruction of value is the deconstruction of intimacy.

In the absence of a shared Story of Value, a story that is an authentic expression of Reality's Eros, a story rooted in *pseudo-Eros* takes center stage and becomes the generator function for existential risk. Our modern pseudo-Eros story is *rivalrous conflict governed by win/lose metrics.* Such a story catalyzes in its wake the second generator function of existential risk: *complicated fragile systems with no allurement or intimacy between the parts.* It is in that sense that we have argued that the first generator function for existential risk is the success story.

- The failure of intimacy is precisely the impotent experience that there is no shared identity between the interior of the human being and Reality. **There is no shared identity in the sense of any kind of common participation in a field of shared intrinsic value.**

- **But only a shared Story of Value can arouse the global will required to engage catastrophic and existential risk.** For it is only global political, moral, and social will—and we can even say *erotic* will—that can generate the most Good, True and Beautiful world that we have always known is possible.

THE EVOLUTION OF LOVE IS THE TELLING OF A NEW STORY

Coupled with the Intimacy Equation is the scientifically grounded realization, in both the exterior and interior sciences, that Reality is a progressive deepening of intimacies, or, said slightly differently:

Reality is Evolution. Evolution is the evolution of intimacy.

- The evolution of intimacy requires—both personally and collectively—a deeper, more accurate discernment of the nature of our universe, ourselves, and our beloveds.
- This new discernment generates a new global Story of Value.
- The new global Story of Value generates an emergent, heretofore unseen global intimacy and heals the global intimacy disorder.

The new Story of Value is the direct hit that takes down the Death Star and replaces it with the hope that invokes the memory of our best future.

Global intimacy facilitates global coherence, which facilitates global coordination, which activates the possibility of our creative and effectively coordinated global responses to the global meta-crisis in its entirety and its specific expressions.

To solve Bertrand Russell's challenge—the apparent argument for the subjectivity of ethical values—**we have to reground value theory in eternal yet evolving First Principles and First Values, and articulate a new Story of Value.**

This is what we call CosmoErotic Humanism.

CosmoErotic Humanism—together with other emergent strands—**needs to become the ground of a world religion as a context for our diversity**. We need religion, even as we need science, to articulate a shared global grammar of value.

As we said at the beginning, our choice is simple: love or die.

- To love means to participate in the evolution of love, which is the evolution of the human Story of Value.
- To love means to evolve and activate a new cultural enlightenment—rooted in a new narrative of identity, a new narrative of value, a new narrative of intimate communion, a new narrative of desire, a new narrative of power—all of which will birth new narratives of economics and politics.
- The evolution of love is the telling of a new story.

The new story that must be told is a love story, for in fact that is the deepest truth of Reality, rooted in the best exterior and interior sciences, that we have at this moment in time:

- Reality is not merely a fact. Reality is a story.
- Reality is not an ordinary story. Reality is a love story.
- Reality is not an ordinary love story. Reality is an Outrageous Love Story.

Story doesn't mean it's *made-up*.

It means doing the hard work of integrating the validated insights of the traditional world, the modern world, and the postmodern world.

This is the intention at the heart of telling the new Story of CosmoErotic Humanism.

ABOUT THIS VOLUME

We are in a time between stories, a time between worlds, standing at the edge of either devolution or evolution, destruction or creation. The choice is stark: Love or Die.

This book is an invitation to play a larger game—to become *Homo amor*, the new human, and to participate in the evolution of love. It offers a path forward, drawing together the best insights of the premodern, modern, and postmodern eras into a vision that births the next stage of human becoming.

The stakes could not be higher. We are facing a meta-crisis driven not merely by political dysfunction or environmental collapse, but by a far deeper cause: a global intimacy disorder. Along with this disorder is the murder of Eros that occurs when we lose contact with our own deepest sense of value, beauty, and aliveness. The world today is insane but claims to be sane. We wake up when we reclaim the deeper mad love that is at the heart of Reality.

This book reclaims Eros, power, and desire as intrinsic values of the cosmos that have been split off. It introduces a new grammar of value grounded in First Principles and First Values—the interior structure of the universe. To live aligned with these principles is to become a post-tragic hero—not the old hero of conquest, but a new, tender, fierce lover of value. The post-tragic hero lives with open eyes and an unguarded heart, not in spite of heartbreak, but because of it. Heartbreak is a form of holy revelation, and it opens us to shadow work—where the disowned parts of the self become portals to deeper wholeness. To step into the story of *Homo amor* is to claim your *holy and broken Hallelujah*, and through it, incarnate your true identity as a unique configuration of intimacy and desire that Reality has never seen before.

With the realization of your Unique Self comes obligation: you carry a unique gift, and with it, the unique risk that only you can take. To hold back is to wound the world. To show up is to write a new chapter in the unfolding love story of the cosmos. You are not an extra on the set of Reality. You are a word in the evolving scroll, a voice in the Unique Self Symphony.

This book is a map, a prayer, a transmission. A call to stop contributing to a culture that murders Eros—and instead become an embodiment of the genuine Eros of *Homo amor*.

The universe is intimate. Reality needs you. Are you ready to answer the call?

Volume 36

These oral essays are edited talks delivered by Marc Gafni between October 2020 and December 2024.

CHAPTER ONE

FROM THE MURDER OF EROS TO *HOMO AMOR*: LOVEPOWER IS THE WORD, AND THE WORD IS GOOD

Episode 208 — October 4, 2020

POWER HISTORY AND LOVE HISTORY: RECOGNIZING THE MURDER OF EROS

Our intention is to participate together in the evolution of love.

At this moment between utopia and dystopia, when unimaginable suffering lurks at the door, our intention is to find our way in, to articulate together a new vision—not based on New Age declarations or fundamentalist reclaiming—based on the deepest integration of premodernity, modernity, and postmodernity.

In every generation, there is what I would call a power history and an *amor* history, or a *love history*. There's the history of power and the history of love—although power and love are not opposites, and we need to reclaim power in its integrity, and love itself is filled with power. This is true.

For the moment I want to talk about power as surface power and love as depth love. Of course, there is also depth power and surface love, but for now let's just access love as the depths—not as ordinary love but the

1

love that literally moves the sun and other stars, the love that is alive in me and is finding its way, that is self-organizing Reality, guiding, moving, constellating, opening us up. Love as the pathfinder, guide, compass, and North Star.

It's the love that is literally holding your body together this very second, all thirty-seven trillion cells. An unimaginable number of neurons are moving in you. Slightly fewer than the number of stars in the sky is the number of neurons inside of you, with a level of interconnectivity that's unimaginable, in which every neuron knows what every other neuron's doing in every second. So you're a galaxy.

That connectivity between neurons is based on allurement, based on an instant knowing, based on love, based on Eros. That interconnected galaxy that you literally are right now, if you could feel it pulsing and throbbing inside of you, is animated by desire and love. The neurons seek each other. They're allured to each other. The protons and the neutrons, hadrons, leptons, muons, and all the rest are in configurations of allurement. This is the power of love. And you come together yourself as a unique configuration of Eros, intimacy, desire, allurement. You're literally, as am I, a force of love unlike any other.

UNDERSTANDING THE MURDER OF EROS

Our topic today is going to be the murder of Eros and what that means. When you get distracted, we call that pseudo-eros. **When you get *really* distracted you seek to murder Eros.** When I'm distracted, I try to find something wrong. And there are all sorts of small ways we move to murder Eros.

The murder of Eros is a fundamental force in society:

+ It's one of the shadows of cancel culture, for example.
+ It's the shunning, the excommunication, that happens in the religious world. It's the sense that *we are right and they are*

damned. There's no redemption, said Augustine, *outside of the Church*. Everyone else is outside.

- It's the pluralistic level of consciousness that lives both on the left and the right that says, *we pretend to be pluralistic, but really we've got it right and you've got it wrong, and you guys are so bad.*

That's the source of polarization: you murder the Eros, the aliveness, and the life vision of those people who seem to be so close to you. The murder of Eros is very deep, and we're going to talk about how it works and what it means. **Until we recognize the murder of Eros, we can't move beyond it.**

EROS HISTORY AND POWER HISTORY

But let's find each other now. There's the history of Eros, erotic history, but by erotic history we don't mean sexual history. We mean the history of Eros, the history of love—love as Eros, as *amor*. Then there's power history in the sense of surface power. Those are two different histories and two different stories. **The story that our colleague Yuval Harari tells in *Sapiens* is the story of power history.** It's driven by narrow, egoic self-interest or ethnocentric self-interest.

> *The story we're telling is the story of Homo amor. It's the history of love. It's the story of Eros.*

Those stories are happening right next to each other. They're not as separate as they seem. Sometimes dimensions of power history enter love history. And love history is always playing, in its own way, in power history. But at their core, there are these two movements in Cosmos, part of the larger One, and we need to bring those movements together.

LOVEPOWER: COSMOS IS A FIELD OF ALLUREMENT AND WE ARE EACH ITS UNIQUE EXPRESSIONS

We need to bring power and love together where love is animated with such power, and power is animated with such love, that they become not two separate histories but one history.

That is our vision. That's what we're about.

We can't do that by declaring it. Declarations are always suspect; you declare something when there's nothing behind it. That's why when the conquistadors came to the New World in the Americas, before they would massacre and rape and burn and pillage, they declared the demands of the King of Spain and his sovereignty. Those were called the *declarations of the conquistadors*.

Google *declares* its right to gather all of your personal data, to organize it based on machine intelligence, and to sell a predictive analysis of what you'll do to advertisers all over the world without your permission. Google does this based on six declarations, where they just say they have access. Simply because no one has declared a law against it, they declare that they have a right to all that information.

So this is not a declaration we're talking about here. This is based on the deepest knowings we have in the interior and exterior sciences, from the great wisdom traditions, modernity, and postmodernity. We bring all these insights and weave them together. We don't declare this truth. This is the deepest knowing of science today:

> Love and power come together. And we're unique expressions of *LovePower*. Let's create a new word together: *LovePower*. Let's access that. Can we just access *LovePower* together? I'm a unique expression of *LovePower*. That's who I am.
>
> I'm a unique expression of *LovePower* that never was, is, or will be ever again.

We are One Love and One Communion. We're the communion of *amor*. In some sense, we're One Love and we're One Power. We're One Communion. In the twelfth century, the Cathars called their church the Church of Amor, and they had a hidden *Book of Love*. Wow!

- We take a dimension of the Cathars.
- We take a dimension of the great Sabbatean movement that declared love at the center—and we leave the shadows aside. The Cathars had shadows. The Sabbatean movement had shadows.
- We claim the Shakti of Kashmir Shaivism, which is the love particles that animate and drive Reality, in Abhinavagupta's great thought.
- We claim the love implicit in Vajrayana Buddhism.
- We claim the love implicit in particle physics: the realization that Reality at the subatomic level is driven by allurement.

The subatomic level is not the only place where quantum reality plays; it plays in the macroscopic world as well. We're learning that more and more. We know that allurement is the driving force of Cosmos.

Cosmos is a Field of Allurement: LovePower.

That's our intention here, to realize this.

WE'VE BEEN TOGETHER BEFORE, AND OUR INTENTION IS TO GO THE WHOLE WAY IN THIS LIFETIME

I want to say something audacious, with your permission. I want to bring in a term that's been rejected, but rejected by a superficial mainstream. But a much deeper cut of Reality, a new mainstream, is emerging that—without a blithe or arrogant or supercilious rejection—is realizing there's an enormous amount of data which speaks about what Ian Stevenson at the University of Virginia called reincarnation, and that soul groups reincarnate as well. They reincarnate and they come together again.

There's an enormous amount of evidence for this that didn't exist 120 years ago. It has nothing to do with woo-woo. It has nothing to do with New Age. **It's hard data, science, our best explanation we have of Reality, which tells us it's not over when it's over, for lots of reasons. Reincarnation is part of that.**

I want to make a suggestion to you that I can feel in my body. See if you can feel it with me. *We've been together before*, friends. Can you feel that?

We've been together before.
We've done this before.
We've tried this before.

It hasn't always gone so well—because of the murder of Eros.

- Think about the Cathars.
- Think about the Sabbateans.
- Think about all the radical movements towards love.
- Think about the utopians in different generations.
- Think about the people who were ahead of their time in Kashmir Shaivism, Buddhism, Christianity, Taoism, Confucianism.

There have been bands of Outrageous Lovers throughout history. But this time, my friends, for the first time, *everything* is at stake. Wow!

- We've got to bring everybody with us.
- We've got to create a large tent.
- We've got to go the whole way in this lifetime.

That's the intention, with your permission, with tears in my eyes. If you can feel the tears, you can cry them with me, but they're tears of joy and tears of urgency.

I want to set an intention. Can we set an intention together, with everyone's permission? **Our intention is to go the whole way in this lifetime.** Our intention is to participate in the evolution of love and to go the whole way in this lifetime.

THE EVOLUTIONARY IMPULSE WHERE LOVE AND POWER COME TOGETHER

We are the communion of *amor*. *Amor* is that which animates the Cosmos and which lives in us, as us, and through us. **We are the leading edge of *amor*, and we can take responsibility for the whole thing—even as we're held in every second.**

Here's the question.

+ Are we ready to play a larger game? Let's step in.
+ Are we ready to go the whole way in this lifetime? This is our lifetime.
+ Are we ready to step in, to feel the ecstatic urgency of the evolutionary impulse living in us?

The impulse of evolution is the thrill, the responsibility, the urgency, the delight of creating the future, of accessing the memory of the future, of taking responsibility for the future. We're going to take responsibility in the best way we can, held by forces unseen and mysteries much larger than us. And yet those mysteries live in us. **The mysteries are within us. The sacred texts are written in our hearts and souls.** We are evolution.

+ I am the leading edge of evolution.
+ I don't live in the world; the world lives in me.
+ I don't live in the Intimate Universe (although I do); the Intimate Universe lives in me.

To be evolution, I've got to feel the full power of the evolutionary impulse. Being the evolutionary impulse is where love and power come together. That's *LovePower.*

At the deepest place, the power of love and the love of power are the same.

You want to know what the evolutionary impulse feels like on the inside? It doesn't feel like love; it doesn't feel like power. That's an old binary, a false split imposed on us by those who claimed the name in vain. It's not true. It's not *love against power.* Jimi Hendrix was awesome on the guitar at Woodstock, but he got it wrong. We're not waiting for the day when *the power of love overcomes the love of power.* That's true only in the superficial way that we started, when power is surface power and love is depth love.

At the deepest place, the power of love and the love of power are the same. **Love inheres with power.** Love is not weak; love is strong.

Love is the most powerful force that ever was, is, or will be. It's real. That's power, LovePower.

I'm a unique incarnation of LovePower. Wow!

It's the greatest privilege of my life to be with you, for us to be with each other, for us to love each other, and to be this band of Outrageous Lovers, this band of committed ones. We invite anyone to join us. There's no dogma. This is not pre-personal commitment; it's not pre-personal loyalty. It's transpersonal.

- ◆ We share a vision.
- ◆ We honor the individual irreducible autonomy and uniqueness of every human being.
- ◆ And we come together in a larger vision that we're radically committed to for the sake of alleviating suffering, for the sake of every child knowing that they have a song to sing and a

poem to write, that their life matters and that their story has to be lived and told and honored and celebrated.

That's the world we need to live in. It's the world we can create.

THE MANY DISTRESSING DISGUISES OF THE MURDER OF EROS

This week's Evolutionary Love Code:

Radical aliveness is life.

We yearn for life, but when we are deadened, we move to kill life as a shortcut to genuine aliveness.

The murder of Eros is sourced in the failure of Eros.

We cannot become *Homo amor* until we transcend the impulse to murder Eros.

To transcend that impulse, we must first fearlessly recognize it.

The murder of Eros is the desire to murder life force. That desire to murder life force comes from our own failure to experience our own aliveness.

When I'm not experiencing my own aliveness what happens is that I attempt to murder life force.

That expresses itself in many ways, but it's a fundamental dimension of Reality, and we've got to recognize it. It's hidden. This is esoteric. The reason we're studying this is because we can't get home until we get a sense of how this works. The New Age world, for example, doesn't recognize this possibility, but it exists everywhere.

This notion of the murder of Eros hides in many distressing disguises. For example, the people who murder Eros never announce, *we're out to murder Eros.* The people who murder Eros always hide behind a disguise. What's the disguise? The disguise is some form of counterfeit. The fig leaf is always a noble cause. *I'm standing for a cause. I'm making sure everything is pure.*

The murderers of Eros are always standing for purity. They always disguise their own sense of being not enough, their own sense of not being seen, their own sense of feeling deadened in their hearts. Scott Peck had a word for this: *people of the lie*. But people of the lie always disguise themselves very well; they're always very hidden. The great fear of people of the lie is when someone shines a light on them and their motives are exposed. That's really important to get. You've got to search and realize, *oh, that noble cause isn't really a noble cause.*

There's something in psychology called the Karpman Triangle, sometimes also called the *victim triangle* or the *drama triangle*, which talks about there being a victim, a persecutor, and a rescuer. On the surface, you think that you know: *that's the victim, that's the rescuer, that's the persecutor.* But what's often true is that the persecutor is hiding as a victim or a rescuer:

- The rescuer who says, *I'm standing for victims*, is often the persecutor.
- The victim who's claiming victimhood is often using the claim of being powerless to wield unholy power.

That's a very common structure in modern culture. It's the false hijacking of a victim identity. It's the exaggeration of hurt and the deployment of malice.

The murder of Eros virtually always deploys the tool of malice.

This is important to understand: malice seeks to murder Eros. The motivation or the methodology of malice is projection. I project my own ulterior motives, my own viciousness that's split off, my own rage that's disowned, and I stand for purity on the side of the ostensible victims.

Now, we have to defend and hold every true victim.

- We stand on the side of the vulnerable.

- We stand on the side of the oppressed.
- We stand on the side of the powerless.

But we have to watch very carefully for the victim triangle. We have to watch very carefully, and we realize that often the most ulterior motive of all is the motive of purity. Beware of those who can't hold irony. Beware of those who forget to laugh about the whole thing.

Beware of those who can't hold complexity, who are battling for purity, who are engaged in all forms of demonization. I remember reading an article a while ago that someone had written—let's call them Person A—who was attacking and demonizing another person, let's call them Person B. It made all sorts of claims and it said, *I began to look into B, and I came with an open mind.* A wrote this very dramatic article, essentially calling B every form of evil. A had never met B. **They'd never met each other.** Although B happened to be living in the same city as person A at the time A wrote the article.

I happen to know someone who hated B—let's call them C. And I had an intuition that A, the author of the article, must know C. So I Googled their names, and *it turns out that A and C are best friends.*

- They've been in the same group for ten years.
- They know each other very well.
- They live close to each other.
- They're involved in many activities together.

But the *righteous* person, A, who's quite well known, wrote this attacking article and lied. He hid the malice.

The article comes across as this noble defense of victims, *but he doesn't know anything about the story.* It was a complete lie from beginning to end.

I was a bit shocked at the audacity of it. But that's the nature of the murder of Eros. The murder of Eros gets very audacious. What drives it is the sense *that someone has aliveness or Eros that I don't have.* Actually, it's a form of evil. **The murder of Eros is evil, without question**. Evil is *live* spelled backwards—the failure of aliveness turns into evil.

THE FAILURE OF ALIVENESS TURNS INTO EVIL

I'll give you a couple of examples. In *Othello,* Iago is driven completely insane by the aliveness of Othello, so he goes to demonize Othello. Now, is Othello perfect? Of course Othello is not perfect. We're all imperfect vessels for the light. But Iago is not concerned with genuine imperfection. He's not concerned with helping Othello be more whole. He's only concerned with—and driven insane by—the experience that in some way Othello possesses an aliveness that he doesn't have.

I'll give you another example, a popular cinematic take of a historical situation. It's not completely accurate, but we'll use it for the sake of this image now: the movie *Amadeus,* about Mozart and Salieri. Salieri is a composer in the great court of Austria. He's a decent composer—he's competent, he's even pretty good—but Mozart's got something else. Mozart's got a gift of grace that's unimaginable. Mozart is post-conventional and wild. He lives outrageously. He's complex, and he's imperfect. When Salieri hears Mozart's music, he's driven insane.

He feels the transmission in it.

He feels the aliveness in it.

Instead of just opening up to it and being delighted in the Unique Self of Mozart, which is different from his Unique Self, Salieri feels this sense of greed and envy coming together. It moves him towards what Joseph Berke, a major psychoanalytic writer in the peer-reviewed journals on malice, calls *annihilating behavior.*

The demarcating characteristic of malice is the move towards annihilating behavior.

I want to read you a section from an essay at the end of the book *Return to Eros*, called The Murder of Eros. It cites this notion of annihilating behavior:

> That's how you know. The way you know that you're actually dealing with the murder of Eros and not with an authentic movement of love is this sense of this annihilating behavior. It's this sense that *if I don't destroy that person, somehow I'll be in some fundamental way not alive in the world.*

Wow. That's the experience of Salieri, who spreads rumors that Mozart is sleeping with teenage girls—his students. So Mozart can't get a job, because he lives from the patronage of people who hire him to tutor their daughters in music. That's actually what happened, and Mozart died young, in poverty, writing his *Requiem*. Wow!

CLAIMING MY UNIQUE LOVEPOWER IS NOT A PSYCHOLOGICAL MOVE

So, I must take responsibility for the Eros of my Unique Self, feel the unique quality of Outrageous Love moving through me, claim my place as *LovePower*, and know that my *LovePower* is different from yours. But I don't claim it psychologically. This is not a psychological move.

- ◆ I claim the quality of *Amor* moving through me.
- ◆ I realize that when I get through my contractions and my blocks, Divinity lives inside of me.

I want to recommend a great movie called *Lucy*. People are like, *Oh, it's a great movie, fun, a lot of action*. No, *Lucy* is about one thing. *Lucy* is about apotheosis. It's about the feminine, but the feminine that lives in all of us, claiming the truth that Divinity, that Infinity, lives in me, in each of us.

It's about unclenching. **When I unclench, I become Outrageous Love incarnate**. I become Ultimate Love and Ultimate Power. In one scene, Lucy is talking to Morgan Freeman, and says, *My only concern is that I want to transmit to the next generation; I want to participate in the evolution* *of consciousness.* The movie ends with Lucy exploding beyond human constraints. And this French police captain who's the ultimate male Eros, and who obviously loves her by this time, says, *Where is she?* She writes into his phone, *I'm everywhere.*

She's become Divinity. She's become Outrageous Love exploded into Reality.

You can get a sense of it. There are different ways to get a sense of this, to expand, to feel this:

- You can feel it through dance.
- You can feel it through prayer.
- You can feel it through journeying in different plant forms.

There are many ways to get to this place. It's not mediated. The church is not going to take you there. There is no organized religion that can claim this. This lives in every generation.

---

*You can awaken this truth in you,
this Eros in you, and become a unique
configuration of Eros and desire with
a unique gift to give, so that literally
all of Reality leans over and yearns to
hear your words, and yearns to feel your
feelings, and yearns to receive your gifts.*

It's not about a public or private stage. Your gift can be given fully in private, in an exchange with a bus driver, with a clerk, in a transformation that takes place in you which you offer up for the sake of the whole.

You become Lucy.

Outrageous love flows through you.

WE'RE GOING TO STOP MURDERING EROS, AND WE'RE GOING TO CELEBRATE EACH OTHER

That is *Homo amor*. That's what we're coming together to do.

Now I just want to ask a hard question. Can you find in yourself that place where you murder Eros? Can I find it in myself? This is not just the people who organize smear campaigns. This is not just the people who write articles and hide their true motivation. There are ways that we *all* murder Eros.

We all seek to murder the person who feels like they're holding a particular kind of life force that I want to have, so I go to murder them in a thousand ways in my mind.

How many of us have in our hearts and minds murdered Eros in a thousand different ways? We always claim noble motivations for it. It hides behind all sorts of fig leaves of piety and purity. Who can find that? So we've got to recognize it first. That's what the code says. *If we don't recognize it, we can't move beyond it.* Wow!

We're making this commitment in this synagogue of *Amor*, in this church of *Amor*, in this atheist center of *Amor*, in this Buddhist dharma center of *Amor*. Whatever it is—it's Native American, it's Aboriginal, it's secular, it's religious—in this gathering of *Amor* that is us, this One Love, One Communion, we are making a commitment together.

We're going to stop murdering Eros. We're going to celebrate each other. The opposite of the murder of Eros is the celebration of Eros.

+ I'm delighted by you.
+ Blow me away.
+ Show me what you can do that I can't. Let me be in devotion to you, and let's be in devotion to each other.

There are many guises for the murder of Eros. If you're saying to yourself, *I don't do that*, you're probably wrong.

Can we go the next step? *There's a place for everybody around the table.* Not all positions are equal. Not everyone is equally right. **People have different skills, different talents, different qualities, so there's a natural hierarchy of talents and skills, but we all have equal value.**

We all have equal fundamental value if we're living from *the celebration of the unique configuration of Eros that's me.*

And I take up my instrument; I play my instrument in the Unique Self Symphony.

CHAPTER TWO

THE ALCHEMY OF HOMO AMOR: TRANSCENDING OUR PERSONAL PAST

Episode 236 — April 18, 2021

WELCOME TO THE REVOLUTION IN LOVE, FOR THE SAKE OF LOVE, AND FOR THE SAKE OF THE FUTURE

My friends, welcome. Good morning, good afternoon, good evening from around the world. Welcome to the revolution. **This is a revolution in love, for the sake of love, and for the sake of the future.** We're poised between utopia and dystopia. We have unimaginable possibility to, literally, create heaven on earth. We have a level of life that we've never had accessible or available to us before.

There are 7.8 billion people, going on eight billion, on the planet; that's an explosion of life. And life is value. We had half a billion people some 150 or 200 years ago. That's unimaginable.

At the same time, precisely those forces that created an explosion of life from half a billion to eight billion lives—that's eight billion lives thriving, pulsing, throbbing, feeling—the very forces that generated that reality also generated a set of structures which will cause Reality to self-terminate.

We've described those structures in great depth, and at their core, their generator function, their root cause, is a failed story. A failed story of what? Of identity:

Who am I? Where does my story of identity come from? What's it rooted in?

We have a failed story of identity because it doesn't meet the data, it doesn't meet our own deepest experience, the data of the interior sciences. Nor does it meet the objective data of what William James called *radical empiricism*; it doesn't meet the data of the exterior sciences.

We have a narrow, paltry, insufficient, distorted narrative of identity that comes from a paltry, insufficient, distorted Universe Story.

Out of those two broken narratives—the broken narrative of *who am I?* and the broken narrative of *where am I?*—we create existential risk and catastrophic risk, risk to our very existence, what we call here *the second shock of existence.*

- The first shock of existence since the dawn of humanity: the death of the individual human being.
- The second shock of existence: the potential death of humanity.

At this moment, poised between utopia and dystopia, there's only one moral imperative, and there's one joy, and there's one ecstatic urgency, and there's one delight.

There's one unimaginably heartrending and heart opening and blowing open Reality that we can do: we can retell the story.

WE NEED TO RE-NARRATE THE STORY OF WHO AM I AND WHERE AM I

When we say *retell the story*, we don't mean an affirmation. We don't mean metaphor. So we have to answer anew those two questions—based on the best information from the interior sciences, and the best information from the exterior scientists. The questions are: *Where am I?* and *Who am I?*

If I have a narrow identity, which is based on—as neuroscience points out and the great traditions do—repeating again and again the traumas of the past where I keep repeating the same old mind, then I'm stuck in the *Groundhog Day* movie with Bill Murray, and I can't get out. I keep repeating the same day. In *Groundhog Day*, they did a freeze-frame on that experience of living the same day again and again by having it be literally the same day.

But actually, we're living the same day again and again, even if the day looks somewhat different. We're basically doing the same thing.

We're lost in the scripts of yesterday, which are scripts of trauma, and scripts of contraction, and scripts of limited emotions, and scripts of—most importantly—limited identity.

We need to re-narrate the story of *who am I?* and *where am I?*

When I re-narrate that story, I begin to effect a transformation. I generate an emergence. I generate an emergence in myself, and I generate an emergence in Reality. It's the emergence of the new human and the new humanity.

I'm already becoming that new human—I'm already, you're already, we're already crossing over every day to the other side. That's our intention.

Who's willing to cross to the other side? Who's ready to become, in our practice today, the new human and the new humanity, to participate in the evolution of love?

We need to evolve what we call the source code of consciousness and culture, to participate in the evolution of the source code of consciousness and culture, which is the evolution of love.

Not by an abstract and arid process of intellectual analysis, but using intellect and heart and mind and body, and weaving together the best validated insights of all the great wisdom traditions and embodying them.

I AM MOVING FROM *HOMO SAPIENS* TO *HOMO AMOR*

I'm no longer *Homo sapiens*. I'm no longer a separate traumatized self replaying the old stories of yesterday.

> *I'm literally revirginated; and when I'm revirginated, I can be loved open by Reality. But not only that, I can love Reality open. I can allure Reality.*

I am able to generate Reality. That's the truth. The simple truth is, I'm not a small *Homo sapiens*; I'm actually *Homo amor*. And *Homo amor* means that *it all lives in me*:

- I live in an Intimate Universe that's interconnected at every level, all the way up and all the way down.
- I share identity with that Intimate Universe and that entire Intimate Universe lives in me. That's the truth.
- I am, quite literally, an incarnation of the Universe in person.
- I'm a personal incarnation of Divinity in person.

◆ I'm a personal incarnation of the Tao in person.

And therefore I'm a creator. Creation's not a one-time event that happened way back when and *we're the passive recipients of a universal causation in which we have no effect.* It's not a cause-and-effect world. It's a world in which we cause the effect. That's what it means to be *Homo amor.* It means that *I am cause.*

I'm not only acted upon. I'm not only an object, buffeted around; but I am subject.

Who is prepared to say, *I am subject?*

I'm no longer merely *Homo sapiens;* I am subject. I am cause of Reality.

I can *trance-end.* I can end the trance and step into a new world and generate that new world.

◆ All of us step into *Homo amor.*
◆ All of us cross over to the other side together.
◆ All of us step into Unique Self and live as irreducibly unique expressions of True Self, not my Myers-Briggs test but me as a unique expression of the entire field of our awesome desire.

We join hands together. Let's hold hands, friends. Let's circle the globe holding hands. Let's breathe together because we're one breath. We hold hands together, then we begin to generate this next step of the self-actualizing Cosmos, the next step of the self-organizing Universe. We begin to awaken in love. We begin to generate a Planetary Awakening in Love through Unique Self Symphonies. That's our intention, that's where we are, and it's the only choice we have, my friends, the only choice.

I remember my dad used to tell me about the 1967 war in Israel, a strange and terrible war that took six days. Israel was surrounded by ten states that all recited Nazi propaganda and said, *We're going to destroy the state and finish the work of the Holocaust.* Terrible moment and, thank God, there's been new possible evolutions in the Arab world and we're not in 1967, but that was a terrible moment. I said to my dad, and I was five years old or something, *How did Israel win?* And he said, *They had no choice.* It was an existential risk.

We have no choice, friends. There are two choices today: Love or die, but not just loving small. *Love* meaning: *become love in person* and *know the physics of it,* and *know the science of it,* and *know its truth.*

I AM A CREATOR IN THE INTERCONNECTED INTIMATE FIELD OF REALITY

Evolutionary Love code:

> Your Unique Self is an expression of the larger Field of LoveIntelligence and LoveBeauty that is the interior face of the Cosmos.

> We call that dimension of Reality—the seamless coat of the Universe—by many names. One name is True Self. Another name is *the field.*

> Using the name of True Self, we can now speak the sacred calculus of Unique Self.

Amor, its insides are lined with love. *Amor. Homo amor. Homo amor* means I am lived by love, I am lived as love, not as an individual, not as a separate self merely, but I'm part of the actual Field of Love and I affect that field. I'm cause in that field. *Wow!* We're going to take that code to the next level.

One of the things that Barbara and I talked about all the time was this new emergence, this new human, this new humanity. Barbara originally called her version of it *Homo universalis* and I talked about *Homo amor.* Then for a while we did *Homo amor universalis,* but Barbara and I decided about a year before Barbara passed that we needed to bring *universalis* into *Homo amor* and that *Homo amor* needed to hold the center, and we agreed together on that name. Every time we say *Homo amor*, we feel Barbara with us.

As long as I'm stuck in the limiting sense of reality—my limiting belief, my limiting emotions, my traumas of yesterday—I'm lost in quiet desperation. But then I realize that:

- I live in a Field of Intimacy and a Field of Interconnectivity where everything's connected to everything else, where nothing exists independently of anything.
- I'm in that Field of Intimacy in which there's utter interconnectivity all the way up and all the way down, and that field is whole; there's a wholeness to that field. There's a quality of wholeness, and everything is non-locally connected. Just as in the body, for example, every one of the hundreds and hundreds of billions and billions of neurons, trillions and trillions and trillions of cells—and, of course, exponentially even more neurons—they're all talking to each other. **There's a wholeness which underlies the entire field.**

That's the exact nature of the Field of Reality. And that field is intimate. That field has a third-person quality—so there are forces that move through it, that drive it: electromagnetism, the strong and weak nuclear, gravitational—but all of those forces are animated by the Infinity that's manifesting as the drive for intimacy.

Infinity desires intimacy, and Infinity drives the field towards ever more wholeness and ever more intimacy. That's the nature of the field. That's the arc of evolution. **The arc of evolution moves towards the Intimate Universe, even when the arc of evolution's very long.** That's always true. It's always happening. *It's never about just this reality.* There's this lifetime, and there's this dimension, but there's a multidimensional Cosmos.

There's a continuity of consciousness, and there's this long, wider field, and in the wider field, in the great arc of Reality, we're participating in the evolution of love.

We are lived as love. We live in an Amorous Cosmos; that Amorous Cosmos lives in us. And the way we would describe that field is as the Infinity of Intimacy. So, God's not just the Infinity of Power; God both holds us and lives in us.

- The New Age meditations got it wrong. It's not just *God lives in me*—God holds us.
- The old religions got it wrong. It's not just that *God holds us*—God lives in us.

Those are both true. At the depth of the Human Potential Movement and at the depth of the classical traditions, this understanding lives at the leading edge, and it's absolutely true. **She lives in us, and as us, and through us, *and* She holds us.**

In prayer, I show up as God kissing God, as God kissing Goddess, as the feminine kissing the masculine, or God kissing God, and Goddess kissing Goddess. I show up as a unique expression of the intimate field yearning for and turning to the field itself, and saying, *Hold me, help me, love me open.*

IN PRAYER I CLARIFY AND RECOGNIZE THE DIGNITY OF MY DESIRE AND MY NEED

I come with my need. I come with everything that I need because *what I need matters,* because I am a unique configuration of intimacy.

I'm not a small self. I'm not a contracted self.

I'm a unique node in the networks of Infinity, with unique needs, and those unique needs are not an accident.

The intention of Cosmos is to manifest me, thee, as unique configurations of intimacy and desire with unique desires and needs, and I've got to clarify my needs.

I have to know, *What do I really need? What's my deepest heart's desire?*

Once I can access my deepest heart's desire and I know that it lives in me, it lives in me *revirginated*—and it's so powerful, and it's so intense that it undoes the sticky power, the pseudo-intensities of addictions and traumas.

My ecstasy, my presence, has to be so powerful that it undoes the pseudo-bonds, the pseudo-intensities of the old dramas, and the old addictions, and the old traumas. The new presencing of this moment, the new creation in this moment, in which *I am cause* and *I am creator* and *I am Homo amor*, has to be so deep, so profound.

As *Homo amor*, the intensification of experience, the transfiguration, needs to be so real that I break out of the bonds of yesterday and I'm free. I'm literally born free.

That process is not a metaphoric process. Some version of that process was described by all the contemplative traditions. They got a lot of things wrong, but they got this core right, and it's validated in the best technologies that are emergent from the new sciences: I can actually break free, and it begins with prayer. I don't isolate into myself.

I turn to the field. I turn to the Infinity of Intimacy that knows my name and holds me even as She lives in me, as me, and through me.

I know the dignity of my need.

I know the dignity of my desire

I clarify my desire.

It's not about a red car. Who wants a red car anyway? Blue. It's about something so much deeper. **It's about being able to show up and, literally, be God in person, be Infinity in person.** There's no greater pleasure, my friends.

When I realize:

- I don't need to be buffeted anymore.
- I'm no longer a side effect in my own life.
- I'm no longer the subject of all sorts of forces moving against me, and on me, and through me from all of the yesterdays that I can't have any impact or transmuting effect on.
- I'm an alchemist.
- I'm a transformationalist.

That's what I was born for. That's not an accident of Cosmos. That's the very intention of Cosmos, that I should be the great *alchemista* of my life.

That transformation, my transformation—my own unique personal transformation for the sake of the whole— is the greatest pleasure of my life.

But I can't do it myself. I've got to turn to Source that lives in me and holds me, to God who's the Infinity of Intimacy and who knows my name, and say, *Please, please, hold me. I need you. I love you madly. Divinity, and I need you.*

Divinity looks at you and says, *I love you madly and I need you too.*

You say, *One second, but I asked first.*

And Divinity says, *Okay, what do you need?*

Then you ask for everything, because prayer to the Infinity of Intimacy affirms the dignity of personal need. You bring to the altar of the Divine, to the altar of She, your holy, my holy, our holy and our broken *Hallelujah* because *there's a blaze of light in every word—it doesn't matter what you heard, the holy or the broken Hallelujah.*

Every place we've been, we needed to be, and nothing was an accident. Every detour is a destination, and all of it's part of the unique configuration of allurement and winding desire that's the particular node in the network of Divinity that is me, that is my unique incarnation.

So let's chant, and when we go into Cohen's *holy and broken Hallelujah*, do it as a meditation, because that's why we're doing it.

You're not listening to a song.

We're not doing blessings to Girl Scouts.

We're going inside and offering on the altar of She our holy and our broken *Hallelujah* and then coming back and praying. Not to the cosmic vending machine god. Not to the mythic, premodern god who's ethnocentric and homophobic, but to the Infinity of Intimacy that courses through me and that holds me and knows my name, and my holy and broken *Hallelujah*. And let's be virgins, my friends. **Let's revirginate: let's be loved open again for the very first time today.**

Hallelujah, and we ask for everything because prayer affirms the dignity of personal need. *Homo amor.* Let's ask for everything, friends, like we never have before.

Oh my God, and let's take all these prayers and let's impress them like a bouquet on the lips of She. She kissing She. We're held in this moment. The Infinity of Intimacy knows our name, and the word is good, and obstacles are melted away, and it's already happening right now. Oh my God.

YOUR UNIQUE SELF IS THE UNIQUE FEATURE OF THE SEAMLESS COAT OF THE UNIVERSE

Let's take a look at this week's evolutionary code. I want to read the code with you, and then I'm going to do a meditation with you on this code. Here's this week's code:

> Your Unique Self is an expression of the larger Field of LoveIntelligence and LoveBeauty that is the interior face of the Cosmos. We call that dimension of Reality the field, the seamless coat of the Universe. The coat of the Universe is seamless, but not featureless, and your Unique Self is a unique feature of that seamless coat of the Universe. You're an irreducible incarnation of that unique field. Using the name True Self, we can speak of the field, and the Field of True Self generates Unique Self.

Now, what does all that mean? Today we're going to talk about the five selves. We're not going to talk about all of them, but we're going to focus on two or three of them. So, we've been doing this *dharma* of the five selves for 11 years, and the first self is the emergence of self, of an experience of self.

When I move from pre-personal to self, I individuate. Margaret Mahler called it *Separation-Individuation*; that's the emergence of separate self. And **the separate self is a blessing; it's a beautiful blessing: I have a sense of agency, a sense of identity**.

Here I am. This is me. I can show up.

I've got a sense that *I've got a unique destiny*. I begin to realize *I'm not my mother*, and *I'm not my surroundings*, and *I'm in relationship with them in some way*. So there's some distinction, some individuation; that's separate self.

The shadow of separate self is when I think *That's all I am*. That's the shadow of this notion of individuating. I think *I'm, ontologically, genuinely separate from the larger field in a fundamental way*. That feeling, that sense of aloneness, that sense of contraction, that's what we call, in the negative sense, the ego.

The healthy ego is the healthy, integrated sense of self, but the ego in its shadow form is a contraction. It's a coiling of Infinity into a finite point and then that finite point dissociates from the larger Field of Infinity.

In that dissociation, in this attention fixation on the contraction where I think, *That's all I am*—that's the source of pain, that's the source of suffering. If my attention is stuck on that materialist contraction, then I keep looping again and again. I loop. I keep looping through yesterday and looping through the old traumas and I can never get out of them, and that's called "false self." False self is all the distorted forms of separate self, which we're not going to talk about today.

The beginning of the transformation is to actually give a better answer, a more factual answer, a more accurate answer, an honest answer, a true answer to the question of *who are you?*

The only way to respond to existential risk, which is sourced in a broken answer to that question, out of which comes a broken story—a success story governed by win/lose metrics that drives extraction models, and exponential growth curves that self-terminate—is to answer the question, *Who are you?* in a more accurate way.

Now, stay close and let's step into this meditation. Let's see if we can access in this moment the answer to the question of *who are you?*

Who are you? Is it true that you're a separate self? **We know that it's not true that I'm a separate self because we know that I *yearn to move beyond myself.***

We know that if I live on an island by myself, even though I have all of my needs taken care of, I'm fundamentally devastated. We know that I yearn for contact; I yearn for interiority, to touch interiority. I yearn to create. We know, based on the deepest realization of the interior sciences and the exterior sciences, that I'm not separate self, but I'm actually True Self.

True Self: I am consciousness, and I am in intimacy with the whole

---

When I really understand the realization of True Self, I awaken to the realization of Unique Self. When I really understand the realization of uniqueness, I awaken to Evolutionary Unique Self.

TRUE SELF, UNIQUE SELF, AND EVOLUTIONARY UNIQUE SELF

So, let's understand: *what do we mean by True Self?* The way True Self is usually understood, my friends, is *I go inside, and I meditate on my inner nature.* I realize, *Oh, I have a hand, but I'm not my hand.* I have a hand, so I'm an *I* that has a hand. Beautiful.

Then I realize I have emotions, but I'm not my emotions because I have emotions.

Then I realize I have thoughts, but I'm not my thoughts because I am having thoughts.

So, *Who am I?*

- I'm the *I* that's aware of my emotions.
- I'm the *I* that's aware of my body.
- I'm the *I* that's aware of my thoughts.
- I'm aware of my awareness. And that's considered, in some deep way, the *summum bonum* of meditation.

And that's important; it's important to know that the essence of who I am is consciousness, is awareness, because then I realize the power of my intention.

But awareness of awareness is insufficient; that's just the beginning of True Self. You see, when we define anything, my friends—what is something made up of? Something's made up of something that's deeper than its parts. The parts come together and there's a *synergy*, and a synergy means that there's a new whole greater than the sum of its parts. You can't define something in terms of the sum of its parts. You can't even define it in terms of the sum of its qualities. There's a new wholeness that's actually generated. This new wholeness means that there's an intimacy between the parts and the parts share identity. So the subatomic particles come together, and they form an atom:

- The atom is a new identity. It's a shared identity.
- There's mutuality of pathos when it's healthy; all the parts can feel each other.
- There's mutuality of recognition; all the parts recognize each other.
- There's mutuality of purpose; all the parts move together towards a shared destiny.

This is going to take us into what True Self means and into what Unique Self means. In this guided, meditative moment—this is what my friend the Dalai Lama called an "analytic meditation"—in which we go inside to contemplate the true nature of Reality.

THE WHOLE UNIVERSE GIVES RISE TO AN ATOM

So, if I asked you, *Do atoms exist and are atoms real?* Well, yes and no. What does exist mean? What does it mean to be real? If you frame it in a classical, limited scientific way, you'd say, *Well, of course atoms are real. That's a silly question.*

Why are atoms real? Well, because the atom has different dimensions, different properties, and those different properties allow us to predict, to know what the atom's going to do. An atom has proton radius, an atom has atomic radius, an atom has molecular properties; but actually when those properties come together, they're greater than the sum of the parts. They share an identity, but that's not the entire identity of an atom. That's not what an atom is by itself.

If the parts were what an atom was, an atom would not exist. An atom would not be real. There's something else that defines an atom. There's a wider field. The atom also has a larger context, which is part of the atom's identity:

- For example, there's no atom without the Higgs field.
- There's no atom without the electromagnetic field.
- There's no atom without the fine-structure constant, or without the strong force, or without gluons.

Without all those fields, there's literally no existence, there's no reality to the atom. And we could add almost ad infinitum to those dimensions that *seem to be outside the identity of the atom*. And we realize that *without them, there's no atom*.

Let's begin to understand what we're saying. **If I begin to understand that the whole universe gives rise to an atom, that ontologically the atom is inseparable from this wider field, then I can say that the atom's real**. But I need to understand that there's no way to approach the identity of the atom without the Higgs field, without the electromagnetic field, without the nature of the subject that's perceiving the object of the atom.

Then I begin to understand what Einstein meant when he said it's an optical delusion to believe that there are separate things at all. I begin to understand that to understand anything, you have to start with understanding everything. I begin to understand what Master Dogen meant when he said, *Enlightenment is intimacy with all things.*

ALL OF REALITY EXISTS IN INTIMACY, ALL THE WAY UP AND ALL THE WAY DOWN

I begin to understand what we mean in our First Principles and First Values when we say that intimacy is not just a feeling. Intimacy means something. **Intimacy means shared identity with the larger field.** *I'm a free, generative unique node in the Field of Intimacy and Desire.* Let's feel this for a second. Let's feel this in relationship to myself. I begin to understand something which is wildly beautiful and insanely profound: I cannot talk about myself in a limited way.

Yes, there's a boundary of my self-organized experience; there's something to be said for my personhood. But my personhood includes a much wider Field of Identity.

Yes, there are certain genetics that lives in me. Yet there's also this wider field of bacteria, and viral movements coursing through me, and molecules coming from plants. All the stuff that's outside of me, all that stuff outside of my self-organizing boundary, is also me.

If I go into my body, I realize:

- ◆ I've got organs, and I've got organ systems.
- ◆ Then I've got tissues, then I've got cells.
- ◆ Then I've got molecules, and I've got atoms, and I've got subatomic particles.

I realize all of that; all the fields that live in them are part of the very definition of who I am.

Then from the interior perspective, all the various movements of Spirit are part of my identity:

- All the various movements of desire
- All the various allurements
- All the various configurations of the divine field
- All of the various Fields of Consciousness

All of that is part of my identity.

I understand that my identity goes down to the very foundation of Reality itself, beneath quantum mechanics, and I can't speak of self without that.

At the same time, I understand that there are quantum phenomena interacting to create the emergent property of classicality around the level of atoms that generate me, and that there's a profound ontic emergence all the way up and all the way down.

None of me and none of thee exists independently of all these top-down and bottom-up forces—and without all of it, I quite literally would not exist. So I am, if I understand the true nature of myself, not merely a separate self. I am True Self, and True Self means that I am a unique interactivity in the seamless coat of the Universe.

> *I'm not just True Self. It's not just a Field of Interconnectivity. I'm a unique node; I'm a unique feature.*

The seamless coat of the Universe is seamless, but not featureless. There's a standing wave and there are nodes in that standing wave.

I AM A FREE, GENERATIVE NODE IN THE FIELD OF INTIMACY

I'm a part that's part of a larger whole, that itself is part of a larger whole, which is in turn part of a larger whole. I'm part of this larger Field of Interconnectivity and Intimacy that's defined by the experience of allurement and desire. I'm not just in the Field of Intimacy and Desire, but *I'm a unique node in that field.*

I *uniquely* stand at the very center of that field. There's not one center, but there are multiple centers in mathematical cosmology today. I am one of those multiple centers and I'm not just affected by the universal causation, which generates me, but *I am cause.* That's what it means to be a Unique Self. It means that my unique node in the middle of that field is generative and free.

All of the fields acting on me all the way up and all the way down—that hold me, that are part of my identity, that seem to cause me and that do cause me—are also moved by my central node in the midst of it all, which is my irreducible uniqueness.

And my irreducible uniqueness is cause. **I'm both generated by the entire cause and effect, which is part of my very profound, intimate identity, and I cause the effect.**

I am, literally, cause of Reality.

To be a Unique Self is to know that *I'm not just an object affected by cause and effect, but I am subject, which is cause.*

To be a Unique Self is to know that *I'm the irreducibly unique cause of all of Reality.*

And I am not just Unique Self; I'm *Evolutionary* Unique Self, meaning the entire process of evolution moves through me. I'm not transcending my ego; that's not the focus. **I'm aligning with the evolutionary impulse, which is the unique configuration of the intimacy, Eros, and desire that lives in me, as me, and through me, which causes Reality.**

In that precise sense, I am not merely created, but I am the creator. I am not merely caused, but I am cause. That's the new mind that's birthed in me in every day, in every moment, and I have but one question.

> *There's one question, which is the ultimate Unique Self practice, and the question is: what does Reality need me to cause in the very next moment?*

I am True Self. I am part of the field. The field moves in me. I'm not an isolated or discrete atom. I'm made up of trillions and trillions of atoms which are held by the Higgs field, and which are held by the electromagnetic field, and which are held in the field of the gluon, and which are held by all of those properties, and all of the quantum reality, all the way up and all the way down, all of the biosphere generated by the quantum reality—all that lives in me.

All of evolution, quite literally, lives inside of me. And the Divine voice turns to me and says, *na'aseh adam, let us, you and me together create Reality in our image*. I literally become Divine; I literally become *Metatron*.

This is where the reality of the interior sciences meets the reality of the exterior sciences, and we realize *it's all one*. There's no separation; there's no split.

And anything less will leave me devastated, pained, contracted. It's the pain of my clothes not fitting; it's the pain of experiencing myself coiled and contracted so much smaller than I am.

The great truth of Cosmos, my friends, is who we really are.

When I know who I am and I cry out, *Here I am, I'm ready to be*—and I link hands with other Unique Selves, and we join together and we create and generate the next stage of the self-actualizing Cosmos, the next level of the self-organizing Universe—then we unleash a cascading force of love, of Eros, unlike any of the top-down, command-and-control systems could have ever dreamed of.

That's how we respond to existential risk: not just by avoiding dystopia, but by becoming utopia in person ourselves.

Homo sapiens becomes Homo amor.

That's true. That's real. It's the most accurate understanding of Cosmos we have. That's the way of the heart, the one heart, the one love that beats uniquely in each one of us, allowing each one of us to be cause of Reality.

CHAPTER THREE

BECOMING THE NEW HUMAN, HOMO AMOR: STRATEGIES OF SEDUCTION AND UNFURNISHING THE EYES OF CONSCIOUSNESS

Episode 294 — May 29, 2022

REALITY IS A LOVE STORY, AND WE ARE THAT STORY: BETWEEN UTOPIA AND DYSTOPIA

Welcome, everyone!

Every week we do a recapitulation of the *dharma*—the First Values and First Principles that we are articulating in this moment poised between utopia and dystopia:

- A utopia that's unimaginable. A level of human depth, and human thriving, and human joy, and human capacitating of goodness, truth, and beauty—unrivaled in human history.
- And dystopia, a degradation of humanity. A degradation so intense that it becomes existential risk—the death of humanity.

Existential risk has been termed as such by Nick Bostrom at the beginning of the 2000s. It was a good term to

39

describe something that had been well articulated in the 50 years before by people like Robert Jay Lifton, in a book called *Facing Apocalypse*. Existential risk—in other words, risk to our very existence.

At this moment in time, there is a *catastrophic risk*, which causes suffering to billions of people, and particularly to the least advantaged, to the half of the planet, or to two-thirds of the planet, that are vulnerable in a very radical way.

Now, we are all vulnerable, and the illusion of safety is just an illusion. But the vulnerability of a third of the planet at the lowest socio-economic level, and then even the next third, is intensely more stark and more dangerous, than the upper third or fourth or fifth of the planet.

Catastrophic risk means a devastation to the billions of the most vulnerable.

But existential risk is a threat to the existence of humanity itself, which is real.

Over the next, let's say, 100 to 800 years, according to the best crunching of the numbers, the actuarial tables of human continuity, there's a very significant possibility of us disappearing.

And it will not happen because a meteor strikes the Earth.

The disappearance will happen because of the *animating algorithm* we have created at the center of our culture.

It's an algorithm of the interiors—an algorithm that's running our interiors—which means *story*. **The interior algorithm of humanity is a story** because we live, and think, and are animated by stories.

THE ANIMATING ENERGY OF REALITY TODAY IS
THE ALGORITHM OF A SUCCESS STORY

This story at the center of our culture is a success story. We called it Success 2.0 in a conference we did six years ago.

Success 1.0 is the classical success of the premodern, medieval period: success within my religion, and obedience to God.

Success 2.0, the modern story of Reality, is **rivalrous conflict, governed by win/lose metrics,** in which I have to get ahead and self-commodify in order to exist—and it's win/lose metrics all the way up and all the way down.

For example, there's a race to the bottom. It's called the tragedy of the commons, or a multipolar trap:

- We know, for example, that there are certain kinds of artificial intelligence that we should not develop, and we should make an agreement not to develop it.
- But because win/lose metrics are the animating ethos, or story, of Reality, everyone's afraid that someone else is going to break the agreement and do it.
- Since they're going to do it, since they're going to secretly create that kind of artificial intelligence—and therefore they will dominate and destroy and control us—then we have to do it as well.
- And so, even though we all know that kind of artificial intelligence, for example, should not be created, we create it anyways because of the multipolar trap that *if we don't, they will.* (That's just an example of one existential risk.)

Because the animating energy of Reality today is the algorithm of the success story. That's what drives the system in a thousand ways that we've talked about many times here.

What we understand is that there's only one response that's actually effective from a human perspective, and the response has to be the telling of a new story.

A new algorithm is a new story of intrinsic value. We have to actually download a new algorithm. Not an exterior science algorithm, but, if you will, an interior algorithm. I'm using the word *algorithm* in the interior sense, *mytho-poetically*.

A new algorithm is a new Story of Value, rooted in First Principles and First Values, that tells a different story about who we are and ushers in a new human and a new humanity.

In response to what used to be called *Armageddon*, and is now called *existential risk*—we offer a Messianic vision. Not the old Messianic vision, not the old vision of *Messiah* as a response to Armageddon. But rather— the new vision, the new human and the new humanity: *Homo sapiens* becoming *Homo amor*. The new story of what it means to be a human being.

A new way of being human—which becomes the new source code of Reality itself and its interior rhythms—is the single most effective response we have to existential risk.

That means it's the single greatest and most potent and most necessary response to the possible advent of the greatest suffering for the greatest number of human beings that's ever been known in history.

That's what we're doing here at *One Mountain*. If I sound urgent about it, I *am* urgent about it. But it's an ecstatic urgency—because what a privilege it is to be a human being, and to be in this conversation, and to be working together to evolve the source code. It's an ecstatic urgency—because in the end, in whatever dimension, however Reality plays out in its multi-dimensionality, I understand that **Reality is a love story**. That it's moving, ultimately, towards ever greater and ever deeper forms of goodness, truth, and beauty, to ever greater and ever deeper forms of love. That we participate in that story.

We are not living *in* the story; we *are* the story. We are both the storytellers of Reality—so we *tell* the story—and we are creating the story, so we're actually *enacting* the story. It's so insanely beautiful.

We have to tell the new story by gathering new information and reweaving that information into a new whole. That's what the new story is—we are gathering the best strands of validated gnosis (information) from premodern traditional, modern, and postmodern knowing, weaving it together in a new way to enact a new Story of Value.

Then we don't just *enact* that Story of Value, we don't just *tell* that Story of Value, we *are* that story. We become the new human, and we actually cross to the other side.

WE ARE HERE TO ENACT A NEW REALITY

In one of the original texts of civilization, when they tell the story of one of the crossers to the other side, they name him the Hebrew, *Avraham ha Ivri, Abraham, the Hebrew*. The word Hebrew means *le'avra akher ivri, he crosses to the other side*.

That's what we are here to do. We're here to cross to the other side. **We're here to tell the new Story of Value, and to cross to the other side.**

So, who's up for it? Who wants to cross to the other side? That's what we are here to do.

It's not just a podcast, although I guess it *is* a podcast. It's not just *One Mountain, Many Paths*, although it totally *is One Mountain, Many Paths*.

But we are here as revolutionaries.

We are here to enact a new Reality.

We are here to move from *Homo sapiens* to *Homo amor*. *Homo amor*, a human being who is the unique configuration of Evolutionary Love; a human being who is an irreducibly unique expression of the LoveIntelligence and LoveBeauty that's the initiating and animating Eros of All-That-Is, that lives in us, as us, and through us.

So, who is ready to cross to the other side?

Let us set our intention. Are we ready to cross to the other side? Who's ready? I am ready. Can we do this together? Can we cross to the other side together?

Who is on the other side? **Let's go the whole way in this lifetime.**

My beloved evolutionary partner, Barbara Marx Hubbard, used to say, *Marc, are you ready to go the whole way in this lifetime?* Barbara, who is with us today—because there's continuity of consciousness, and all the dimensions are related to each other—Barbara, who passed three years ago, *I am with you and you are with me, and there is continuity.*

Let us hold hands, and let's turn to each other—all of us. Are we ready to cross to the other side? Are we ready to go the whole way in this lifetime?

Are we ready to be the evolutionary impulse in love that stands at the abyss of darkness? Are we ready to say, *let's tell a new Story of Value, let there be light?* Yes, we are excited about it.

UNBEARABLE TRAGEDY AND UNBEARABLE JOY

We are wildly excited about it; we are ecstatically urgent.

And we cry out of one side of our eyes at the unbearable tragedy of someone shooting children.

What does that even mean, that someone shoots children, in the United States, in Texas?

The unbearable tragedy in the Sudan.

The unbearable tragedy in Ethiopia.

The unbearable tragedies playing out in Russia and the Ukraine—and any place, and every place in the world.

Yet, understand: at the same time that there's unbearable tragedy, there's exponentially more unbearable joy.

> *Human beings are committing billions of Outrageous Acts of Love every second. Human beings are breathing and living love, despite the fact that the story is breaking down.*

We need to now reanimate the story, and we need to up-level.

We need to participate in the evolution of love.

But human beings are gorgeous; human beings are beautiful.

We need to articulate, as humanity, the next vision of what it means to be human.

That's what we are here to do together. Oh my God, what a crazy, insane joy and delight, to be here together! Thank you, everyone.

We're going to talk about *seducing yourself*, and we're going to talk about music, and we're going to talk about how we see, and how we arouse, and how we awaken, and what that means, and how that changes my life and my relationships, and how I *be* in the world literally forever and ever.

BECOMING LINEAGE HOLDERS IN THE GREAT TRADITION

We have a group of people who are lineage holders. We have been studying together for—some of us over a decade, some of us a little less or a little more—and we have been deep in these First Principles and First Values.

These First Principles and First Values are an expression of a lineage that we are creating.

By *lineage*, we mean:

It is rooted in the depth of the validated insights of the ancient traditions, and integrated with that depth:

- And in the depths of the best gnosis of modernity
- And the best insight of postmodernity
- But grounded in all of the depth of gnosis that's actually *moving within the community*

Someone who steps into that, and who masters a piece of it and studies intently, becomes **what the great traditions called a *lineage holder*.**

It's very different from the Human Potential Movement, or the New Age world, or the fundamentalist world. We're actually borrowing a page from the great traditions, which spoke in terms of lineage, meaning we are creating this body of knowing.

We're going to talk today about how we create that body of knowing.

That's what today's topic is: **how do you seduce yourself into this gnosis, into this body of knowing?**

That's the same thing as *how do you become the new human,* which is the same thing as *how do you become Homo amor,* which is the same thing as *how do I become an Outrageous Lover?*

That's how I respond to existential and catastrophic risk, which is how I evolve the source code of consciousness and culture, which is the evolution of love. It's all part of the same fabric.

But we're calling that a lineage holder. What that means is:

- There's a depth of lineage.
- There's a depth of transmission.
- There's a depth of rigor.
- There's a depth of commitment.
- There's a depth of study.
- There's a depth of practice.

To be a lineage holder means that I actually step in—often I have the privilege of doing what we call Holy of Holies (private study), and we study also in a group context—and I become a master of one piece of this new meta-theory, this new lineage, this vision of First Values and First Principles.

Of course, anyone is welcome.

In this lineage, it's all about individuating as the most powerful and gorgeous and magnificent version of your Unique Self, to play your instrument in the Unique Self Symphony. Articulating that is what we're about.

At the festival this summer—we have been wanting to do this for the last three or four years, but we ran into Covid and other challenges—for the first time, we're going to have an empowerment ceremony for lineage holders.

Claire Molinard is one of those lineage holders, and she's in the lineage of the entire set of First Principles and First Values, with a particular concentration and focus on Unique Self:

- The Unique Self teaching
- The Unique Self enlightenment teaching
- The Unique Self theory
- The Unique Self psychological theory
- The Unique Self coaching

We are partnering and enacting a Unique Self Institute, which will be the holder of this Unique Self, this particular piece of First Values and First Principles.

WE ARE A BAND OF OUTRAGEOUS LOVERS

Everybody is welcome.

At the center of the community is a revolution—a revolution of love, in response to present and potential suffering, in response to existential risk. This community is evolution awakening to itself.

And the one ground rule of the community is Outrageous Love, meaning, we don't get lost in politics. In other words, we work things out.

There are issues that come up, but, to the best of our ability, we do it with an enormous sense of sincerity, clarity, joy, laughter, and hopefully with strategy and with skill and with wisdom. **We don't bypass issues; we work through them.**

This is a place—I hope and pray, and I am super proud of our community—where the inside of the community and the outside of the community are the same. There are no backrooms filled—as they often are—with all sorts of things that violate what is being spoken in public.

We're doing our best to *be* the new human, to be lived as love, which is what we need to do to invoke this new human and the new humanity.

I just wanted to explain what a lineage holder is. I just wanted to share a little bit of a fragrance of what our lineage is.

Perhaps one more thing. We are saying:

- At the center of the community is not one person.
- At the center of the community are the First Principles and First Values.
- At the center of community is the vision.
- At the center of the community, yes, there's hopefully strong teaching, and there are strong students, and there are new emergent teachers.

Because this revolution is going to happen when there are twenty strong and powerful teachers, who then raise up themselves twenty more strong and powerful teachers, who are committed, who are rigorous, who are uniquely creative, playing their Unique Self instrument in the Unique Self Symphony.

Transmission is critical.

Living presence is critical.

The transmission of the inner quality of the *dharma* is critical.

The articulation of it is critical.

But in the end, it can never be dependent on one person. Different individual people hold it at different times, but then it's transmitted to people. **Lineage holders receive the teaching, and they mediate and refract it through the prism of their Unique Selves.**

There is a radical commitment, there is a Unique Self creativity, and there is a higher individuation beyond ego. And what emerges is a planetary awakening in love through Unique Self Symphonies.

Does it get much better than that? I don't think so.

REALITY NEEDS YOU TO SEDUCE YOURSELF TO YOUR OWN GREATNESS

This week's Evolutionary Love code says: there's no love without seduction.

Our topic this week is *seduce yourself*, and we are in a series of talks around this topic. The Delphic Oracle said: *Know Thyself.* But this *know* is carnal: *Adam knew his wife Eve.* It's sensual.

Sensemaking is sensual.

To know yourself is to make sense out of yourself, even as we stand before the mystery.

Carnal knowledge, the sensuality of sensemaking—in the CosmoErotic Universe, in the Amorous Cosmos, which is a love story—requires *seduction.* Because seduction itself is a First Principle and First Value of Cosmos.

Two weeks ago, we talked about these two kinds of seduction:

- We talked about an *unholy* seduction, in which I seduce someone to break their appropriate boundary for the sake of my greed.
- It is juxtaposed with *sacred* seduction, in which I seduce someone to break their contracted boundary, the boundary of their limitation, for the sake of their own deepest need.

Of course, that applies not just to the seduction of other, but even more profoundly, to self-seduction.

Seduce thyself is the new Oracle.

The *Homo amor* oracle says: Seduce Thyself.

This means **I have to seduce myself to break the boundary of my limitation and the boundary of my contraction—because that is my own deepest need.**

It's not only my own deepest need, but as Meir ibn Gabbai, a great interior scientist of the 16th century, writes, *avodah tzorech Gavoha*, *"Reality needs your service."*

We are going to talk about that deeply this week, because that's going to lead us to next week, which is about *confessing your greatness.*

Two weeks ago, we said wisdom is to distinguish between holy and unholy seduction—holy seduction seduces upwards; unholy seduction seduces downwards:

- Unholy seduction: I seduce you to violate your appropriate boundary for the sake of my greed.
- Holy seduction: I seduce you to transcend the boundary of the limitation of your contraction, for the sake of your and Reality's deepest need.

Let's add to that.

If the ultimate human self is a separate self, **if separate self is the end of the whole story—a separate self defined by their boundaries—then** *don't violate my boundaries.* That's how a separate self defines itself. If that is the ultimate human—which is how Western society generally understands the human being—then, if I seduce you to violate your separate self, I am causing you to regress. Because if separate self is the ultimate—that's the personal—then the only place to go is *down*, to the pre-personal.

But if I understand that there is a larger Field of Existence in which you live, and **the larger field in which you live is your True Self**—you actually participate in the seamless coat of the Universe, you participate in the Field of Desire, or True Self. The total number of True Selves is one (as Ervin Schrodinger, the physicist, wrote: *the singular that has no plural*), then you seduce yourself even more deeply into your Unique Self, which is your irreducible unique individuation of the Field of True Self.

Unique Self is the unique set of eyes, the unique quality of intimacy, and the unique capacity, that individuated expression of the Field of True Self, of the Field of Consciousness and Desire, that is you and that is me, that's your Unique Self. Then **I locate that Unique Self in an evolutionary context**, this wider evolutionary context in which I realize I am uniquely *evolution*, and evolution is throbbing and pulsing in me. That's Evolutionary Unique Self.

Then, as an Evolutionary Unique Self in this larger evolutionary context—I am a unique expression of the Eros of Cosmos; I am a unique expression of Evolutionary Love—I then take up my instrument and **play my music in the Unique Self Symphony,** this self-organizing and self-actualizing Cosmos through Unique Self Symphonies, in which each of us, individually and together in groups of Unique Selves, address the unique needs in our unique circle of intimacy and influence.

Then we generate *Homo amor*. That's what *Homo amor* is; that's the new human and the new humanity.

If *that's* seduction, if you seduce yourself to that—then seduce thyself!

Then we have to seduce each other to our True Self, we have to seduce each other to our Unique Self, and we have to seduce each other to our Evolutionary Unique Self. We have to seduce each other musically to join the Unique Self Symphony.

That is our context.

SEDUCTION TO INVOKE THE NEW HUMAN AND THE NEW HUMANITY

These are meditations on seduction to invoke the new human and the new humanity, meditations on seduction to seduce ourselves from *Homo sapiens* to *Homo amor*, to cross to the other side.

Let me introduce something about this topic that we all know intuitively. And I would call that topic *music*.

The most powerful instrument of seduction is clearly music. Music seduces. Music changes our mood. And the move from *Homo sapiens* to *Homo amor* takes place when we change our mood, and then when we change the mood of culture.

Heidegger was not wrong when he said *everything's about mood*. Mood is the fundamental category of Reality itself.

So we have to change our mood.

We have to deepen our mood.

Music changes our mood at its core. It was Aldous Huxley who reminded us that music discloses the blessedness that is at the heart of all things. It has been here from the beginning of time.

The preponderance of music—its rhythms, melodies, and lyrics—speak of love. **Music is about love songs.** It may be personal love, or its loss. It may be the love of spirit, of nature, of country, or their loss. But music is always about love: its agonies and ecstasies, its devotions and demands, its rapture and ravaging. That's always at the center of music. Music is love songs in all of their myriad forms.

And music itself is the inner form of mathematics. The avowedly anti-materialist, transcendentalist woman, Margaret Fuller (a close colleague of the New England Transcendentalists)—she died at age 40, a brilliant woman—she echoes the pre-Socratic Pythagoreans when she writes:

All truth is comprised in music and mathematics.

But music itself does not exist before the manifest world of matter emerges. There is no music before there is matter, for **sound itself is made of matter.** Sound is an expression of one of the earliest forms of matter, gravitational waves.

Gravitational waves—disclosed by Einstein's mathematical formula, but discovered experimentally only in 2015 with the help of a three-kilometer-long tuning fork, if you will—the gravitational waves that form music are an expression of time.

Music is an expression of time—which is not separate from space, as disclosed in Einstein's theory of relativity—and rooted in mathematics.

So we live in, and we are composed of, the space-time continuum. Music, at its core, is made up *not* of notes of sound. Rather, music is made up of what sound *is* at its core.

MUSIC IS MADE OF ATOMS OF TIME

If you go back to the Big Bang, when the single point of the Singularity stretches itself out in a line, time is birthed into Reality. Within that line of time, there is continuity. Moments distinguish themselves. It is the distinction of moments that allows for chords and harmonies.

It is in the distinction of moments, in the break in the continuity of time, that rhythm and melody are born.

Now this gets wild. Once we realize that music is the stuff of time, and that we ourselves are made of time, then we further realize that **we are made of music.** Let me say that again.

We ourselves are made of time, because time is part of the space-time continuum. It is part of matter. That original matter in the first nanoseconds of the Big Bang, when the space-time continuum is born, lives in us. We are composed of it.

Once we realize that music is the stuff of time, and that we ourselves are made of time, we further realize that we are made of music. So, the music that seduces us lives inside of us.

CLEANSING THE DOORS OF PERCEPTION: UNFURNISH YOUR EYES

That was the end—and now let's go back to the beginning.

How do we seduce ourselves? **We seduce ourselves by knowing the true nature of Reality.**

Seduction is knowledge—carnal knowledge. It's *Know Thyself*, which means: love yourself open, make love, and birth your highest self, through knowing your true nature and knowing the nature of Reality.

When I know the nature of Reality, what do I know?

- I know that Reality is Eros at its core. Reality is love. Not love which is mere human sentiment—but love which is the heart of existence itself. Love is Eros, the heart of existence itself, that lives uniquely in me.
- I am a unique configuration of Eros that participates in the Field of Eros.
- I know that Eros is real, that Love is real.
- I know that Reality is not merely a fact; Reality is a story.
- I know that story is a First Value and First Principle of Cosmos, and that story is a love story.
- It's a story of Eros and the evolution of Eros.

I have to seduce myself to that knowledge. I have to seduce myself to that *gnosis* that lives in me.

To do that, I have to unfurnish my eyes.

How did Emily Dickinson write it?

Not Revelation—'tis—that waits, but our unfurnished eyes.

If I would but *cleanse the doors of perception*, then I would realize that *everything I look upon is infinite*, wrote William Blake.

So I've got to unfurnish my eyes. But what eyes do I have to unfurnish?

Barbara and I talked about this a lot, and I'm going to talk about them in a completely new way.

THE EYE OF THE FLESH, THE EYE OF THE SENSES

The first eye is what we might call *the Eye of the Flesh*, or *the Eye of the Senses*.

The Eye of the Flesh, or the Eye of the Senses, is *empirical*—meaning I have direct access to gnosis, or knowledge.

- I want to know if it's raining outside—I go outside and I put my hand out. *Oh, there's rain. It's raining. Okay, got it, it's raining.*
- I do an experiment, or what Thomas Kuhn called an injunction. I get a result, an illumination, a new gnosis, a new piece of knowledge.
- Then, as Karl Popper said, it's verifiable, because I can ask someone else to do that same injunction or that same experiment, and if they do it consistently and rigorously, they'll get some version of the same result.

That's the Eye of the Senses.

Now, scientism made a claim—not modern, true science, not classical science, but the dogmas of modern science. It said, the only real empiricism on which valid science is based is the empiricism of the Eye of the Senses, and another eye that we'll describe in a moment.

They call it sensory empiricism: *It's only true if I can see it under a microscope, if the Eye of the Senses reveals it to me.* The Eye of the Senses might be my eyes, it might be a telescope, it might be a microscope, it might be an fMRI machine charting the waves of the brain, or it might be the Hubble telescope.

But the Eye of the Senses, or the Eye of the Flesh—that's the first eye—operates together with a second eye. The second eye can see dimensions of Reality that the first eye can't see.

Now, you need the Eye of the Senses; you can't move without the senses, and you have to develop them very deeply, but they're insufficient, because there are all sorts of things you can't see with the Eye of the Senses. For example, the Eye of the Senses can't see mathematics. They can't see logic. They can't see moral reasoning, or classical political reasoning.

THE EYE OF THE MIND, THE EYE OF REASON

Moral reasoning, mathematics, and logic are available, not to the Eye of the Senses, but to the second eye, and we'll give it two different names. We might call that the Eye of the Mind, or the Eye of Reason.

Those two eyes (flesh and mind), though, cannot tell me anything about that which matters most to me.

They can tell me only what lives in the world of the measurable (or at least, that's the way it's usually understood).

- Because they can't tell me about love, and surely, they can't tell me that love is real.
- They can't tell me about loyalty.
- They can't really tell me about spirit.
- They can't tell me about value.
- They can't tell me about the immeasurable;
- They can't tell me about the priceless.

So the Eye of the Senses and the Eye of the Mind tell me important things about the measurable, and they tell me important things about the commodifiable. They allow for modern science. They give me massive empirical information.

The Eye of the Senses gives me sensory empiricism, and the Eye of the Mind gives me what we might call mental empiricism.

It's beautiful, but they can't tell me about consciousness.

THE EYE OF CONSCIOUSNESS

I want to introduce a third eye, and I want to call it the Eye of Consciousness.

The third eye has four expressions.

1. One is **the Eye of the Heart**: that which I see through the heart. The Sufis use that word a lot.
2. The second, used more often by, let's say, the Buddhist world or the Vedanta world—let's call it **the Eye of Contemplation.**
3. A third word, which I coined a bunch of months ago, we'll call it **the Eye of Value.**
4. A fourth word, used by Christian mystics, is **the Eye of the Spirit.**

These are four expressions of the Eye of Consciousness. Now, we are articulating this new understanding in First Values and First Principles. There's an Eye of Consciousness, and it has four expressions.

But what's the difference between these four expressions? Are these just overlapping or inter-included? Well, they are all expressions of the Eye of Consciousness.

But **each expression of the Eye of Consciousness involves a somewhat different practice,** a somewhat different injunction.

I'm going to do this just very loosely in two minutes, although this takes several hours to unpack. But just to get it for a second, let's say the Eye of

Contemplation might involve meditation. The Eye of the Heart might be opened through the practice of loving.

- In the Eye of Contemplation, you might sit Zazen in Buddhism; you might *meditate your way to enlightenment.*
- In the Eye of the Heart, you might do what I like to call *loving your way to enlightenment.* The actual injunction, the practice is to be an Outrageous Lover. The practice is not meditating; the practice is to love.

Now those eyes, of course, can live together with each other. But the question is, *what's the primary practice?*

The primary practice in the Eye of the Heart is love.

The primary practice is to become an *Outrageous Lover,* to write *Outrageous Love Letters.*

It is not *cute.*

It is not *sweet.*

It is not *lovely.*

It is the ultimate practice.

It is the injunction that opens the Eye of the Heart—that you actually love your way into being *Homo amor.*

The Eye of Value, the third expression of the Eye of Consciousness, means you actually *see value directly.* You see goodness, and you identify goodness. And you understand that goodness is a discernment of the Eye of Value.

So, you say, *Reality should be fair.* Why should Reality be fair? Because your Eye of Value discerns that fairness, or justice, or Lady Justice, is an expression of the Field of Consciousness.

You discern Reality through ethics, and there's kind of an ethical mono-pantheism. Ethos suffuses Reality; value suffuses Reality. Reality is a Field of Value, and you're able to discern value directly, so you enter through the door of value.

Finally, the fourth expression of the Eye of Consciousness, the Eye of the Spirit, comes from *doing ritual*. I actually do ritual in a particular tradition: I do ceremony, I study sacred texts. In other words, I engage in the classical expressions of the spiritual, which give me direct access to the Field of Spirit, or to the Field of Consciousness.

So these four eyes have different practices, and each one opens a somewhat different quality of the Field of the Infinite, the Field of the True Self, or the Field of Consciousness.

REALITY ALL THE WAY UP AND ALL THE WAY DOWN IS PAN-INTERIORITY

Now we're about to make the leap. It's about to get crazy beautiful. This is a big huge next step. I have been thinking about this day and night for the last two weeks—to try to clarify this, so we can actually move First Principles and First Values forward.

We are used to thinking in the way that premodernists thought about it. Although they didn't use these terms exactly, but in the medieval period, they thought that the three eyes were distinct from each other—to the extent that they understood these three eyes. Although they didn't use *the Eye of Consciousness*—they didn't have the breakdown into the four expressions of the Eye of Consciousness—but they had the general distinction between, let's say, the Eye of Flesh, the Eye of Reason, and the Eye of the Spirit.

But what did they think? They believed in the great chain of being. The great chain of being is a partial important truth of Reality. Arthur Lovejoy wrote a very important book on the great chain of being.

It's the understanding that there's this movement in Reality from matter (the inanimate), to life (the biological world), to mind (the world of culture), to the soul (the ensouled expression of the human being, which is more individual), and then to Spirit:

- Matter: the physiosphere.
- Life: the biosphere.
- Mind: what de Chardin, the Jesuit paleontologist, might have called the noosphere, or the world of mind.
- Soul: the spiritual quality of the individual human being.
- Then, Spirit: the Field of Spirit.

Now, here's the thing.

What the medievalists assumed, and most of the great religions still assume, is that matter is at the bottom, and soul and spirit are on top. That means if science, for example, talks about matter, then science talks about the bottom stuff. Or if science talks about life, that's number two towards the bottom. Or the social sciences might talk about mind. But the real stuff and the high stuff, soul and spirit—that's for religion.

That's a mistake.

It's not that matter (exteriors) is at the bottom, and then spirit or soul, which we might call interiors, are at the top. That's a mistake, not true.

It's interiors and exteriors all the way up and all the way down. I call that *pan-interiority* (a new name created about a year ago, late at night):

Reality is interiors and exteriors all the way up and all the way down.

That's why, for example, you can take a medicine journey. You can decide to take a certain kind of psychedelic journey, and—I'm not suggesting this—you might ingest a certain plant, and that plant might affect your physiology, and then your physiology will open you up to the Eye of Consciousness. Well, how could that be true? If matter is at the bottom, and soul and spirit are on top (exteriors are at the bottom, and interiors are on top), then they have nothing to do with each other.

We have to re-vision the great chain of being.

Reality all the way up and all the way down is pan-interiority. It is interiors and exteriors all the way up and all the way down. Now, this is really important. **So, what that then tells me is that it's one Field of Reality.**

It's one Eros.

It's one heart.

It's one consciousness.

It's one world.

It's one Reality.

It's not a fragmented and fractured Reality.

Therefore, if that's true, then:

+ These three eyes are not separate from each other.
+ These three eyes are inter-included with each other; they're interdigitated.
+ These three eyes are really three expressions of one eye.

It's not true that in order to seduce yourself, you have to transcend the world of matter.

It's not true that you have to transcend (end the trance) of the body, and play a harp. No. Music itself is of the world of matter. Harps are not in heaven. Harps are an expression of the material Universe itself.

When you go to the depth of any of the eyes, they are actually going to show you. If you use all three of them together, you will seduce yourself into the knowing that Reality is a love story.

Let me say that sentence again.

If you deploy all three eyes together as expressions of the one eye, you will actually be able to know directly, in your own being-ness, that:

- The very core of Reality is Eros.
- You participate in that Eros.
- Eros is real.
- Eros has a narrative arc and a story.
- Story is a love story.
- You participate in that love story.

To seduce myself, it is not enough to deploy the Eye of the Senses, or the Eye of the Mind

But you don't know that, for example, by studying the new sciences.

A NEW PARADIGM IN SCIENCE DOESN'T GIVE YOU THIS KNOWING

You don't say: *Oh, let me study the new physics, or let me study systems theory or complexity theory* (Systems theory is the beginning, and then complexity theory is systems theory plus the new mathematics that became possible when computers were introduced).

You don't say: *I'm going to study the new physics* (which are now a hundred years old), or *I'm going to study general dynamics theory*, (which later becomes *systems theory* and *complexity theory* and *chaos theory*), and I'm going to therefore have this understanding that Reality is a love story. No.

You can study systems theory, chaos theory, or the new physics and still be dogmatically committed to the world being materialist. Even though you see that the world is, for example, a system, you say *it is a system of interconnected flatland "its."*

There were many theorists of the Western world enlightenment who were materialists, who said the world's not atomistic—it's not atomized; it's not separate parts. It's all one system.

They were arguing about whether the material world is constructed from atomized separate parts, or is it a system? They said *it's a system*, but it's a system of reductive materialist *its*.

You can open up the Eye of the Mind, you can be an expert in muons and the mathematics involved with muons—as Steven Weinberg was, for example, or as Hawking was, in other dimensions, studying black holes and more—and be a complete materialist, completely amoral, and have no sense of the Universe being a love story. That's really important.

The myth that there's a new paradigm in science that gives you the Universe: A Love Story is not true. Now, that doesn't mean we don't critically need the Eye of the Senses and the Eye of the Mind—we do. But the three eyes inter-animate each other.

Take Ramanujan, the great mathematician from India. Ramanujan says:

> Mathematics doesn't exist for me unless it lives in the mind of the Infinite.

So Ramanujan—who opens the Eye of Contemplation and the Eye of the Spirit and the Eye of the Heart—when he looks at the field of mathematics, he sees the shimmering Field of Eros.

When I look at complexity theory after I have opened the Eye of the Heart, I have direct access to a trans-logical field. I have direct access, not to pre-rational, but to a trans-mind field, where I'm actually living in the Field of Consciousness.

I have opened the Eye of Consciousness, and the Eye of Consciousness is pulsing with the heart of the Cosmos. I have removed the blocks and I have realized that at my core, I am the substance of love, which is the fabric of Reality.

Once I have that direct realization, I'm not speaking *about* it; **I *am* it.**

I'm writing Outrageous Love Letters, so I'm opening the Eye of the Heart. It's our core practice: I write Outrageous Love Letters to myself, to trees, to Reality, to a moment in time.

But once I've opened the Eye of the Heart, let's say through Outrageous Love Letters and chants. Or once I've opened the Eye of Contemplation through deep Zazen meditation. Or once I profoundly engage in practice ritual, and I read sacred texts, and I open the Eye of the Spirit. Or once I live in the vivified sense of the very goodness of Reality, the pulsing goodness, the eye of intrinsic value.

Once I open those eyes, when I then turn back to the Eye of the Mind, and I look at complexity theory, I realize that complexity theory is not a system of interconnected *its*; **complexity theory is the mathematics of intimacy, and intimacy is the interior of interconnectivity.**

We live in an Intimate Universe. And complexity theory is the mathematics of intimacy, and intimacy is the interior of interconnectivity. In other words, when I use the eyes together, then I seduce myself to the knowing that Reality is a love story.

THE PLAYER OF MUSIC BECOMES THE MUSIC

Let's go to sex for a second.

When I open the Eye of the Heart, then sex becomes love in the body.

When Krishna and Radha merge in ecstatic union, that's because sexing is love in the body. In other words, let's say *sex is the Eye of the Senses*. It's one of the five senses; it's touch. But when I open the Eye of the Senses (touch), merged with the Eye of the Heart, then I realize that sex is love in the body. Sex is cosmic Eros performed in the flesh.

That's the same thing that happens in music.

What is music?

Music is not merely sound. Music is sound which is itself atoms of time, and time is part of the space-time continuum. So we are made of time, and music is made of time, which means we are made of music. It's not just that music affects us; music lives in us.

Music is the Eye of the Senses in its most exquisite form, which then collapses into the Eye of the Heart, the Eye of Contemplation, and the Eye of Spirit.

Take a look at the Book of 2 Kings, Chapter 3, Verse 13, Benjamin and Elisha.

Elisha, the prophet, turns to his colleague and he says, *I want to open up the Eye of the Spirit, the heart.* He says, *we-atah qekhu li menagen*: take for me a player of music, *vehayah kenagen ha-menagen*: and when the minstrel (the music player) plays music.

That's the literal translation.

But in Hebrew, it means *when the player of music becomes the music.* So in the interior sciences, we say the player of music becomes the music, because I am the music. **Music seems like the Eye of the Spirit, but it's actually the Eye of the Senses and the Eye of the Spirit together.**

Pythagoras already pointed out that music and mathematics are actually the inner and outer face of each other.

Mathematics is the Eye of the Mind. Music is both the Eye of the Senses and the Eye of the Spirit. We are made of music, and music is made of matter. Sound is made of matter. We are music; we are sound. It lives in us.

The space-time continuum, which is the structure of music, lives inside of us. Music is mathematics. It's the Eye of the Mind.

Music is what awakens the prophet in me, what awakens *Homo amor* in me.

To seduce myself, it is not enough to deploy the Eye of the Senses, or the Eye of the Mind. I have to deploy the Eye of Consciousness, in all of its four forms: the Eye of Spirit, the Eye of the Heart, the Eye of Value, and the Eye of Contemplation.

But the key is, I've got to deploy them together, with that understanding that it's inter-included.

It's one eye.

It's one Reality.

It's one heart.

It's one Cosmos.

It's one field.

I seduce myself by seeing, by unfurnishing my eyes, by cleansing the doors of perception, by deploying all of the eyes together. I perceive sex as love in the body.

I perceive music as the very quality which discloses, if we go back to Huxley, *the blessedness at the heart of all things*. Blessing is an interior, but music, which is made of matter, discloses that interior.

What we tried to lay out today was the path of seduction: How do we seduce ourselves?

Now we finish with prayer. Prayer is Leonard Cohen being King David, and King David writes the Psalms, and they are music. *I heard there was a secret chord that David played, and it pleased the Lord.* That's the music. He plays with it, Leonard Cohen; he's in the mystery of it.

We pray from that place of the music that opens the Eye of the Heart. So we pray to seduce ourselves. **Prayer itself is self-seduction.** We seduce ourselves into *Homo amor.*

We seduce ourselves into our unique configuration of intimacy that's known by the Field of Intimacy, by the Infinity of Intimacy that knows our name, and *we become the music.* When we become the music, we become the prophet, as Elisha did in the book of Kings, and we become *Homo amor.*

That's why all music is love songs. Music is love songs because music is one of the great seductions of Reality that lives inside of us. It tells us that Reality is not merely a fact, discerned by the Eye of the Senses, or even the Eye of the Mind.

Reality is a story discerned by the Eye of Consciousness.

- ◆ It's not an ordinary story; it's a love story.
- ◆ It's not an ordinary love story; it's an Outrageous Love Story.
- ◆ My story, as an Outrageous Lover, is chapter and verse in the Universe: A Love Story.

That's how we open up.

I actually want to make a different suggestion. This act of opening the eye is an act of opening up. So, instead of going to Leonard Cohen, we'll just do the practice of opening up. My dear friend Yogananda had a take on it, so I'll give you a take on it, and we'll actually offer prayer from the place of this practice of opening up.

So the words are:

I am opening up in sweet surrender

To the luminous love light of the One.

Once I know it's a love story, I know that every place I fall, I fall into the hands of Outrageous Love, into the hands of She.

So even when I fall, I rise. I always rise again like a phoenix from the fire.

We are rising up like a phoenix from the fire.

Brothers and sisters, spread your wings and fly higher!

CHAPTER FOUR

ATTACHMENT THEORY AND BEYOND: *HOMO AMOR* EVOLVES THE BLESSING OF THE FATHER

Episode 297 — June 19, 2022

THE BLESSING OF THE FATHER: REALITY IS PROUD OF US

The Blessing of the Father is: *I am proud of you. I'm just really proud of you.*

We all need to know that, actually, Reality is proud of us. And we need to do things to make Reality proud. We *should* want Dad to be proud of us.

Yes, there are pathological ways in which that occurs. And there's very, very important work that's done in healing the pathologies of the fathers who weren't fathers and children who got caught up in broken attachment models.

One of the great innovations of the last hundred years is understanding where this goes wrong, where mothers and fathers go wrong, and where we're shaped or mis-shaped by early attachment. That's a very critical field.

One of my closest friends, a board member and a close friend, Lori, is one of the most brilliant trauma therapists

in the world, and she is a great healer in this realm of trauma. So, deep recognition for that dimension.

But the reason there's trauma is because mother and father *matter* **so much.** A mother and father matter so much.

Sometimes we've got the exact right father and the exact right mother, and it worked perfectly; but generally, it's imperfect. Generally, there's a lack of attunement.

For many of us, it was hard. We were hurt, and maybe our parents were hurt; our parents had parents.

We need to know that the role of fathering and the role of mothering, in the new emergent world and a new world of evolutionary intimacy, is not just the mother and the father. We need to be mothers and fathers to each other.

So, with permission, everyone, just with complete humility, if you'll give me permission to give you the blessing of the Father: *I am so wildly proud of you, and proud of who you are and proud of what you do!*

Just so much pride, and I am so proud of all of us. It's something that I don't say often enough.

We're here taking responsibility for the evolution of the source code.

We're here taking responsibility at this time between worlds, at this time between stories, poised between utopia and dystopia.

I'm so proud of the way we are stepping in and the way we're taking on this commitment.

I'm just so overwhelmingly filled with joy and pride. And when I say *pride*, it's not arrogance. It's what the Tibetan Buddhists called *Divine pride*. We are proud of each other, and we give each other the blessing of the Father. There's nothing like it.

WE NEED TO BE FATHERS AND MOTHERS TO EACH OTHER

I want to go into the energy today on Father's Day of the Blessing of the Father, and we're going to watch a clip. I'm going to ask everyone if you can, just to watch the clip, watch the faces, watch the relationship. It's a short clip of about three and a half minutes. Don't worry about the words so much. The words are beautiful, but they're not the key. The key is the music. The key is the faces. It's a father and son. It's called *Fall on Me.*[1]

The father's face just lit up! Who could see that? He just lit up. And this is a complex relationship between the two of them; it's not an easy relationship. It's got *lions and tigers and bears, oh my!*

Andrea Bocelli is a larger-than-life human being, and he is calling his son to perform with him, and creating great demands on his son. There was a whole question about whether they should make this clip or not, because he was in the middle of his music studies, and his father didn't want him to take any time off and he wanted him to actually show up in his musical studies in this very radical way.

It's not easy.

It is not all sweetness and light:

- There's the demand of the Father, and there's the pride of the Father. The blessing of the Father is: I'm proud of you.
- There's this way in which the father and the mother are the very air we breathe. It's so deep—it's the very air we breathe.

---

1 Andrea Bocelli and Matteo Bocelli, "Fall On Me," https://youtu.be/ChcR2gKt5WM?si=Qdja2P7urREr5fW3.

For so many of us, this is indeed a bittersweet day. It's a day with so many dimensions: we may have lost our father, we may have lost our mother, or we may have never quite had them.

So let's hold this moment, and let's be fathers and let's be mothers.

BEYOND THE ROOT OF ALL HUMAN SUFFERING

Now holding the space of the blessing of the Father and the blessing of the Mother, I want to take two steps with you.

Here's this week's Evolutionary Love Code:

> We all need the blessing of the Father. We all need the love of the Father.
>
> We all need the blessing of the Mother. We all need the love of the Mother, because the Universe is a love story, and at the beginning of our lives, we experience our parents as the entire Universe.
>
> And your mother and father are not limited to your biological mother and father.
>
> We all have the capacity to give each other the blessing of the Father and the blessing of the Mother. We are all mothers and fathers to each other. We can also be mothers and fathers to ourselves.

We all need the blessing of the Father. We all need the love of the Father. We all need the blessing of the Mother. We all need the love of the Mother.

Because the Universe is a love story, and at the beginning of our lives, we experience our parents as the entire Universe. Okay, you get that? Wow!

Now I want to add something to the code, part two of the code. We're writing this code together.

I want to just say one word. If you are new to *One Mountain,* and you've never been here before, one of the things that we do here in *One*

Mountain is that we work out the next steps of the great Story of Value, the *dharma*, which is rooted in First Principles and First Values, in order to actually evolve the source code of consciousness and culture. Because we understand that the root cause of catastrophic risk and existential risk, and the root cause of what we call ordinary suffering—from obesity, to suicide, to mental breakdown, to evil in all of its manifold forms—the root cause of all of that is a breakdown in a Story of Value.

We don't live in a Story of Value rooted in First Principles and First Values, and that's the ultimate root cause of all the generator functions of existential risk.

The root cause of the generator functions of existential risk is precisely the breakdown in the Story of Value. So I want to see if we can, together, evolve this notion of Father's Day and Mother's Day, and this notion of parenting, and root it deeply in this larger Story of Value.

PEOPLE OF THE LIE

In the first hundred pages of a book called *People of the Lie,* Scott Peck wrote very beautifully about the tragedies of evil that appear within families. It's actually one of the greatest books ever written. It was little noticed and misunderstood. The first hundred pages of the book are about the people of the lie, within families when parents go pathological, and they don't love their children—but also within social groups.

Spiritual teachers can be *people of the lie.*

Bloggers can be *people of the lie.*

Cultural critics can be *people of the lie.*

This happens when people have this fundamental core emptiness inside them, and that emptiness is driving everything. In other words, underneath the surface personality, there's a fundamental emptiness, because the person was, in some sense, violated.

They didn't receive the Blessing of the Father or the Blessing of the Mother, and then something got so contracted, so shriveled, so frozen that the person froze into a mask in which survival and looking good—or survival and a certain kind of public recognition—became everything.

In order to achieve that, they're willing to do almost anything. That's what underlies jihads in all of their forms, and all "holy wars"—whether it's in their Joseph McCarthyite forms, or whether it's all of the ways that people move to hurt each other under the guise of being a rescuer.

In the Drama Triangle we looked at in Chapter 1, you've got a persecutor, you've got a victim, and a rescuer—but actually, the roles are often confused:

All of the pathologies that happen that are the root of all human suffering—the root of all war, the root of all breakdown, mental breakdown, social breakdown, of the worst kind—come from people who somehow lost their capacity to act, and be, and feel out of the Field of Value and Love.

They got empty inside at a certain moment, and they lost themselves, often at a particular moment; and then they began to loathe themselves, and to hate themselves, and eventually they became what Peck called *people of the lie*. Then they express themselves in malice.

Joseph Berke, a key student of R.D. Laing, and a dear colleague, wrote a book called *The Tyranny of Malice*, about the pathological versions of the father and the pathological versions of the mother. So that's real.

And, at the same time—oh my God—there are so many gorgeous fathers, and we can be fathers for each other, and we can be mothers for each other.

We can give each other the blessing of the Father, and we can give each other the Blessing of the Mother.

WE MUST BE BELOVEDS TO EACH OTHER

Let's look at this week's Evolutionary Love Code again:

> We all need the Blessing of the Father. We all need the love of the Father.

> We all need the Blessing of the Mother. We all need the love of the Mother, because the Universe is a love story, and at the beginning of our lives, we experience our parents as the entire Universe.

> And your mother and father are not limited to your biological mother and father.

> We all have the capacity to give each other the blessing of the Father and the Blessing of the Mother. We are all mothers and fathers to each other. We can also be mothers and fathers to ourselves.

I want to evolve this notion of the Mother and Father. So, the first evolution, the next part of the code is:

> *And your mother and father are not limited to your biological mother and father.*

This is unbelievably important! **We all have the capacity to give each other the Blessing of the Father and the Blessing of the Mother.** That's the first evolution. We are all mothers and fathers to each other.

In the Hebrew mystical tradition, if you read the Song of Solomon, the Beloved is sister, brother, father, mother; the Beloved has many faces.

We track the Beloved in the classical romantic relationship, but actually **we need to be Beloveds to each other.** That's what we call Outrageous Lovers. Part of the emergence of *Homo amor* is that we are Beloveds to each other.

But *Beloveds to each other* doesn't mean that it's frozen in a romantic context. That's one context, and it's an important context. But too often, that's ordinary love. Too often, the romantic context is a strategy of the ego, seeking comfort and security, which is reactive to that which happens to it. But **love that's not ordinary love, that's Outrageous Love, emerges from within and takes on many wondrous guises.**

So we can be everything to each other at once:

- We can be Beloved.
- We can be lover.
- We can be brother.
- We can be sister.
- We can be father.
- We can be mother.
- We can be uncle.

We need to be many things to each other.

When we lock ourselves in one relationship, we lose the power of the Universe: A Love Story.

That's why the Song of Solomon, the Song of Songs, if you look at Chapter 8, for example, moves between the lover and Beloved. In the Song of Songs, they move between brother and sister, and father and mother.

> *I wish you were my brother,*
> *who nursed at my mother's breast; then,*
> *if I met you outdoors,*
> *I could kiss you,*
> *and no one would look down on me.*
>
> *- Song of Songs, Chapter 8*

I just want to invite us now, at this moment: *Let us be brothers and sisters to each other.*

But particularly today, let us be fathers and mothers to each other. We can give each other the blessing of the Father and the blessing of the Mother. It's huge!

Can we feel that?

Who's willing to be fathers and mothers to each other? To show up in that stunning way for each other and with each other? Wow!

YOU ARE WELCOME IN THE UNIVERSE!

Most of us on this call, and most people in the world, are the product of imperfect parenting.

Because parenting is imperfect, and some of us may have been the product of really brutal parenting. So, do the work:

- Do the psychological work.
- Do the therapeutic work.
- Do the traumatic work.

That's critically important, and there is no bypass road.

But actually, it's not about that. You have to liberate yourself from the notion that there's this one person, your mother or father, who's the pharaoh in your life, and if they did it wrong, you can't liberate yourself.

That's not true. You are a Unique Self, and you can recover your Unique Self.

Your Unique Self is the realization that:

- I'm not just called by the past.
- I'm not only defined by the memory of my past.
- I'm called by the memory of my future.
- The memory of my future is in the faces of all the mothers and

fathers who call me forward, who are desperate to be proud of me, and who need my service, and who see me, invite me, recognize me, choose me, desire, and adore me.

As mothers and fathers, we have to adore each other. It's not enough to love each other; we have to *adore* each other. What do we say to each other? We say to each other what the mother and father need to say to their child in the ideal world, which is: *Welcome! You're welcome in the Universe.*

You see, the reason mothers and fathers matter so much is because the Universe is a love story, and that love story is a Story of Value. It's a story of evolving value and evolving love. It's an Evolutionary Love Story.

But love is not just a social construction; love is the central value of Cosmos.

So mother and father transmit to us two things:

- ◆ One, the experience of love, of being held, of being welcome.
- ◆ Two, the experience that we are irreducibly valuable, but in a Field of Value; we are irreducibly valuable in a Field of Value which is Cosmos. Cosmos is a Field of Value, and to be a Unique Self is to be an irreducibly unique expression of that Field of Eros and Value.

In the ideal world, that is what mother and father remind us of. We look at the faces of mother and father, and we see our value, and we see the *welcome sign*.

But that welcome sign, brothers and sisters, fathers and mothers, friends and lovers, **that welcome sign is not actually hung around the neck, in a limited way, of my biological mother and father.**

So yes, do the work. It is critical to do the work; you can't bypass the work. Any spiritual path that says you can do a spiritual bypass, and not do the deep work is wrong. Do the deep work—the attachment work let's call it, the re-fathering and the re-mothering work—which is the best that modern psychology has to offer in its best forms.

There are a lot of corrupted forms of it, but its best forms are brilliant, shamanic, stunning, utterly necessary.

But once you've done that work, give it up!

In other words, let go of your attachment to reliving that story again, and again, and again. Not in a way that's healthy, but in a way that you get into a recursive loop that you can't get out of.

Because **going through the story again and again becomes not your Eros, not your healing, but your pseudo-eros.** It becomes an addiction.

Step into the realization that you are Unique Self, and you are called by the future itself.

The Welcome Home sign is not chained to the neck of your mother and father biologically. The Welcome Home sign is actually posted all over Reality.

It's posted in beauty.

It's posted in color.

It's posted in elegance.

It's posted in ethos.

It's posted in creativity.

It's posted in your unique ethos and your unique creativity.

Your very uniqueness, your very experience of yourself as an irreducibly unique expression of the larger Field of Value, is itself a Welcome Home sign!

We can come to understand:

- Your infinite importance
- Your unique contribution
- The unique quality of intimacy that you bring to Reality
- The unique quality of being and becoming that you bring to

Reality

- The unique gift that you have to give to your unique circle of intimacy and influence, that can be given by you and you alone

Then you realize that the very experience of being a Unique Self and recognizing yourself as Unique Self is a Welcome Home sign in Cosmos.

That actually, not only are we all mothers and fathers to each other, but we can also be mothers and fathers to ourselves.

Oh my God! We can also be mothers and fathers to ourselves. Let's add this to this week's Evolutionary Love Code:

We can also be mothers and fathers to ourselves.

THE WELCOME HOME SIGN IN COSMOS IS THE FIELD OF VALUE ITSELF

Now let's go even deeper. Let's see if we can take this another step. Happy Father's Day, everyone. Happy Mother's Day, for those who missed it. We're going to do Mother's and Father's Day together here. Let's go to the next step.

And the Welcome Home sign is not only from us to each other. It's not only us to ourselves. It's not only that we can be mothers and fathers to each other—and we do need to be mothers and fathers to ourselves.

But actually, the Welcome Home sign in Cosmos is the Field of Value itself. The Field of Value has many disguises, but the blessing of the Father begins with the recognition that as a Unique Self, you, my son, you, my daughter:

- You have a unique contribution.
- You are a unique value of Cosmos that's needed by Cosmos.
- You are part of this larger Field of Value, and we need you to show up.

- ◆ You are part of the team; you are part of Team Humanity.
- ◆ You are part of Team Human, and Team Human needs you deeply!
- ◆ We are on Team Human, and Team Human needs you deeply.

In other words, it's not enough to have a good father and mother.

I had a beautiful night a few nights ago with a close friend, a brother of mine who's literally my family, this past Thursday night, and we were talking. He's a great dad, and I happen to know his son who's a great guy; I'm having a great time studying with his son. I'd have no chance to study with his son without the gorgeous fathering that he did, and obviously the mothering that his wife did.

And, you can be the best father in the world, but it's insufficient. Because if you are the best father in the world, and you send your son or your daughter into a world in which there's no Story of Value and there are no First Principles and First Values, and there's a postmodern deconstruction of value, and there's a deconstruction of meaning, then your son goes off to college—which of course you pay for—and they get downloaded this notion that actually value is not real, and stories are not real, and the only grand narrative is that there's no grand narrative.

Then it gets confusing, and it gets depressing. Then addiction sets in, and breakdown sets in.

So we need a second form of fathering. That's what we're doing.

Here at the Center, through the Great Library, we're creating a new incarnation of the father and the mother. The Great Library is about Unique Self recovery. It is about the Story of Value that we live in.

The Field of Value itself, and love/Eros, which is at the center of the Field of Value, is the mother and father. In other words, there's a mother and father beyond the biological mother and father: all of us, and each of us for ourselves.

But then, there's a mother and father beyond individual human beings.

The very structure of the living Universe itself is a Field of Value and a Field of Eros, which is the Mother and Father.

It's not that the father is value and the mother is Eros, but the father and mother are yin and yang: they are interpenetrating Fields of Value and Eros.

So I am fathered by the Story of Value that calls me to my best self, that demands that I confess my greatness.

I'm held by that field, by the mother. I'm held in that field, which is not just a Field of Love. It's not enough to have a Field of Love. Love by itself doesn't do it unless love is a value of Cosmos.

You have to recognize and feel that love is not a social construction of Reality; it's not an egoic move. This love that I am experiencing, that's flowing through the Story of Value, is the Eros that drives all of Cosmos.

We live in a CosmoErotic Universe. Eros animates the Field of Value, and Eros animates the Field of Love, and it generates in us the Field of Dreams.

Can you feel that, everyone? Wow!

WE HAVE TO LIBERATE OURSELVES FROM THE IDOLATRY OF MOTHER AND FATHER

Part of evolving the source code of consciousness and culture is that we have to liberate ourselves from the idolatry of mother and father. For 2,000 years, we didn't take mother and father and what happened in those early relationships seriously enough, and then attachment theory burst forth as a great revelation, as an evolutionary breakthrough, as a critical new understanding.

That's beautiful and necessary, but then, we can idolize that new breakthrough and say everything is about the mother and father. No, it's not, and everything is not about one lifetime.

It's not about one mother and father. Not only can *we* re-parent each other, and re-parent ourselves, but:

- Reality re-parents us.
- Goodness, Truth, and Beauty re-parent us.
- The Story of Value re-parents us.
- The Universe: A Love Story is actually holding us.

My teacher Mordechai Leiner of Izbica wrote:

Every place you fall, you fall into Her arms.

Can you feel that, my friends? There are ways that we have to re-parent each other, and there are ways that this structure of value lives in culture. How are we doing so far? Who can feel this? Wow, we can feel this!

There are different vehicles of transmission. So I want to just *feel* one thing together with you.

What we're doing here in *One Mountain, Many Paths*, at this moment in which we're poised between utopia and dystopia, at this moment of existential and catastrophic risk and massive ordinary suffering, is:

- The recognition that as ordinary suffering is happening, and as human brutality is happening, there is also unimaginable beauty.
- There's so much more beauty than there is ugliness; we only recognize it's ugly because it's contrasted with beauty.
- There are actually billions of people who are working and toiling and efforting and pouring themselves into goodness.

People need hope. Hope is a memory of the future, and hope comes from the realization that Reality Herself is the Mother and the Father. We need

She, the Goddess, the Great Mother, who holds us, and we need *Avinu Malkeinu*: the Great Father, who holds us.

For 2,000 years, we distorted the Father in all sorts of exoteric versions of religion, in which you only got the blessing of the Father if you fulfilled a particular set of ritual requirements, and you alienated yourself from your body, and you denied that which was essential to you in multiple ways. **Religions hijacked the authentic, human, cosmic structure of the blessings of the Father.**

Then in many ways, today, in the new age, we've gone for the blessing of the mother.

We have rejected the father entirely, and we've adopted the blessing of the mother.

But the blessing of the mother is about unconditional love, without any expectation—without the demands of value, without the demand of living my Unique Self and giving my unique gift and confessing my greatness. We need both.

WE NEED TO UP-LEVEL THE BLESSING OF THE MOTHER, AND WE NEED TO UP-LEVEL THE BLESSING OF THE FATHER

We need to evolve the source code of consciousness and culture, which means we need to evolve the Blessing of the Father, and we need to evolve the Blessing of the Mother.

The mother loves, not with ordinary love. The mother's love is the expression of the Outrageous Love of Cosmos moving through the mother, whether it's the biological mother, or it's the Field of Reality itself.

The Blessing of the Father is the value and love of Cosmos moving through the father, whether it's the biological father—or it's the Field of Reality itself.

Reality Herself is the Mother and the Father.

86

So when Cohen sings his prayer about *the holy and the broken Hallelujah*, he's singing to the Mother and the Father, to the Field of Cosmos that holds us. The reason we come back to that song every week is because he's not only speaking about the biological. Cohen is actually emerging from his lineage (that I share with him), which speaks about this; Kashmir Shaivism does it in its way, and Sufism does it in its way, and mystical Christianity does it in its way.

We need to evolve those traditions, because in order to tell the new Story of Value, we need to integrate the best of the traditional world (the premodern world), the best of the modern, and the best of the postmodern world, into a new Story of Value in which God and Goddess, the Father and the Mother—not as Mr. or Mrs. Santa Claus, although Mr. or Mrs. Santa Claus would be human expressions of that field—calls us and lives in us.

- Gaia Herself as the living Mother,
- The Field of Value as the living Father.

In the old world, and much of the world we would watch in the Westerns, you'd see kind of the lone, rugged individual, the man, or the woman who was in the homestead holding the children.

So let's liberate those worlds from their gender stereotypes. And let's also reclaim them:

- We need the Mother and the Father, and they need to live in us.
- But they also live in Reality Herself; Reality Herself is the Mother and the Father.
- Abba: Father, Father, Father, my father, my father! I've got to be able to turn and cry out to my father, and I can't exhaust my father in the biological father.
- And I've got to be able to cry to my mother. Mother, mother, mother! Mother, carry me! Mother, hold me! Hold me, mother!
- I've got to know that every place I fall, I fall into His arms,

and every place I fall, I fall into Her arms.

That's what Unique Self Recovery is about. It is why we're creating a Unique Self Institute. It's why we're creating Unique Self Recovery, which we have been working on for seven years. It's an expression of the Unique Self Institute and an expression of *One Mountain*, because to recover my Unique Self is to realize that my father and mother love me madly, and my father and mother are the Field of the Living Universe itself.

The Universe is magical. The Universe is alive, and it's alive with the quality of the Infinity of Intimacy.

The Infinity of Intimacy is not just lover. It's not just brother and sister. Oh my God, the Infinity of Intimacy is the Mother and the Father that hold us in our holy and our broken *Hallelujah*.

Wow!

OUTRAGEOUS LOVE FESTIVAL IS A LABORATORY FOR THE DHARMA

Friends, we're going to get together this summer.

The Outrageous Love Festival is our laboratory for the *dharma*, where we spend seven days together and we go deep in an ecstatic field of practice, of integrity, of Unique Self.

There's no guru; we're standing against the guru, with all due respect for the guru. But the guru has to be the Field of Value itself. At the center of our community is not Barbara Marx Hubbard, and it's not Marc Gafni. At the center of our community is a Field of Value and a Field of Ethics, which calls every Unique Self to play their instrument in the Unique Self Symphony. Just feel that!

We've all got to work on this through our own sacred autobiography, and we're going to work in the summer also on sacred autobiography. Every one of us has to do the work with our own particular mother and father, step one. Then we have to actually emerge as we do that work, to actually become mother and father ourselves, whether or not that's biologically.

I just spent an incredible four-day trip with my son, Zion; we did a father-son trip in San Francisco, which was just beyond imagination beautiful. We'll get to The Five Principles of Baseball Dharma another time, and we'll get to Confessions of Greatness another week.

But for now, I just want to be with you in this mother and father moment. We need to be Mother and Father to each other, and we need to be Mother and Father to ourselves. But we also need to realize that in telling the new Story of Value, in writing the Great Library, and creating *One Mountain*; in being the revolution, we're weaving the Field of Mother and Father, which is the quality of Reality herself.

In other words, we actually become part of the field that holds us: the Field of Mother and Father, which is the Field of Gaia Herself, which is the Field of Value Himself, which is God/Goddess which holds us, which is beyond us.

Not a kind of trite New Age, *I am God. Just relax, buddy!* God is God; Goddess is Goddess. **God is so much larger than us, and—not in contradiction, but paradoxically—I participate in that field, that's actually true, and I weave the field.**

On this Father's Day, we're weaving the Field of the Father. We're crying out to Father, and Father cries out to us and says: *be Father with me*. When we write this new Story of Value, rooted in First Values and First Principles, we're reweaving the Field of Value: the Field of the Mother and the Father.

That's what we're going to do this summer at the Outrageous Love Festival, and I'm insanely ecstatic to be with you.

Today we celebrated Father's Day together. We did not only celebrate, but we evolved Father's Day; we evolved Mother's Day. Oh my God, thank you! Happy Father's Day. Happy Mother's Day! All of us, mothers and fathers to each other, to Reality, and as part of the Field of Father and Mother.

CHAPTER FIVE

THE NINE GREAT STATIONS ON THE JOURNEY OF TRANSFORMATION

Episode 317 — November 7, 2022

IN THE HUMAN JOURNEY, THERE ARE NINE STATIONS OF TRANSFORMATION

Here is today's Evolutionary Love Code:

Human life is not an event; it is a journey. In all of the interior and evolutionary sciences, the journey is understood to be a journey of transformation. In the most advanced understanding of the human journey, there are nine stations of transformation. These are what we term *the seven selves*. The journey through the seven selves, to the best of our understanding, is the purpose of human life in the manifest world.

This is an insanely exciting week in our evolutionary sensemaking, and I am madly delighted to be with you. An insanely exciting and important week! We are going to talk about the nine stations in the journey of self—**the seven selves and the nine stations in the journey of self, an answer to the question of** *who are you?*

We are going to dive in, and to look at this question. *Who am I?*

It is my hope, my prayer, and my trust in our promise that we're going to have a sense of *who you are* that exponentially exceeds who we understand ourselves to be right now. Some of us have studied, and we've articulated and developed this understanding of identity—but **what we're about to present is the best understanding of identity, I believe, that exists in the Cosmos today.**

At least on planet Earth. And this is our job on planet Earth.

The way we become a resonant beacon for the larger galactic unfolding is by evolving who we are, to the best, the deepest, the truest, the most good, the most beautiful that we can be.

Okay, so let us see if we can do this, and let us make da Vinci proud, because we *need* to be da Vinci in this generation—but we need to be da Vinci *exponentialized*. We need to move way past Leonardo and create this new Renaissance—because the alternative is dystopia, meaning no future, or a dystopian future. Let us create the most beautiful world, the most good world, the most true world that we already know is possible.

So here we go. Okay, are we ready? Let us dive in. Let's see if we can set the tone and address together one of the key questions, which is the question of *who are you*, the question of *identity*.

We want to integrate the best leading-edge validated insights of all the wisdom streams: premodern, modern, and postmodern will *all* be resonant in this unpacking. We're going to unpack it at the level of *second simplicity*, meaning simplicity *after* complexity, in relatively clear terms. We're going to look at these nine stations, which address the great question of *who am I, who are you?*

STATION ONE: PRE-PERSONAL

Station one is what we might call the *pre-personal*. **Before the self comes online, there is the pre-personal.**

At the level of the baby, before the baby goes through what Margaret Mahler calls *separation-individuation*, the baby is fully *absorbed*, in some sense, in the mother; the baby is *identified* with the mother, and **the baby doesn't have any sense of being separate.** That absorption, that *oneness* between the mother and baby—we would call that *pre-personal*.

That is a necessary and beautiful stage of life, in which the baby nurses at the breast of the mother and hasn't yet individuated—but when you *arrest* on that pre-personal space, you get distortion. You get pathology.

The pre-personal space lives:

- Not only in ontogeny, not only in the personal unfolding of human life
- But also in phylogeny, in the stages of humanity's unfolding

Because the *who are you/who am I* story of human being is also the *who are you/who am I* story of humanity. Ontogeny and phylogeny recapitulate each other. **The story of humanity's unfolding and the story of the human being's unfolding are embedded in each other.**

So the first station is the pre-personal. Now, where would the pre-personal show up, let's say in shadow form, in the unfolding of humanity? It might show up in a cult, in a pre-personal cult, in a negative cult—a cult in the negative sense of the word. In a cult where you have one person or a little group of people who are dominating the space, in which:

- There's no sense of the dignity of the distinct separate personal self.

- There's no sense of autonomy.
- There's no sense of freedom.
- There's no sense of choice.
- There is a complete absorption in the cult.

And there's something very powerful about that, and there's something very attractive about that, and there's something very *alluring* about that: I lose my sense of individuated self; I'm reabsorbed in a cult—and that's a great and tragic unfolding.

Now, it doesn't mean that it's a tragic unfolding to be absorbed in a beautiful, gorgeous community, and in a gorgeous intimate communion with a larger community where my identity is part of—and is, in part, defined by—the larger communion. That's *not* pre-personal; that's *transpersonal*. We're going to get to transpersonal later.

Pre-personal is when you haven't yet individuated—or you regress. It's a regressive move. The pre-personal shows up in a cult, it can show up in a gang, and it can even show up in some moments of a company or a religion, where I become so entirely defined by the company, or the religion, or the organization, or the nation that I actually lose a sense of my individuated dignity and personhood.

That's the pre-personal, the first station. That station is important, and we are formed and shaped in a wildly gorgeous, stunning, beautiful, positive way in that station.

When Sinead O'Connor sings "This Is To Mother You," she is talking about that experience of being held in the arms of the adoring mother *before* I am even conscious, and knowing *I am welcome*. That experience of nursing at the breast of the mother, before I am even conscious as an individual, downloads into the very source code of my being the experience of being welcome in Cosmos. And so, that pre-personal experience is critical and beautiful—but when it *arrests* or appears later in this arrested form, when we regress to it without any sense of the personal, it pathologizes. That's station one.

STATION TWO: SEPARATE SELF

Station two is the first emergence of separate self.

Separate self emerges—and **separate self is not to be demonized**, as in so many of the Eastern Buddhist and other mystical traditions in Judaism and Christianity and Hinduism. The mystical traditions demonize the separate self. Bad mistake. **Separate self is a beautiful emergence.**

It is an emergence in the history—*his*-story, *her*-story—of the individual, and of the story of culture. The emergence of separate self explodes in the world with the canon of biblical thought, when the human being is addressed as *homo imago dei.*

Every unique individual human being is participatory in the image of the Infinite, in the image of infinite value, in the image of God.

That's the notion of the dignity of the individual.

That notion is strong in Hebrew wisdom, but it doesn't become utterly central in culture until Christianity and Islam, each in their own ways, liberate some dimensions of Hebrew wisdom and bring them into the world. And that ultimately comes together, in Europe at least, in the Renaissance—and really in the sixteenth century, for the first time, the word *self* appears in the dictionary. **The word *self* doesn't appear in the dictionary before the sixteenth century.**

And *self* is separate self, rooted in the great traditions, but not fully crystallized. In Hebrew wisdom, not fully crystallized. In Christianity, in part. In Islam, in part. In part for a simple reason:

- In Christianity, there's no dignity to the individual unless they accept a certain set of tenets. If you don't accept Christ in a particular way, you are damned, and that doesn't speak for the dignity of the individual.

- It's not sufficient either in Hebrew wisdom, because it is limited to too narrow a group of people, the chosen people.
- In Islam, again, there is a sense of chosen people: it's either us or them. There's not the innate dignity of the individual per se.

But those are *proto-versions* of separate self. **The full separate self appears in the Renaissance.** Every human being has dignity. Every human being, independent of the larger context, simply as a separate self, has dignity.

That's the emergence of the modern citizen, the modern separate self. And separate self is real. I want to say it in classical nomenclature: **separate self is a real construct in the mind of God.**

Separate self is real. Separate self is the moment in my life when I say:

- This is my story, and this is my life.
- My life isn't anybody else's life
- I can't be anyone else.
- I can't be born at a different time.
- I can't look a different way.
- This is me, and I'm embracing my story, and I'm embracing the dignity of my separate self, and I am standing in that inherent dignity, and I step out of all co-dependencies. Not interdependencies, but I step out of all co-dependencies, and I feel the inherent dignity of me being a separate self.

Okay, wow, that's a very big deal. Separate self is hugely important. It's an evolutionary leap that cannot be ignored, cannot be pathologized, cannot be demonized—and yet, that's only station two.

Because the separate self *by itself*—when the separate self or the *ego* self is the end of the story—then, by definition, **I am going to be lonely and alienated, because I am in violation of my deeper nature.**

Because separate self is *a dimension* of my nature, my ego self is a dimension of my nature, and I never want to evolve beyond it. **You never want to *evolve beyond ego***. When I hear teachers teaching, *I'm going to teach evolution beyond ego*, I get scared. Because anyone that says they've evolved beyond ego is lying, and anyone who says they've evolved beyond separate self is violating the structure in the mind of God, which is separate self. It is real.

So I never evolve beyond ego, I never evolve beyond separate self. But what I do is **I have to evolve beyond my *exclusive identity* with separate self.** Does that make sense?

I am not just separate self.

I am not just ego self.

I am something more.

STATION THREE: SOCIAL SELF

Now, the third self I want to introduce is one attempt to talk about what that *something more* is, and it's an attempt that has a partial truth. It's true, but partial. But when it becomes the *totality* of self, it fails.

That third station of self is very strong today. It's being taught at the MIT Media Lab. It was taught by B.F. Skinner at Harvard for six decades. Chomsky and others rejected B.F. Skinner, the great behavioral psychologist for good reason, but Skinner's thinking has reemerged in what we might call—Auguste Comte coined the term—"social physics."

Social physics is the theory that underlies the entire web-plex, that pretty much everyone on this call participates in. The social self, rooted in social physics, suggests that who I am is:

- The sum total of my social interactions
- The sum total of the social influences on me
- The social network incentives that shape and form me

The web is built around those—likes, and views, and this complete bubble in which I'm *defined* by this very tight network of social interactions, which can undermine my sense of being a separate self and undermine my *autonomy*, undermine my *free will*. **As a social self, I actually become the object of manipulation through social nudges and social cues.**

That's an understanding that lines the web-plex.

Mark Zuckerberg pretty much believes this—if you study him carefully, it's his default belief. And Larry Page and Sergey Brin over at Google pretty much believe this. And Satya Nardella over at Microsoft pretty much believed this. And they're all influenced by a guy named Alex Pentland, in the MIT Media Lab, who very clearly believes this and has articulated it in probably two hundred papers, and he has dozens and dozens and dozens of doctoral students who have all achieved their doctorates and have started companies embedded in the tech plex.

The sense that who I am is not a separate self—I am a *social* self. I'm the sum total of all my social interactions, and I'm *defined* by social cues and social pressure—that's the social self. Now, that's not wrong. I am absolutely impacted.

The social self *is* part of who I am.

I am not *just* a separate self. I'm not *just* autonomy, my autonomous separate self.

The value of separate self is *autonomy*. The value of social self is *communion*. But they mustn't ignore each other; **autonomy and communion have to live together**.

So let's take a look. Our third station is what we're calling *social self*. Social self exists throughout history, but it's now becoming the dominant self in the tech plex:

- It might be in China, where the social credit system is built on a totalitarian version of the social self.

98

- It might be in the United States which has its own oligarchy of tech plex, what I would call TechnoFeudalists, who are also selling a non-totalitarian, non-overtly totalitarian, a non-Orwellian version of the social self, but one that's equally insidious, that equally undermines free will, that equally undermines the inward space of meaning in which the glory and nobility of self is formed.

Because the social self, especially in the tech plex, speaks to *the lowest common denominator.*

The social self ignores *intrinsic value.*

The social self says that the only thing that really exists are loops and loops of social interactions, which are all in the end driven, as Skinner said and as Pentland writes, by survival.

That's the social self. Now, there is *some* truth to it. The truth is that we *are* social beings, embedded in social systems—we *are* social selves. But it's just a piece of who we are; it's far from *all* of who we are. **We're actually something much deeper.**

Let's recapitulate:

- We've got a **pre-personal self**, which exists, again, both in the human being and in humanity.
- We then transcend (we end the *trance* of, if you will, speaking poetically) the pre-personal self. We get to **separate self**. Separate self is a reality in the mind of God. The dignity of separate self, the embrace of my story at the separate self level, is critical. Yet separate self doesn't exhaust my identity. I'm *more* than a separate self; I'm more than just autonomy.
- Third station: we have this realization of **social self**. That's a true realization, but it's true but partial.

When I embrace and *apotheosize* the social self by itself—I make it as if it were *godlike*—and **when I make communion the *ultimate* value, then I create a distortion**. I create a pathology that exists on the web today, and that sense of a social self which is the pathology also exists in some of the meta-theories of classical communism, in which only the social body exists—and the individual doesn't exist at all.

That's the social self, both in its beauty and its limiting pathologies. That's station three.

STATION FOUR: FALSE SELF

Station four, which I'm not going to spend a lot of time on—I'm just going to mention it, because it's really the higher stations we want to get today; that's where the game is. But we need to know the steps along the way; we're doing a full theory. We are going to try to articulate the best, most advanced theory and understanding and realization, embodied realization in our lives, of this experience of responding to the question of *who am I?*

And all of us, as you listen, if you can, friends, notice:

- Where are you in **pre-personal self**? Where are you being pre-personal? Where have you *regressed*, where you want to be just in the arms of the mother and actually *give up* that individuation? That's beautiful, and that's good, and that has a place, and there are places we should actually let ourselves fall *into the arms of*. It's just *insufficient*. So, find the pre-personal self, and find it in yourself, and give it place, and give it honor.
- And then, friends, find your separate self, **your dignity as a separate self**, your classical identity as a citizen, and see the goodness of just embracing your individuated story, and the beauty of that.
- And then see in your life where I am a social self, and *to what extent* I'm a social self—what's the truth of that? **Where am I**

100

the sum total of my network of social influences, and why that's beautiful, and why it therefore *matters* what social context I locate myself in? And why that doesn't *exhaust* me, and why I have to be careful to find a deeper strange attractor, North Star of value, so I don't get ultimately *defined* by my social self—which would pathologize me.

Those are the first three stations of self: pre-personal, separate self, social self.

The fourth station, which we're going to talk about briefly, is *false self*. **False self is a distortion of either separate self or social self.** So in some sense, we've already addressed false self:

- When I'm *only* a separate self, when that *exhausts* my identity, that's a distortion that becomes false self.

- When the social self becomes—in the formulation of MIT TechnoFeudalist Alex Pentland—the sum *total*, when I am the sum total of materialistic social interactions—that's a distortion of social self. That's another version of false self.

- The third version of false self would be when my attention fixates early in life in a distorted form. I come into the world and I experience the shock of separation. Here I am, and I have to find my way in the world, and I am shocked by my existence in this world. I'm shocked that the world is not *attuned* to me. I was in the mother's womb and all Reality was attuned to me, and all of a sudden, there's this discordance between me and Reality. And very early on, I cannot blame Reality, because that will crush me; it will make me suicidal to Reality, so I, in some sense, fault *myself*, and I begin to live within a false core.

And that false core—because we live in a world of language—formulates itself in a sentence, so I will have a false core sentence, and the false core sentence might be:

I am too much, I am too much, I am too much.

I am not good enough.

I am ugly.

I am bad.

I am not lovable.

I am not safe.

I will always be alone.

I am not trustworthy.

Who can feel those?

That's a third version of the false self, and that's when I generate Reality from the place of my false core, which formulates as a false core sentence.

As long as I am creating and generating my Reality from within that false core sentence, my Reality is going to be distorted, and I am going to generate a pathologized Reality.

What we do is **then *cover up* our false core with a false self**. Let's say my sentence is, *I am not safe*. What I will do, since I am not safe, is:

- I will take unimaginable and foolhardy risks, because I am not safe anyways—so it just doesn't matter.
- Or I will do the opposite: I'll retreat so deep inside that I'll never take the appropriate unique risks that I *have* to take, because I'm so trembling and fearful because I'm not safe.

There are a lot of strategies to do it. And the courses being offered now by Claire Molinard and David Cicerchi at the Unique Self Institute include practical strategies for working with the false self. It's unbelievably important, where we unpack this in great depth. So that's the fourth station, the fourth self.

PUZZLE PIECES WITHOUT ORIGINAL PUZZLE

Now, see if you can picture this for a second.

Imagine that the separate self is a *puzzle piece*.

The puzzle piece is looking for the puzzle, but the puzzle piece is told that **there is no puzzle**. There's no puzzle, not at all. No puzzle, it doesn't exist.

That's the separate self—so the separate self walks a little funny. Because if you are a puzzle piece, it's hard to walk. It's very idiosyncratic—look at the edges of a puzzle piece! It wants to fit into something, but there is nothing there to fit *into*. That's the experience of a puzzle piece. **The separate self experiences itself as a puzzle piece disconnected from a larger puzzle.**

The social self experiences there being *lots* of puzzle pieces, tons and tons and tons of puzzle pieces—but when those puzzle pieces come together, they don't form the true wholeness of an original vision of a puzzle. They just randomly fall together, they shape together, and however they happen to fall together, *that* becomes the puzzle. **As social selves, there's no original puzzle, there's no intrinsic vision they are trying to fulfill.** However the pieces happen to fall together, that's the puzzle.

To recap:

- **Pre-personal**, that's pre-personal self.
- Then **separate self** is now no longer in the pre-personal; separate self is in the *personal*. It's the personal. It's the personal, though, which isn't related to a larger field. So it's the puzzle piece with no larger puzzle.
- Then you go to **social self**, and social self is still the personal, but it's the *personal social*. So it's not the *individual* personal, it's the personal *social*. It's lots of individual personals, coming

together in the social. It's lots of individual puzzle pieces that do not *cohere* in the vision of an original puzzle that's intrinsic to Cosmos, that seeks to emerge. They are going to fall together randomly with each other, and however they fall together, they're going to call that the puzzle. That's social self.

- **False self** is still in the realm of the personal. It's a puzzle piece, but it's distorted. It's been twisted. It's been misshaped. It is a misshaped, twisted puzzle piece, still in the realm of the personal. That's the fourth station.

Those are the first four stations—and now, massive takeoff!

STATION FIVE: TRUE SELF

Now we are going to take a momentous leap into the fifth station, and the fifth station is this dramatic, exponential up-leveling of self, where something *new* happens.

- We are laying down, we are *evolving,* the source code of consciousness and culture itself right now.
- We are literally participating in the evolution of love. We are doing the hard work—but it's ecstatic work.
- We are putting together, weaving together, the deepest validated insights of premodernity, modernity, and postmodernity. We are weaving them into a larger whole, which is a full vision of self.

Now that's going to translate in lots of *second simplicity* ways. We have to download it into culture. But first we have to *get it*. Let us see if we can get this, if we can *access* this. Are we ready for this huge leap?

We are now getting to station five, which is **the fifth self, which is the leap beyond the personal into the *impersonal*, or we might even call it the *transpersonal.***

104

We're moving *beyond the personal*. We're moving from separate self, social self, false self, that cluster of selves—they're all in the realm of the personal.

We're moving *to the impersonal, to the transpersonal*, and it's a more true, deeper version of self. And it's called actually *True Self*.

True Self is wildly important, and it's also been misunderstood even by the great traditions that talked about it. We are not *restating* ancient truths—we are *drawing* from ancient, modern, and postmodern, but we are *evolving* them; so let us say this in the evolved and the deepest way it can be said:

- True Self is the Field of Consciousness, but it's not *just* the Field of Consciousness.
- It's the Field of Desire.
- It's the Field of Value—in which everything is connected to everything else.
- **True Self is the Field of Intimate Consciousness. It's the Field of Intimate Value. It's the Field of Intimacy with all things.**

I just had a beautiful conversation this morning, with a beautiful new friend, if I can be so bold, who is a profound teacher in the Zen tradition, and we were talking about this statement by Master Dogen, great Zen master, *Enlightenment is intimacy with all things*. And we were looking together at the original Japanese, which I wanted to do for a while to make sure that was a correct translation. **And this notion of *enlightenment is intimacy with all things*, that's True Self.**

But it's not just that there's a Field of Consciousness. There's a Field of Consciousness in which:

- I'm completely *lost*—and completely *found*.
- I'm completely *deconstructed*—and I'm completely *reconstructed*.
- I've *given up* all of my self—and I've *found* all of myself, and my self is not separate from the entire field.

And that *interpenetration*, that *interdependent co-arising* of the correct form that happens in True Self—that is the deepest sense of who I am.

Who am I? I am essence.

Who am I? I am True Self.

Who am I? I am inseparable from the Field of Consciousness.

Who am I? I am indivisible from the Field of Value.

Who am I? I cannot be in any way disambiguated from the great Field of Desire.

I am desire. I am consciousness. I am value.

I Am that I Am.

All of us participate in the same one True Self. The total number of True Selves in the world is one. True Self is the singular that has no plural.

I am speaking to you, friends, **not from the constructs of the mind—but the constructs of the lived realization of my own body, heart, and mind**, and the lived realization of the most subtle and speculative minds, hearts, and bodies. We need to integrate all of that knowing, the best understanding we have at this level, station five.

Now, many of the great traditions, if they get here (and they usually don't get here), claim **True Self as being one with** *consciousness*. We just did a much deeper vision of True Self.

They *stop* here and say:

- *This* is the accomplishment.
- *This* is enlightenment.
- *This* is the mystical realization.

- *This* is attainment.
- *This* is Satori.
- This is it.

No, it's not. This is a critical station, momentous leap, the beginning of the change that changes everything. **But we are not home yet.**

Because True Self is the experience—in terms of the puzzle piece image— that **there *is* a puzzle, it is one whole—there are no separate puzzle pieces.**

One second, you think there *are* puzzle pieces, you *see* these lines separating, there seem to be puzzle pieces. That's an illusion. Die on the cushion, sit, meditate, or however you practice, like a whirling dervish, and you will realize that there is no separation at all—it doesn't exist. And there is no distinction, there is no uniqueness. Those are all illusions; we are all part of the same one True Self, one Field of Consciousness.

That is precisely true and not true. And when you claim it as a *whole* truth, you devastate the human body, heart, and mind, which is what mystical traditions have done forever.

Because actually, friends, there is no True Self anywhere in the manifest world—it doesn't exist. Every True Self sees through a unique set of eyes— and **uniqueness is not separateness.**

STATION SIX: UNIQUE SELF

Separateness is a Reality of Cosmos. We are *supposed* to have an experience of separateness. Separateness is a true reality, a real experience—but ultimately, separateness *dissolves*. Ultimately, Einstein wasn't wrong when he said separateness is an optical delusion of consciousness.

But after separateness dissolves, and I realize I am indivisible from the Field of True Self, the one consciousness, and one heart, and one desire, and one love. I then individuate not into separation; I individuate into *uniqueness*.

I actually *am* an irreducibly unique expression of True Self.

There is no True Self in the manifest world, and the attempt to locate True Self in the manifest world is doomed to failure—because every one of us is an individuated expression of True Self. Every one of us is a distinct expression of True Self.

True Self is the realization that we are all part of the seamless coat of the Universe. **The seamless coat of the Universe is *seamless* but not *featureless*, and you and I are its distinct features**. Actually, the experience of my enlightenment is *not* True Self. It's stunning, my friends! **The experience of my enlightenment is Unique Self.**

Who are you?

You are an irreducibly unique expression of the LoveIntelligence and LoveBeauty and LoveDesire that's the initiating and animating Eros of All-That-Is, that lives in you, as you, and through you, that never was, is, or will be ever again, other than through you.

Can you feel that?

And as such:

- You have an irreducibly unique *perspective*.
- You incarnate an irreducibly unique *quality of intimacy*.
- This comes together to foster your *unique gift*.
- This allows you to respond to a *unique need* in your unique circle of intimacy and influence.

That's Unique Self.

There is a beautiful apocryphal story of a child.

> *The teacher asks the children to draw trees. And the teacher comes over and looks over the child's shoulder and says, "You didn't draw my tree. You are drawing a purple tree."*
>
> *"Yeah, I did."*
>
> *"But there's no purple trees."*
>
> *"Yes, there are. I just drew one."*
>
> *And the teacher says, "But I can't see it."*
>
> *And the child looks and says, "Isn't that a shame?"*

Everyone's got a purple tree.

Everyone's an irreducibly unique expression—and that irreducibly unique expression is *not* your talent.

It's not your Myers-Briggs test. It's not your personality test.

It's *not* your talent—it's your gift.

It's the Field of Value, the Field of Consciousness, the Field of Desire. That's the Holy Trinity: value, desire, and consciousness. **Those fields, *uniquely individuated in you, as you, and through you,* as the intention of Cosmos—that's your Unique Self.**

Your Unique Self, my friends, is the sixth station, the sixth expression of self.

Your Unique Self is a puzzle piece that completes the puzzle.

The puzzle piece that completes the puzzle is *located*. The puzzle actually *holds* the puzzle piece, and the puzzle piece intimately *fits* gorgeously and perfectly. **And as the puzzle and the puzzle piece merge, there's this gorgeous explosion.** Oh my God, oh my God, yes, yes, yes! I'm completing. I'm needed.

Only my idiosyncratic puzzle piece can complete this puzzle—that is the experience of Unique Self.

So far we have:

- The first station: pre-personal self
- The second station: separate self
- The third station: social self
- The fourth station: false self
- The fifth station: True Self
- The sixth station: Unique Self

STATION SEVEN: UNIQUE SHADOW

Now, the seventh station I am going to talk about just for a moment. And it's not a quality of self; it's actually *a quality of consciousness*. It's a distortion, if you will, of self. It's a distorted quality of self, and that's what we call *unique shadow*.

Unique shadow is related to unique wound, but they are not the same. Every person has a unique way in which they are wounded, and everyone has a unique expression of shadow. The way my story wounded me, the trauma of my life—that's my unique wound. That's *one part* of this next station, of this seventh station.

And then there is my unique shadow.

People usually understand shadow as being as Robert Bly defines it in his book called *The Little Book of the Shadow*, which gets it exactly wrong, in which shadow is your jealousy, your rage, your contraction, your anger. That's not shadow. Those are shadow *qualities*.

Shadow is rather the part of your light which is not visible.

Light—your light, or your illumination, or your enlightenment—is your unique expression of True Self, your Unique Self, your unique story. Now your story is coming on board again. Now, in this place of Unique Self, we are not in *just* the personal.

Now, stay close for a second, we are in this new structure of consciousness.

Pre-personal is where we start, then we get to separate self, which is *personal*, then we get to True Self, which is normally understood as *impersonal*.

Then when you go to Unique Self, now you are the personal beyond the impersonal. You are back at the personal; it's the personal again. **Unique Self is absolutely radically intimate and personal, but it's the personal *after* the impersonal.**

Your Unique Self personal is your light—*ner Elohim nishmat adam*— *the candle of the Divine is the soul of the human*—that's why light is such an important image. The sense of being *enlightened*, the sense of being *illuminated*, means I have a unique frequency of light. I am a unique frequency; I have a singular frequency of light.

Imagine there's a circle, and in that circle is the uniqueness of my life that participates in the larger field. In that circle, to the precise extent that I *cut off* a quarter or a half—or most of us, four fifths of the circle, **I cut off four fifths of the circle of that light. And it's shrouded, obscured, not realized—it's in darkness. That's called *shadow*.**

Shadow is the part of my Unique Self that's in darkness. It's the part of my Unique Self that's unlived or distorted.

My Unique Self distortion, or my soul-print distortion, or my unlived Unique Self—that's shadow. But of course, it's *unique*. There's no such thing as *generic* shadow; it has to be unique because it's a distortion of my Unique Self. My unique shadow is a distortion of my Unique Self.

If you would, friends, look for the place where you—or I—*always mess up.*

It's a place you always get caught, where you *always* mess it up, always fall, where you keep effing it up again and again, and again and again—that place is a confluence of your unique wound and your unique shadow. **It's not just your woundedness—it's also that there is a particular dimension of your light that's unlived and you keep blowing it again and again.**

But in the unique way you're blowing it, you're actually expressing, or showing, or disclosing the pathway back to your Unique Self. Because you follow your unique shadow all the way home to your Unique Self.

WHY SHOULD YOU INTEGRATE YOUR SHADOW?

I'm going to give an example because we really have to *get* this. And afterwards, we have only two more stations. But I'll give you an example, and this is a true story. I was in Germany, and I had just begun to teach this idea of unique shadow, and it's a critically important idea. Because the entire conversation around shadow is distorted in a very tragic way, in which shadow is understood as your rage or anger. And when everyone tells you your anger is your shadow, then **why should you integrate your rage and anger?** I mean, you want to be *aware* of it, but why should you *integrate* it into your wholeness?

Inappropriate rage and inappropriate anger you should work with.

There's appropriate rage and appropriate anger—*that* clearly has a place.

But pathological rage and pathological anger—which is what shadow is—why would you want to integrate *that*? That's what the shadow world teaches. And it's a mistake, of course. Because those are your shadow *qualities*. Your shadow is your unlived Unique Self.

It's your Unique Self distortion that you have to integrate, because **that's your light that's been placed in darkness and has to be integrated in**

order for you to be *whole*—and uniquely whole, because you can only be uniquely whole.

I'll just tell you just a very brief story, a true story.

> I was in Germany with my friend, Diane, and we were teaching this Unique Self teaching, Unique Self and unique shadow, and it was maybe 2010. And there was this very lovely man, a German man, at the event.
>
> We are teaching this Unique Self idea. And this guy was this charismatic and attractive personality, and he was with us. And as soon as I started talking about unique shadow, he clearly got agitated. He raised his hand and he said, "This is ridiculous, this notion of unique shadow! I'm a therapist and I work with shadows; this notion of unique shadow is just not true."
>
> I said, "Okay."
>
> He says, "Just okay?"
>
> "Yeah, okay."
>
> "Well, talk to me about it."
>
> I said, "Okay, we can talk about it. You are a therapist, so what would you say your shadow is what I would call your unique shadow?"
>
> "Well, if I would think about that, I would say I do an enormous amount of meth and fisting. Meth and fisting." (And fisting is a quite graphic experience in which an entire fist is inserted into an orifice as an expression of sexuality.)
>
> So he said, "I do meth and fisting." And here is this very urbane, refined person. And there's a big shudder in the room, as I'm sure there is now in you, a big shudder.
>
> He said, "If you want a unique shadow, that's my unique shadow."
>
> I said, "Wow!"

He said, "What does that have to do with my Unique Self? That's got nothing to do with my Unique Self. Okay, it's my unique shadow; it's the way I mess up all the time."

So first off, I said to him, "Why is that a shadow?" Everybody laughed, and he laughed too, and we softened a little bit.

He said, "Well, it's a shadow because I do too much of it. I do too much of it, I don't want to be doing that much."

I said, "Okay, so you're a therapist, so what do you do as a therapist?"

Now he got really open and he said, "I hold people."

I said, "Wow, that's fantastic. You hold people. That's a great thing to do. But what if the person has a really challenging issue, do you challenge people as well?"

"I think therapists challenge people too much. I really hold people."

"Wow, that's great. You hold people. That's so beautiful. But what about when some issue needs to be broken up and someone needs to be kind of penetrated, we need your penetrating insight?"

"Nah, my job is to hold people."

And gradually, the room got quiet, and he got quiet.

I said, "Wow. So you're a therapist, and your Unique Self is being a therapist. People come to you and trust you, and they desperately need your penetrating insight, and they need you to challenge them. And you just hold them, and you refuse to penetrate their consciousness with the depth of your insight. Wow, you're a brilliant therapist. ***But your Unique Self, your penetration, your ecstatic penetration to illuminate something is in shadow.*** *And so it emerges as your unique shadow: meth and fisting."*

He started crying, and we all got quiet. We could see it.

Everyone has a place which is not just shadow—it's *unique* shadow.

And that is, my friends, that's the seventh station. It's not a self, but it's a *distortion* of self. It's like false self in that sense, so we could call it a self in the same way we could call false self a self. It's a particular expression of self. It's a quality of consciousness. Let's call it a self the same way we've called false self a self.

STATION EIGHT: EVOLUTIONARY UNIQUE SELF

So we've got pre-personal self, separate self, social self, false self, True Self, Unique Self, as well as unique shadow and unique wound, which constellate together to form this distorted expression, this shadow self, this unique shadow self. That's station seven. Okay, we've got two more, two more to go!

We are actually re-sourcing Reality. We are participating together, in this moment, in evolving the source code in response to the meta-crisis, in generating the best and deepest vision of self, weaving together the valid insights of premodernity, modernity, and postmodernity, into a new Story of Value.

This new Story of Value has to address three questions:

+ Who am I? Who are you? Who are we? That's all part of the same question.
+ Where are we, and where are we going?
+ What's there to do? What do we desire?

We are looking at the first question here, and we are now at station eight. And station eight, my friends, is Evolutionary Unique Self.

Evolutionary Unique Self is Unique Self in an evolutionary context, where I experience that I am an irreducibly unique expression of the evolutionary impulse itself.

I'm an irreducibly unique expression of the evolutionary impulse itself, that lives *in me, as me, and through me.* **I am no less than the personal face of the evolutionary impulse.** And evolution is desire. The desire of evolution lives uniquely in me, as me, and through me.

So who am I? I am evolutionary desire. But I'm not just *generically* an expression of evolutionary desire. I'm an irreducibly unique expression.

- I'm an irreducibly unique expression of the LoveDesire of evolution.
- I'm the love story of the Universe, incarnate in person in me.
- I'm the personal face of the Universe: A Love Story.
- I've evolved from *Homo sapiens*, and I've become the new human. I'm crossing to the other side; I become *Homo amor.* *Homo amor* is when I've crossed to the other side—I am now *Homo amor.*
- **I'm an irreducibly unique expression of the evolutionary impulse itself. All of evolution throbs in me. All of evolution pulses in me.**

Your desire—your *clarified* desire, not your *surface* desire but what we call, together with my evolutionary partner, Barbara Marx Hubbard, **your Deepest Heart's Desire—is the desire of evolution awake and alive in you**. That's why you can't *tell* it; that's why you have to *listen* to it. That's why we have to listen to the murmurings of the sacred that live in the whisperings of desire, that call us to live and incarnate Evolutionary Unique Self.

Evolutionary Unique Self is not just a puzzle piece that *completes* the puzzle. Evolutionary Unique Self is a puzzle piece that *evolves* the puzzle.

There is *more* puzzle. The puzzle *expands*, and it gets deeper, and wider, and more good, and more true, and more beautiful. That's Evolutionary Unique Self.

Evolutionary Unique Self stands for the core equation of the new Story of Value, which integrates the best of premodern, modern, and

Postmodern. And that core equation, which we talked about last week: infinity plus finitude equals more infinity (finitude is the manifest, this world, the evolutionary world, the world of becoming).

Infinity plus finitude equals more infinity.

Now, the rules of logic can't wrap around it—but actually, trans-logic does.

It's a lived realization.

It's the truth of paradox that—in some paradoxical sense—you can realize in your own body. You can actually find this in your own body literally right now.

- Find your own sense of yourself. Do you matter? You do. What do you think about all the time? Yourself? Why? Because you're a narcissist? No, because when you're thinking about yourself all the time, you're eavesdropping on Infinity thinking about you. Because you are Infinity becoming more of itself. **God plus you equals more God.**

There is literally more God to come.

Infinite value plus your unique incarnation of value equals *more* value.

You are, quite literally, *more God to come.* You're more value to come.

There is more goodness and more truth and more beauty when—when what? *When you clarify.*

Does everyone understand? That's actually, quite literally, how it works—when I *clarify* my story.

This is now not my story at the level of separate self, which is the level of the personal. I get from the personal to the impersonal, and at the impersonal, I'm True Self, where I leave my story behind. And then I rise to the personal that is beyond the impersonal, which is my Unique Self—and then my Unique Self in the evolutionary context. Then my story comes back online, roaring back online, and I realize that **my story has ultimate dignity,**

because my story is chapter and verse in the sacred autobiography of the Infinite.

My story is chapter and verse in the sacred autobiography of the Infinite.

My story is chapter and verse in the sacred autobiography of the Divine.

My story is chapter and verse in the sacred autobiography of God.

STATION NINE: UNIQUE SELF SYMPHONY

And from that place, my friends—and here we crescendo—we get to the ninth station.

The ninth expression, or quality, where Self plays, is **Unique Self Symphony**—a new structure of intimacy, which responds to the root cause of the meta-crisis.

The root cause of the meta-crisis is global intimacy disorder. And global intimacy disorder expresses itself as rivalrous conflict governed by win/ lose metrics. It expresses itself as complicated systems in which the parts don't know each other, and therefore the system becomes fragile. But these complicated fragile systems, and these rivalrous, complex, success-story win-lose metrics—those *generator functions* of existential risk—are rooted in a *deeper root cause*, which is the global intimacy disorder.

We have to respond to the global intimacy disorder, which splits us off and blocks us from achieving what we need—which is global intimacy, which achieves global resonance, which achieves global coherence, which achieves the possibility of global coordination, which allows us to respond to global challenges.

How do we actually get to that place? How do we realize that? We have to overcome, we have to solve, we have to resolve at a higher level of consciousness, the global intimacy disorder.

This means we need to generate a new structure of intimacy, and **a new structure of intimacy can come only from the deepest new structure of Self**. Because intimacy means intimacy between selves.

Now, here's the last step:

- Separate selves can't create intimacy, because they're ultimately *separate*.
- False selves are too *distorted* to create intimacy.
- Social selves create pseudo-harmonies, pseudo-intimacies of the hive mind, which are *depersonalize*d and degraded.
- The total number of True Selves in the world is one, part of the one field, so there's no intimacy; there's no intimacy with the one.
- **True intimacy begins at Unique Self.** Unique Selves create Unique Self coherence.
- **Evolutionary Unique Selves:** I'm intimate, not just with my own uniqueness—my uniqueness resonates with your uniqueness. **I am intimate with the entire evolutionary context.** I realize evolution is moving uniquely through me; we are Evolutionary Unique Selves, and we come together in a new structure of intimacy, in an evolutionary intimacy, which we might call Unique Self Symphony.
- **Unique Self Symphony is the political social structural image which responds to the meta-crisis. It's the deepest response we have to the meta-crisis.**

Imagine an anthill, in which everyone knows what to do. How do they know? Because maybe pheromones are exchanged—we're not sure scientifically. That anthill is, in some dramatic sense, pre-personal. **Imagine an anthill or a beehive, but exponentially more conscious at the human level, in which the strange attractor to perform my great mission is my uniqueness.** It's not pheromones that are being exchanged between the ants, but it's every human being actually *listening*:

- To their deepest desires
- To their deepest *unique* desires
- To their own unique set of *allurements*

Through this, they can enact goodness, truth, and beauty as an expression of their unique gift, their unique qualities of value, and unique qualities of intimacy. That's what it means to play your instrument in the Unique Self Symphony.

When I am in the Unique Self Symphony, there might be seven or eight of us, or a thousand of us, each uniquely playing the *same* instrument. But we *each* have a unique *take* on that instrument, and it's a Unique Self *jazz* Symphony.

And there is a moment in time in my particular corner of Reality where I can look into un-love, I can look into the eyes of un-love, and I can say, *let there be light!* **And I can give a unique gift that no one that ever is, was, or will be in the history of Reality can give, in the unique way that I can give it.**

That's what it means to play my instrument in the Unique Self Symphony: I am listening to the score of music. There's a shared score, and we each have our own jazz section in that shared score. We need all the other instruments, and we are all moved by the original Eros of Cosmos, the original love, Evolutionary Love, and Outrageous Love of Cosmos that lives uniquely in us.

The vision is a planetary awakening in Eros through Unique Self Symphonies, a planetary awakening in love through Unique Self Symphonies.

Can we feel that together—a Planetary Awakening in Love through Unique Self Symphonies?

That's the ninth station.

That's the new emergence.

That's *Homo amor*.

That's the new human.

That's the new humanity.

We just evolved the source code. Thank you so crazy much. I'm so—tears in my eyes—grateful. Thank you for your presence, your instrument in the Symphony, your listening, your participation, your joy, and your beauty.

CHAPTER SIX

FEEL YOU FEELING ME: THE NEW HUMAN AND THE NEW NAME OF GOD

Episode 353 — July 16, 2023

THE MOST EFFECTIVE ALTRUISM IS TELLING A NEW STORY OF VALUE

In this time between worlds, this time between stories, our intention is to participate in responding to the meta-crisis.

> Crisis is an evolutionary driver, and each crisis, at its core, is a crisis of intimacy, and a crisis of intimacy means a crisis of relationship.

There are two generator functions of existential and catastrophic risk, as we have identified, together with our beloved Barbara Marx Hubbard. **The first generator function of existential and catastrophic risk is rivalrous conflict governed by win/lose metrics as the source code structure of human reality, which leads to the second generator, the fragility of the systems.**

For example, one of the things that is tragically likely— and we're doing nothing about it—is the intense heat wave in India. There's an intense heat wave around the

world, which in a place like India could kill 200 million people in a week. We know that's a genuine possibility, and we are doing nothing about it. Why not? Because it doesn't fit into being able to win in our system of rivalrous conflict, even in India, for any number of reasons I'm not going to go into now. This generates a fragile system. Then we're going to cry about the tragedy.

Wow, that's intense! So we look away.

We look away, as we look away from Ukraine.

How do we look *towards*? What does it mean to look towards?

To look towards is to become *Homo amor*.

To look *towards* is to become the new human—and you can look towards only if you can *respond*. If you cannot respond, if you can only *feel* the pain, but you cannot *respond* to the pain, then in the gap between our ability to feel the pain and our ability to heal the pain, we have to close our hearts.

Not because we're narcissistic and egocentric, as many enlightenment teachers—who are all wonderful people, many of them my friends—like to tell us. There's some truth in that, but that's not the core.

The core is not that we feel too little; it's that we feel too much—and if we cannot respond to the pain that we feel so intensely, at some point we simply have to close our hearts.

In order to open our hearts, we have to be able to respond.

To respond means there's something to feel and something to do that can directly shift the course of history. That ability to shift the course of history at this moment, in this time between worlds, in this time between stories, is the most *effective altruism* that we could do. Effective Altruism is what Peter Singer, Will MacAskill, and Toby Ord (all students of Derek Parfit), and others are talking about. Effective Altruism says, don't just handle the person in front of you, but use reason to understand how you can have the most global effect in alleviating suffering. That's beautiful, and that might result in spending lots of money on mosquito nets, which can save more lives from malaria perhaps than anything else.

However, they are missing the core point (and guys, total respect, love, brothers, but you're missing the point): **you cannot do effective altruism without telling a new Story of Value.**

There is a *deeper* effective altruism:

- To shift the course of history
- To raise all boats
- To transform
- To save the future and the most disadvantaged who will be destroyed by catastrophic risk (and all of us by existential risk).

What we have to do is tell a new Story of Value, because story and value are the source code of Reality.

We have to tell a new story but not a postmodern story that's made up. No, value is *real*; the Field of Value is *real*, and **the best, most effective Story of Value is *real*—not because we decided it is so, but because it aligns with the evolving values of Cosmos.**

We have to tell a new Story of Value rooted in evolving First Principles and First Values—and that new Story of Value has to be understandable and accessible to every man, woman, and child, in China, Afghanistan, Iceland, New Zealand, South America, South Africa, Australia, all over Europe and the Americas, and in Asia. There can be no place where this story is not easily accessible and easily understood.

THE NEW STORY OF VALUE LIVES IN US

Who am I?

I'm not just *Homo sapiens*. I am *Homo amor*. I feel the whole, and the whole lives in me.

> I am *omni-considerate* for the sake of the whole.

> I am *omni-feeling* for the sake of the whole.

> I am *omni-responsible* for the sake of the whole.

Not that I have to do it *all* myself—that's the voice of the egoic mind that shuts us down.

So, what do *I* need to do? **I need to respond to the unique needs in my unique circle of intimacy and influence.** That's what is mine to do. That's what it means to play my instrument in the Unique Self Symphony.

This is a core part of the new story:

> Every man, woman, and child is a Unique Self, an irreducibly unique expression of the LoveIntelligence and LoveBeauty of Cosmos.

> We have unique instruments in the Unique Self Symphony, and those are ours to play.

> That's the expression of the *Shakti*—of the Eros that moves irreducibly through me.

> Answering the call of the *Shakti* and committing my unique Outrageous Acts of Love is the plotline not only of my life but of the entire Universe awake and alive in me.

Evolution awake and alive in me is desiring my enactment of its own values, which are Eros, intimacy, dignity, integrity, fairness, harmony, and uniqueness. Those values live in me, and I can enact them in the world in a unique way in my unique circle of intimacy and influence, and that is the plotline of my life. As the Bible says, *Hot damn!* I think that's from *The Book of Psalms.*

We are here to tell this new story. That's the most effective altruism. That's the seat of this revolution. We are going to talk about that in a new way today, and I want to go deeper into these questions:

- How does this new story live in us?
- How do we enact this new story?
- How do we be this new story?
- How do we become *Homo amor?*

ANTHRO-ONTOLOGY: HOW DO YOU KNOW WHAT YOU KNOW?

Here's this week's Evolutionary Love code:

> If there were two children outside of your home, and you saw them suffering on the front lawn, you would stop everything you were doing to help them.

> But if the same children are in another part of the world, even if you were aware of their existence and the fact that they are suffering, all too often the overwhelming majority of human beings go on with business as usual.

> To be or not to be, that is the question. It's a question that every human being must ask in this moment of meta-crisis.

What does it mean to be human?

What's the nature of our joy as human beings?

What's the nature of our tears as human beings?

What are the actions required of us as human beings?

What are the responsibilities required of us as human beings?

What are the rights required of us as human beings?

What are the raptures required of us as human beings?

We ask these questions not from a place of shame and not from a place of brokenness but from a place of wholeness and celebration—from a place of agony but also a place of ecstasy.

We stand together in the nobility and ecstatic urgency of our humanity.

And we invoke the possible human.

The possible human is omni-considerate for the sake of the whole.

The possible human feels the whole of humanity, the whole of Reality.

The possible human feels the truth that the whole includes not only who's visible in their front yard but also every human being in the past and in the future.

The possible human stops business as usual and acts for the liberation of the whole.

The possible human understands that to be is to be *Homo amor*.

Let's see if we can find our way into this. What does it mean to be *Homo amor*? What does it mean to feel the children in the world who are *not* on my front lawn? In other words, **what does it mean to expand my field of feeling beyond my visual field?**

My visual field is right in front of me—but how do I expand beyond my visual field, which is my egocentric field, what's directly available to me, and experience this feeling of radical desire, care, concern, and love for people I cannot see?

I have to find the people who are dislocated *spatially*—they are not near me.

Then I need to feel the people who are dislocated *temporally*—they are not just currently around the world but are either in the past or in the future.

In responding to existential risk, we must respond:

- **To all past generations**, who have labored mightily for the evolution of consciousness and have passed us the baton, and if we drop it, then all of their work, in some sense, collapses. Yes, what they did has value in and of itself, but it collapses. In other words, we are partners: there is a covenant between the generations.
- **To all of the future generations**. We have to feel the future.

So *how* do we feel?

I am going to go to the core of it. Before we talk about feeling across the globe and then feeling the future, I want to bring it down to the most basic:

How do I feel that which is right in front of me?

How do I feel you, even when you are in my visual field?

How do I feel someone else?

I remember I was talking to my beloved brother, Daniel Schmachtenberger, a few years ago. I was formulating for him this notion of allurement as the core structure of Cosmos and what that means. Then a couple of years later, I was in an early formulation of the *Tenets of Intimacy*, the twenty-four principles of the Intimate Universe. Daniel and I were really excited about it, and we were going back and forth, and whenever we go back and forth, it's fructifying: there's always a deeper whole, a deeper delight, a deeper exchange that emerges.

Then at a certain point, Daniel said to me something like, *How the fuck do you know this shit?* Meaning, how do you know this—what's your source?

As Zak always teases me, I never do literature surveys on a topic. Daniel asks, *How do you know?* That question forced me to clarify the principle of Anthro-Ontology: ***I know it because it lives in me.***

How do you know what you know?

> *Anthro*: within my own interiors.

> *Ontology:* the true nature of the world.

Thus, Anthro-Ontology: what lives inside of me, when I clarify my interiors, are the plotlines of Cosmos, and the plotlines of Cosmos are its evolving First Principles and First Values.

THE CORE OF *HOMO AMOR* IS MY CAPACITY TO FEEL YOU

One of the evolving First Principles and First Values of Cosmos is intimacy itself.

There's actually no such thing as *intimacy*—it's **intimacy-value**. Same with Eros. It's not just *Eros*; it's actually *ErosValue*, one word.

What do these values mean?

- *Eros* is the movement of Reality towards a deeper contact. It's the desire of Reality for deeper contact and ever greater wholeness.
- *Intimacy* is the experience of shared identity, which generates and is generated by the mutuality of feeling. We can feel each other; we are in a shared Field of Value and have shared purpose.

I want to deepen this and really understand this deeply. How does *Homo amor* do this?

When Daniel asked me that question, we attempted to deeply clarify this notion of Anthro-Ontology: how we know what we know, the mysteries within us, and this notion of First Principles and First Values.

When we go deep inside, First Principles and First Values are everywhere. They are not in some philosophy book—they are everywhere.

I want to take you on a little ride into a deep understanding of how this works.

I'll tell you a story.

I'm living here in Vermont, where the Center for World Philosophy and Religion has a house. One of the people who lives at the Center, let's make V his initial, is a big hardy guy, and I'm a little less hardy. In the Vermont winters, it's completely freezing, like 20 degrees below. The windchill factor is like 160 degrees below. Now, cold does not work for me, so I had an enormously difficult first winter here. The cold just froze me. I was sick on and off all through the winter, and I was trying to persuade V and other people connected to the Center, "Let's warm this place up."

"No, it's warm," he said. "We've got this heater, and we've got that heater—it's warm."

"Guys, it's not warm. No, it is not warm. I'm telling you, I am freezing."

And they're fantastic, gorgeous people—obviously this is no critique—but I couldn't quite get across that, Oh my God, I am chilled to the bone. It was hard.

Then, a couple of weeks ago, V and my beloved partner both say:

"Oh my God, it's so hot. I can't work. We have to get air conditioning."

And I am like, "Hot? I love the heat. I'm working through 90 degrees, 100 degrees—not a problem."

Then I said, "Wow, that's so interesting. So you don't get me. You can't feel me feeling my experience of the cold, and I can't feel you feeling your experience of the heat."

To truly love each other, I have to feel what you feel like in the heat, even though the heat doesn't affect me at all. And then I can feel *you*, and how am I going to do that? I've got to do it by feeling how I feel in the cold.

If I can feel how I feel in the cold, and I can then project that onto you in terms of the heat, now I can feel you.

And if you can now feel, wow, you can't work today—you're just dead because of the heat—go to that experience, transpose, and actually feel *me* and how I feel in the cold.

Once we were able to do that, we were completely motivated to create this huge coherent plan. We had this deeper resonance between us and this deeper intimacy. We already have a sense of shared identity, but we had deepened our mutuality of pathos, *our ability to feel each other*, and we were able to then resonate with each other—and then able to create coherence, which is a plan: Okay, how do we get the place air conditioning? How do we actually create proper insulation, or whatever we need to create for the winter?

All of a sudden, a shared purpose became much easier because we could actually *feel* each other.

This is a very big deal.

The core of *Homo amor* is our capacity to feel each other.

Homo amor steps out of her/his own narcissistic predicament and has the capacity to *shift perspectives* and to take the perspective of the other—but not just from a mind perspective, an intellectual perspective, a cognitive perspective (*I can think what you think*). No, I can *feel* what you feel. To love you means *I can see what you see.*

It is so deep.

EVOLVING LOVE IS EVER DEEPER LOOPS IN THE MUTUALITY OF FEELING

We have a structure of three levels of evolving love, three levels in the evolution of relationships:

- One level is **role mate**. *I love you* means: I hear your needs, I respond to your needs, and I show up in my role, either as the creator of the home, as the protector, or as the breadwinner. We have roles.
- **Soul mate** means not so much *I need you*, or I see what you need and respond to your need. It's *I see you*. We are looking deeply into each other's eyes.
- But **whole mate**, the third level beyond soul mate, is not just *I see you*, but *I see what you see*. I love what you love. I feel what you feel.

That's the only liberation from loneliness, my friends. The only liberation from loneliness is when we can look into our beloved's eyes—and our beloved might be our close friend, it might be a partner in this great revolution, it might be someone I'm working alongside, my evolutionary community:

We can feel what they feel.

We can see what they see.

We love what they love.

For *Homo amor*, loving happens at the level of whole mate.

I couldn't quite feel you because I'm not bothered by the cold, or I couldn't quite feel you because I'm not bothered by the heat—but through my experience of the heat, I can find your experience of the cold. Or through my experience of the cold, I can find your experience of the heat.

That's what intimacy means.

Here's the intimacy equation again:

Intimacy = shared identity in the context of relative otherness x mutuality of recognition (we recognize each other) x mutuality of pathos (we feel each other) x mutuality of value (we are in the same Field of Value) x mutuality of purpose.

Let's focus now on just one piece, the mutuality of pathos: we feel each other.

How does that work?

- We feel each other means **I feel you**. I feel you. That's the beginning. I feel you; you feel me. That's the first loop. It's a big deal. That's already huge. I feel you; you feel me. I feel what you feel; you feel what I feel. I can shift perspectives. It's huge!

- It goes deeper. **I feel you** *feeling me.* We are sitting together on the porch, and we are feeling each other. It's genuine intimacy and this depth of conversation. But then, I feel you feeling *me*, and you feel me feeling *you*. That's the second loop, a deeper loop.

- Can we take it a third loop? Let's get a third loop. **I feel you feeling me feeling you.** I feel me feeling you feeling me; you feel me feeling you feeling me. It's an even deeper loop.

I remember talking to Bill Harris many years ago. He said to me, "When I do a meditative practice of awareness, first I'm aware of awareness, then I'm aware of me being aware of awareness, then I'm aware of me being aware of me being aware of awareness."

In other words, you do these loops of awareness till you get the very deep realization of awareness. In Buddhism, that's how they find the Field of Awareness. But on the inside of awareness, the inside of consciousness is *ananda*. *Ananda* is bliss-love, Eros, intimacy. **The inside of consciousness is intimacy.**

To be intimate means:

+ Level one: I feel you, you feel me.
+ Level two: I feel you feeling me; you feel me feeling you.
+ Level three: I feel you feeling me feeling you; you feel me feeling you feeling me.

It keeps going to deeper loops, and that's very beautiful.

This is part of what we mean when we say that the human being is an incarnation of the Divine.

THE DIVINE IS THE INFINITE INTIMATE

The Divine is not the God who is *only* transcendent, who is only *other*, who holds all of Reality in her womb. God/Goddess is also *inherent, intimate.*

God/Goddess is *both* infinite and intimate.

A God/Goddess who is *only* infinite gets lost in the infinity of indifference. She is ultimately indifferent, alienated from Cosmos.

But a God/Goddess who is *only* imminent, or inherent, or intimate, without this infinite power, gets lost in the infinity of impotence.

The Divine is the Infinite Intimate. That's the new name of God, the new name of Goddess—the Infinite Intimate. In the interior sciences, in every generation, we have to re-approach and participate in the evolution of God, which is the evolution of how She/He/Goddess lives in us.

Goddess/God is the Infinite Intimate, and the quality of the Infinite Intimate is that He/She feels us.

Isaiah, the great master, writes, *Bekol Tzaratam Lo Tzar*: In every one of your contractions, in all of your brokenness, in all of your pain, I feel your pain.

From Isaiah comes Christ Consciousness. In other words, the Divine says, *I am going to so take your perspective that I am going to be crucified on a cross as you.* Wow!

Believe me, I have a massive critique of classical Christianity. And as Crosby, Stills, Nash, and Young sang so many years ago, *So many people have died in the name of Christ that I can't believe it all.*

And Voltaire, critiquing Christianity said, *Remember the cruelties*, as he began to give voice to the modern enlightenment.

Christianity has many sins, but it also has an originating interior, a profound realization, which is, *the Universe feels* (and Christianity took this realization from the Song of Solomon).

The Universe feels, and the Universe feels intimacy; the Universe feels love. And intimacy means that *I feel you*. It means *I can take your perspective*— so actually, Infinity is not only infinite, but is the Intimate. So Infinity, the Divine, takes my perspective and becomes me. Goddess/God becomes man incarnate, is crucified, has nails driven into him on the cross.

Oh my Goddess! That's the power of the clarified Christ understanding.

Now stay close, my friends, and we're going to close with this: Not only does God/Goddess take *my* perspective and become me, but *I* take the perspective of God/Goddess and become God/Goddess. **Not only does Goddess feel *my* pain, but I feel *her* pain.**

What that means is that I need to become so intimate with She that I can feel, in my finitude, Her infinite pain. That's impossible. Meaning, I am so intimate with the Infinite Intimate, so intimate with the Divine, that I cry *Her* tears—and remember, the tears of the Divine are not finite; the tears of the Divine are infinite. The pain of the Divine is infinite. God is not only the Infinity of Power; God is also the infinity of pain.

What does it mean to feel it?

> To take God's perspective is to be willing to enter into the Inside of the Inside with *She*, to feel *Her* pain, and to cry *Her* tears.

In Solomon's lineage, we call that *litzta'er b'tsar ha Shekhinah*: to participate with the pain of the *Shekhinah*, of *She*, in the broken exile—with all the broken hearts and lepers, with all the broken people, and with all the lonely people.

That's what it means to be *Homo amor*. *Homo amor* means, *I feel you feeling me.*

God/Goddess is part of *Homo amor*.

Homo amor is part of God/Goddess, even as we are held by the Infinite Intimate.

What we have tried to do today was to evoke some of the quality, some of the feeling tone of *Homo amor*.

CHAPTER SEVEN

FROM HOMO ARMOR TO
HOMO AMOR: HEARTBREAK
IS A STRUCTURE OF THE
INTIMATE UNIVERSE

Episode 354 — July 23, 2023

PART ONE: WE NEED TO EVOLVE THE SOURCE CODE IN WHICH WE LIVE

I want to set our intention this week, as we enter into the full depth of this moment:

> The unimaginable joy that lives in this moment.

> The play that's right here.

> The wisdom that's pregnant in this moment and that wants to be born.

> The ecstasy, the subtlety, the caring, the depth, and the preciousness that are in this moment.

We are going to love this moment open. This moment wants to speak to us.

We are also aware of the ways in which this moment is seeded with meta-crisis. We are aware of the ways

that all of the risks which have always existed have now crossed planetary boundaries. We are aware of the systemic breakdown of our systems, which has the capacity to cause unimaginable suffering and risks—catastrophic risk and even existential risk—to our very existence.

We come together in this moment in which opposites are joined at the hip, in the paradox of this moment. We are poised, literally, between utopia and dystopia, between the most beautiful world that we ever imagined possible and a fundamental degradation of Reality which could lead to the end of humanity, to the death of humanity, or to the death of our humanity as we understand it:

- A human being with free will.
- A human being with infinite dignity.
- A human being whose needs and whose desires are sacred.
- A human being whose heartbreak is held in the bosom of the Infinite.

What a moment, and what a privilege!

We come together every week; this is our 354th week. **Every single week, we come together with the intention of revolution.** In this revolution, we have our thumb inside our fist because we don't want to punch anyone—it's not an aggressive fist; it's a fist that's raised in revolution, that says:

We need to evolve the very systemic source code in which we live.

It's not about challenging some cabal that's running an evil conspiracy; it is about challenging something that's gone errant in the essential unfolding of Reality's basic storyline. The plotlines of Reality have become lost to us. We have stepped out of the Field of Value.

As exterior technologies have grown exponentially, bringing unimaginable dignities in modernity, **those same exterior technologies have been divorced or dissociated from an equal evolution of interior technologies.** We've failed to know how to *engage* the exponential technologies—and how to evaluate, infuse with value, and upload value into these exponential technologies which have given us the power of ancient gods.

We have the power of ancient gods, but we have no new Story of Value equal to our power.

We are in this gap between the explosion of unmoored and dissociated exterior technologies and the failure to articulate a new vision of value of what it means to be a human being, a new answer to the core questions:

Who am I?

Where am I?

What is really a *value*?

What needs to *be done*?

What's my *deepest heart's desire?*

What's *the nature of desire?*

What's the nature of who I am and my own deepest self?

Our failure to answer those questions and our *abandonment* of those questions, our relegation of those questions to the whims and caprices of the marketplace (which now, for the first time in the last fifty years, understands itself as being *outside* the Field of Value and is therefore governed only by the success story, win/lose metrics, and the war of all against all) generates *fragility*:

- In intimate one-on-one relationships
- In familial relationships
- In groups and nations
- In all larger wholes

This generates fragile, complicated systems that collapse on themselves when subject to stress.

That's existential risk. That's catastrophic risk.

WE LIVE IN AN EVOLVING AND PARTICIPATORY COSMOS

So how do we respond to this?

We have to articulate a new Story of Value, rooted not in capriciousness and not in old values that claim to be eternal and unchanging but in the Field of Value, which is both *eternal* and *evolving*—a Field of Evolving Value, in which:

- Love is real, and yet love is ever evolving.
- Eros is absolutely real, and Eros is always evolving.
- Intimacy is real, and there is an evolution of intimacy.
- Value is real, and Reality itself is the evolution of value.

We participate in the Field of Value, the Field of Eros, the Field of Desire, and the Field of Intimacy, and yet we understand that value, Eros, intimacy, and desire are always evolving—and we participate in that evolution of love.

It is that evolution of love that tells the new Story of Value, which then generates a new ground from which Reality emerges.

Reality always emerges from inescapable frameworks, and those frameworks are the Story of Value within which we live.

When we change and evolve the Story of Value, we begin to generate a new Reality—because the new Reality always *emerges*. It is an expression of the invisible plotlines of the story from within which we live.

Who can feel that? Who can feel where we are?

We are in the revolution. And what's the overwhelming moral imperative of the revolution?

To tell a new Story of Value but not to *declare* it; we have to validate it in the deepest strains of wisdom—ancient, modern, and postmodern wisdom. **We then have to weave all of these realizations together in a new synergistic whole and a wider narrative, a narrative that reflects the validated insights of all the wisdom streams of reality**, a narrative we can tell to any six-year-old or nine-year-old, on any continent in the world, to any socio-economic class, to all races, creeds, and colors. This is a Story of Value, a universal grammar of value, that will unite us and also serve as a context for our diversity.

That is the only response to the meta-crisis—the realization that **there is a Unique Self Symphony in every religion, that every nation is a unique intimacy, a unique instrument in that symphony, and has a unique gift to give and a unique life to live**. And Unique Self is not my Myers-Briggs test. It's not my separate self formula based on win/lose metrics—Unique Self is my unique expression of the Field of Eros, of the Field of Intimacy, of the Field of Desire.

That's what we're here to do. We're here to tell that new Story of Value—as a revolutionary act, in response to imminent unimaginable suffering. It's an act of *mad love*, as Rumi would say; we love madly. **It's an act of unimaginable love.**

It's an act not of ordinary love, some social construct between human beings—but of Outrageous Love, of the Eros that's the heart of existence. It's not mere human sentiment. The human sentiment *expresses* that ground of Outrageous Love or Eros that is the nature of Reality itself.

My friends, are we ready to do this?

Are we ready to play a larger game?

Are we ready to participate?

It's a participatory Cosmos, the physicist John Archibald Wheeler reminded us—and that's true in exteriors as well as interiors. It's true all the way in, all the way out, all the way up, and all the way down. Are we ready to participate in the evolution of love, in telling this new Story of Value?

We are going to go into a new world today, the world we've talked about many times over the last decade, but we're going to re-approach it and open it up in a new way. I've been in an ongoing conversation with Kristina Kincaid about this for the last decade, and we've talked about it together in many public teachings over the last decade. I had a conversation yesterday with a dear deep study partner, Ohad, with whom I had tragically lost touch for fourteen or fifteen years, and we recently re-established our practice of love and study. We have been exchanging about this over the last day, so I want to thank him and his partner Katara for their part in the conversation.

Let us step in, and let's blow this open. Let us love this open all the way.

INTIMACY IS ALWAYS BROKEN AND THEN RECOVERED

Here's our Evolutionary Love Code for this week:

> The nature of the Intimate Universe is that intimacy is always broken and that broken intimacy is the intention of the Universe.

> The deeper intention, however, of the same Intimate Universe is that broken intimacy be recovered and that the recovered intimacy is more profound, more poignant, more potent, more powerful, and more whole than it was before.

> The journey of the heart—from intimacy to the breaking of intimacy to its recovery at an ever higher and deeper level—is the evolution of love.

> This is the journey that we refer to in CosmoErotic Humanism as the movement from *Homo armor* to *Homo amor*.

Let us find this and feel this: the sense of the intimacy that's broken as part of the structure of the Universe.

Part of the structure of the Intimate Universe is that intimacy is broken and lost, and then it's recovered.

Breaking is part of the structure of Reality itself. That's called, in the lineage of Solomon, *shevirat ha-kelim*, the breaking of the vessels.

Cosmos lives in me: the personal is the cosmic, and the cosmic is the personal.

This realization—that we live in a participatory Universe, that I participate in the current of cosmic Reality, that the current of evolutionary Reality, the current of Eros, which animates all of Reality, lives *through me*—means that **all the events that form Reality happen in me: the Big Bang happens in me, and supernovas explode me, in some deep and real sense**.

When the lineage of Solomon talks about *the breaking of the vessels*, or other lineages talk about *the Fall*, or we talk about *the exile from Eden*, we talk about a *breaking*, a separation of heaven and earth—that takes place, in some sense, very deeply *inside of me*.

I want to talk about this part of intimacy that is unavoidable: the *breaking* of intimacy, which is the breaking of the heart.

Without this, we cannot talk about the One Heart of Cosmos, the Field of Eros which is Reality itself. We have talked about its scientific grounding, time and again. *The CosmoErotic Universe, the Sensual Cosmos, the Amorous Cosmos, the Intimate Universe*—there are many names we use to describe this realization, and it emerges from the closest reading of the *exterior* sciences but also through the closest reading of the *interior* sciences.

We realize that:

- Reality is driven by allurement and autonomy, attraction and repulsion, autonomy and communion.
- Reality is, quite literally, filled with appetite, filled with desire.

- Reality is Eros, moving towards ever deeper contact and ever greater wholeness.

That's the structure and nature of Reality, and in that movement towards wholeness, there's an inevitable structure, and that inevitable structure is heartbreak—the breaking of the vessels.

HEARTBREAK IS THE NATURAL STATE OF AN ALIVE HUMAN BEING

Let us start with the baby.

In the interior sciences of Hasidism (which is this movement that swept Eastern Europe from about 1760 until World War Two), there is a teaching from Isaac of Vorki, who says you can learn three things from a child. And my friend, Ohad, whom I mentioned earlier, likes to cite this text. I am going to cite it a little differently than the way Isaac of Vorki says it, but this is his basic intention:

You learn *play* from a baby. It's not quite natural *joy*; it's *play*. The baby *plays*. The baby is *Homo ludens*, the playing human being. The sense of dance of joy and play for its own sake is natural to a baby.

As soon as a baby has a fundamental need, the baby cries. **The baby is deeply in touch with her need, and that need evokes tears.** She doesn't disown her need, and she responds.

The baby is always open; the baby doesn't close. That openness expresses itself in curiosity, and curiosity is a quality of loving. *Curious* means I am open, and when I'm open, I take in new realities. By taking in those new realities—by ingesting, by sometimes literally swallowing those new realities with radical curiosity—I become *more*. That's what it means to love. *To love* means I am curious about you, and by being curious about you, I take you in, I love you up, and then by loving you up, you love me open. **The baby is open and curious, so the baby is always transforming.**

The baby is always becoming more, the baby never hits a place of being static, of being shut down and stagnant.

Now, let's go a little deeper. That's the *idealized* baby. Hasidism, in its great beauty, didn't quite anticipate attachment theory, which has developed in the last 100 years, and points out that **this moment of the baby is a fleeting moment.** It's an ephemeral moment, and the baby quickly begins to experience a lack of attunement, a lack of alignment between herself and mother and father—and mother and father (or caretaker) represent, for the baby, the entire world.

The baby begins to *feel* this lack of attunement.

The baby begins to feel an experience of their needs *not* being responded to, their tears not quite being seen, their cries not quite being heard.

The baby begins to have an experience, as Winnicott says, of being humiliated in getting her basic needs met.

The baby moves away from this original idealized, *pre-tragic* state of wondrous bliss where the baby cries, and immediately those needs are met, where the baby is in the state of play and is also open and curious. **The baby immediately encounters *the other*, and as soon as the baby encounters the other—the mother—there is a Garden of Eden moment, and then there's an exile from the garden**—the shock of individuation, the shock of the realization that I am another and that ultimately, even mother is not always fully attuned to me. The baby experiences humiliation in getting her basic needs met.

Martha Nussbaum wrote an important book called *The Language of Emotions*, where she gathers the attachment theory research and some important pieces of writing, and really understands this notion of humiliation in getting our basic needs met.

What begins to happen is: I stop crying because I stop actually *feeling* what I need.

There is this experience of the baby, where the baby experiences need, the baby cries, and the need is responded to. That's the ideal state: the heart desires, the heart needs, the heart cries out to have the need met, and there is joy because the need is fulfilled. That's level one, that's the *pre-tragic* level.

Then the baby—and the human being—enters *the tragic*, where my needs aren't heard, where I am humiliated in getting my basic needs met. I begin to *dissociate* from my needs, and I begin to become *alienated* from my needs. I cannot find the depth of my needs. Now we've entered into the tragic.

When I'm split off from my needs, I cannot cry, and when I lose access to my tears—to my ability to cry out in need, which is the natural human experience of longing, the natural human experience of desire— my heart breaks with desire. That heartbreak is not a degraded state, not an unenlightened state. It's not a depressed state. It's not a clinically pathological state. **Heartbreak of not getting my needs met is the natural state of an alive human being.**

What the interior sciences of Hasidism are pointing to is this *pre-tragic* state of the idealized baby who has the experience of natural wholeness of heartbreak—and the natural wholeness of heartbreak expresses itself in tears.

PRAYER AFFIRMS THE DIGNITY OF PERSONAL NEED

This realization is about the dignity of need. The baby understands, in the pre-tragic state, the dignity of need.

The adult who understands the dignity of need is the one who, in the Solomon tradition, models *prayer*.

There is a woman in the Book of Samuel named Hannah, who has this deep and profound desire to bear a child, to be the mother. It is a primal need—not of every human being and not of every woman, but of many women—and of many men to be the father. Again, not all men, not all women; there are some men and women who have other deep, profound expressions of need for creation that don't express in the desire for physical children. But for a huge swath of humanity, the need for a child *is* a need, and we recognize its dignity.

It's a selfless need.

It's a need that's about self-fulfillment but requires sacrifice.

In that sense, it's selfless for a moment.

It's a bracketing of self to be in devotion to the emergence of life.

It's a very powerful need.

This Hannah enters the Temple, *bacho tivkeh*, and she cries. Her tears are seen in the Solomon tradition as the *locus classicus* of prayer—because prayer is about turning to the depths of Reality, to the Infinite Intimate, to the Infinity of Intimacy, and bringing the full depth of our desire and need, the fullness of their dignity, to the table. It is about claiming the dignity of need. As we often say:

Prayer affirms the dignity
of personal need.

Hannah, in her tears, becomes the model of prayer because she is deeply connected to a particular recognizable need, which is not a *pseudo*-need. It's a true, profound, and deeply erotic human need.

The capacity to affirm the dignity of personal need is the place where we begin to reclaim our own dignity and our own divinity.

WE MUST FEEL THE DEPTH OF OUR NEED

When we did a seminar several years ago, we talked about the notion that a person has a *pain threshold* and a *pleasure threshold*. There's a place past which we are not able to feel our own heartbreak and past which we are not able to feel our own pleasure. There is this limitation, this cap. **We don't allow ourselves to feel the depth of our need.**

Whether it's the depth of our need expressed in heartbreak, or the depths of our need for pleasure, for the full Eros and aliveness of Reality, we split off from our needs, and we *refuse to feel*. As we said it then, I refuse to feel my feelings to completion. I *cut off* the need. I *dissociate* from the need.

I'm in *the tragic*. I'm the traumatized baby. I'm the alienated baby. We are all, in some sense, the traumatized baby—not because that's an accident of Cosmos, and not because we were abused by our parents. **In order to individuate, we must feel the gap between us and our caretaker.**

We have to *feel* our individuated needs.

We have to be able to *recognize* them.

We have to claim their *dignity* and *divinity*.

We have to rest in them, letting them be *in us* and us *in them*.

We have to *not* have them assuaged immediately and *not* have them immediately responded to.

The baby has a fleeting experience of heartbreak—and then:

- In an idealized baby reality, those needs are immediately met.
- In the more real, true reality of the baby, those needs *aren't* met.

Then, as the baby begins to individuate, the baby begins to find herself identifying with her own longing, with her own yearning, with her own need. And then the baby can go one of two ways (and when I say *the baby*, I mean the emerging human being).

The general way we go is we split off from our needs because it's too painful to stay in the heartbreak. That's generally a huge swath of life for many years. We realize our needs aren't being met, so we split them off, we dissociate from them, we alienate from them. That's the first part of the path. **We become non-intimate with our own Eros. We become non-intimate with our own needs.**

The process of recovering of self is:

- To recover a relationship with my own needs.
- To recover the experience of the dignity of my needs.
- To heal the experience of being humiliated in getting my basic needs met by encountering a reality in which my needs *are* reimbursed.

I *always* do this recovery through the beloved.

It's the beloved that I encounter later in life. That beloved might be a dear friend, it might be a teacher, it might be a sensual beloved, it might be a creative partner, it might be a depth of *philia*, a profound love between two friends of a completely non-sensual nature—but it always happens in a place where my needs are recognized, where:

- I can bring *my pain* to the table.
- I can bring *my heartbreak* to the table.
- I can *own* the depth of my heartbreak.

NO TWO HEARTBREAKS ARE THE SAME

When I own the depth of my heartbreak, my heartbreak ceases to be a source of depression or clinical pathology and becomes instead a part of my aliveness. For the first time, I have recognized my needs, I have owned the dignity of my needs, and I have been able to recognize their true nature.

I've been able to access *my deepest heart's desires*—not my surface desires that I invented in order to cover over the emptiness—and I can go back and access them. Those original deepest heart's desires are always unique. **There is no generic desire, and there is no generic heartbreak.** Does everyone get that?

In other words, I have a unique heartbreak. My heartbreak is unique, my desire is unique, and my needs are unique. There are certain shared needs that we all have, shared general desires, but we all have unique scripts of desire and unique qualities to our needs.

To be able to own and live in the fullness of my Unique Self is to live in the uniqueness of my heartbreak.

No two heartbreaks are the same. No two deepest heart's desires are exactly the same.

To heal, to recover my wholeness, **I need to be able to recover my capacity to be in the depth of my need, to be in the depth of my heartbreak, to be in the depth of my unique desire.**

Once I'm in that unique need, desire, and heartbreak, I can begin to *meet* that need.

Once the need has been recognized, it's on the table, and I can begin to meet it. I can find my beloveds; I can find my circle of intimates, who bear witness, who are *listening* to the depth of my unique desire.

And they say to me, *your need is my allurement*:

- The way that you want to be touched, I want to touch you.
- The way you want to be held, I want to hold you.
- The way you want to be aroused, I want to arouse you.
- The way you want to be desired, I want to desire you.

Can everyone feel that? ***Your need is my allurement.***

Then, there's **this capacity to have my needs met by being able to live in the heartbreak**, to reclaim the original capacity of the baby.

THE EVOLUTION OF TEARS IS THE EXPANSION OF OUR CIRCLE OF INTIMACY

But I don't go back to being a baby because the baby is *pre-tragic*; the baby is totally self-involved. The baby is not actually an ideal. **The baby is a *symbolic* ideal, but the baby cannot feel the fullness and depth of *other*.** The baby is identified with mother, and just for a fleeting moment, feels the mother holding, and then in the next moment, the mother becomes an alienated other who doesn't feel her full need—and then the baby feels the fundamental breakdown of attunement, and the beginning of early pain:

- The pain of disorganized attachment
- The pain of insecure attachment
- The pain of broken attachment

Very few people have what's called *secure attachment*, which is a formal term. Most people experience some sort of fundamental lack of attunement, in which they are humiliated in getting their needs met.

But that baby is not attuned to the mother either. **That baby is lost in the baby's own very narrow circle of intimacy:** intimacy, fundamentally, with *self*. The baby cannot feel the world. The baby goes through his or her own process of growing up, and that growing up involves:

- Expanding her circle of feeling
- Expanding her circle of attunement
- Expanding the pain of being dissociated and alienated from core needs

This happens until, later in life, we are able to meet the beloved, in all of her disguises, all of his disguises—and again, not just the sensual beloved— who actually turns to me and says, *Your need is my allurement.* Then the dignity of need is recovered.

Can you feel that now?

Let's go even deeper. When I recover the dignity of my needs and the dignity of my heartbreak—and I recover my tears, and I find myself again in the eyes of the beloved who witnesses me, who hears me, who attunes to me and says, *Your need is my allurement; I am allured to meet your need; let me be your woman; let me be your man; let me be your beloved*—that's just the beginning.

The process of growing up, the process of becoming awake and alive, the process of going from *Homo sapiens*, the wise one, or *Homo ludens*, the playing one, to *Homo amens*, the loving one (what we call *Homo amor*) is the evolution of my *heart*:

- The evolution of my *heartbreak*
- The evolution of my *tears*
- The evolution of my *capacity to feel*

The baby's tears begin as the tears of just the baby. **Then, as the baby's heart expands and evolves, the baby begins to actually *feel* the mother.** The baby is attuned to the mother and feels the mother's tears.

The baby then deepens and begins to feel *the family system*, and the baby feels the joy, the goodness, the aliveness, the tears, the brokenness, and the pain—all of the nooks and crevices in the family system. The baby *feels*. In his or her egocentric circle of intimacy, the baby *feels*. And the baby has this intense desire not only to heal *her own* pain, and not only to hold *her own* heartbreak—but to hold *her mother's* heartbreak, to hold *her father's* heartbreak.

Who here knows the intense desire we have—to hold our father's and our mother's tears, and our brother's and our sister's tears? Who knows this?

There is an *evolution* of tears.

There is this evolution, this heartbreak that I begin to hold, which is not *just* my own.

And then, when I go deeper, I move from this first song—this *egocentric* song—and there is this expansion of my circle of intimacy, which is the expansion of my heartbreak and the expansion of my commitment to love because heartbreak and commitment to love come together. All of a sudden, I begin to feel *even more*. I begin to feel a wider group *beyond* my immediate survival family, my immediate family through which I thrive and which holds me directly. **I begin to feel this larger tribe with whom I share a story.**

Of course there are tragic expressions of this; of course there's pathological ethnocentrism. But there's also *the beauty* of the tribe. This is my tribe, these are my people:

- I feel their pain.
- I feel their joy.
- My heartbreak is for the heartbreak of the entire tribe.
- My heart breaks with the heartbreak of the tribe.

Sometimes I am even so committed to the tribe, to its value and its perpetuation, that I live my life for the tribe, and sometimes I even give up my life for the tribe.

And yes, I understand that this has a pathological manifestation. But I am not talking about the pathological manifestation. I'm talking about its *holy* manifestation, where I can feel the larger tribe.

When we don't have a place to feel that, we go to a sports event, to a huge stadium, and we cheer for a team because **we have a fundamental need to feel this larger field, this larger field in which we can play together, in which we can feel each other**. That's one of the sacred functions of a sporting event. It's supposed to point us to *real* ethnocentric intimacy, to real intimacy with the tribe, but it often serves as a form of *pseudo-eros*, instead of opening up the real and wider Eros, which is our wider joy and our wider heartbreak.

That's the evolution of tears.

EVOLVING TEARS FROM *HOMO SAPIENS* TO *HOMO AMOR*

The evolution of tears goes like this.

First, the baby has moved from *my* tears to the tears of *mother* and to the tears of *egocentric intimacy*, to those in her immediate personal family.

Then there is an evolution of tears, and I feel the tears of *the tribe*.

Then I realize that the tribe is too small; it's not big enough. The tribe has too much pathology in it. It's too much *us and them* and the pathologies of ethnocentrism. I realize I cannot be in just *one* tribe. My heart bursts, and I realize that I'm a Chinese child, and I'm a Japanese mother, and I'm a Hindu, and I'm a Jew, and I'm a Muslim, and I'm an atheist, and I live in North America and South America, and I'm an Aborigine.

I live every place. I have always lived, and I am in every face, and I am in every person, and I *participate*. I begin to feel, in my body, heart, mind, both the joy of every human being that ever breathed and lived, past, present, and future, and the pain and the heartbreak of every human being that ever was, is, and will be.

We are the people. We are the people we've been waiting for, and we're *all* the people. **All the people live in us, and we live in all the people.**

All of a sudden, I have moved: there's been an evolution of tears, and I cannot actually sit in my home and eat comfortably when I know that there are so many hungry people. I feel all the hungry people, and I feel all the lonely people, and I can't shut off from them anymore, and I cannot turn away. *Ni punei*, "my face opens," and *face* means to *turn* (*panim*, to turn towards). I turn towards. I'm *panim el panim*, face-to-face, and no one is outside of the circle. **I feel the heartbreak of the whole story, and I feel the joy of the whole story.**

At this point, I begin to move from *Homo sapiens* to *Homo amor*.

My armor begins to break, in many stages.

My armor breaks in the beginning. The baby develops armor when needs aren't met, and so the baby then breaks open that armor—and begins to feel her heart again (when I say *the baby*, I mean *as the baby grows up, as the child grows up*).

The armor that encases and shuts down the heart is broken open in the eyes of the beloved, who meets my needs, who says, *Your need is my allurement*. And as we play together, as we play in sensuality, and we play in the sensuality of the heart, the wetness of the mind, and in the throbbing of feeling each other, that armor is broken.

> *The armor is broken because there's a deeper Eros, a love deeper than ordinary love.*

When we break the armor open, it's because we've actually *moved*: we've begun to move from *Homo armor* to *Homo amor*. We can access this deeper love that doesn't get shut down, the love that's always available.

There is a part of us that's always innocent.

There is a part of us that is the One Heart that always lives under the armor, that's always there. There is a deeper desire:

- No matter how far we feel we have fallen
- No matter how shut down we become
- No matter how deadened our Field of Desire is

There is a One Desire, there is a One Heart, there is a One Love that's always available.

That's what we call Outrageous Love—that's *Homo amor*.

OUTRAGEOUS LOVE MOVES US FROM *HOMO ARMOR* TO *HOMO AMOR*

Even when we start with the baby, when we close down the heart, the heart becomes armored, and we want to break that armor open. This is what Wilhelm Reich called *de-armoring* and what Kristina Kincaid has done for the last twenty-five years in her deep work. When Kristina and I came together, we talked about *moving from Homo armor to Homo amor.*

It means **I access the Outrageous Love that breaks my heart open and allows me to find the Beloved.** We cannot find each other in *ordinary love*—because that gets armored; it gets shut down. But when we access the current of Eros, which is the current of love, the CosmoErotic Universe, and we feel it *living alive* in us, and we realize we *participate* in that Field of Eros and Desire, then we *break open*. Then the baby becomes alive and feels the mother and the family in a new way.

And then I feel the tribe: the same armor is broken open, and I can feel my whole tribe, I can feel my people, and I move, at the ethnocentric level, from *Homo armor* to *Homo amor.*

In most Western democratic countries, there is no sense of genuine identification with the tribe: we are *armored*, closed in, locked in a broken egocentric self. And in many other countries, there is this false and deluded sense of the tribe, which is fascist, totalitarian, and tragic. So, there's either a regressive, pathological identification with the heart of the tribe or a shutdown heart that cannot feel the tribe.

Instead, I have to be able to find the current of Outrageous Love, and realize that:

- My tribe is good and true.
- Reality intended this tribe.
- This tribe needs me.
- Being in devotion to the tribe is unimaginably beautiful.

Then I move to *worldcentric*, and again, **I cannot hold the world in my heart with ordinary love**. I cannot hold the world in my heart with love which is a social construct and an expression of a reductive materialist random universe that has no meaning. This is not the nature of the Universe. Love is not merely an epiphenomenon of evolutionary psychological drives.

Love is the heart of existence itself. That is Outrageous Love.

To hold the whole world in my heart, to feel the whole thing, I have to access that One Heart—the One Heart that lives and pulses in *me* uniquely, the one heart that pulses in *you* uniquely, which allows you to:

- Wrap your arms around every human being alive today.
- We then pick up the baton from every human being that ever lived.
- We hear the cries of the unborn of every human being that'll ever be.

I am in this worldcentric consciousness, the song of the world, of every human being, and I feel the pain and joy of every human being. My heartbreak has expanded, and it has become virtually unimaginable.

But I cannot hold it with a small heart—I can only hold it with the One Heart, with Outrageous Love as *Homo amor*.

And then my heart expands even more, and I feel every lamb, every blade of grass, every cow, every cat, and every mouse, and every rodent, and every insect, and I feel the entire cacophony of the living Universe. I feel the current of life and its feeling and fundamental will.

Stuart Kauffman pointed out, correctly, that there is *will* all through Reality. Biology is not computation. As my friend Perry Marshall wrote in a beautiful academic article, *biology transcends computation*. It's immeasurable. It's the quality of the living Universe, the aliveness of the All-That-Is, and so I feel the pain of Reality.

I feel the pain of the seas that are being destroyed and the fish extracted, and I feel the dead zones in the ocean.

I feel the desertification.

I feel the extraction of resources, their degradation, and their depletion.

I feel the planetary boundaries being crossed.

I am madly in love with Reality. It's not that I am just worried about my own survival.

My love of the biosphere is not: Oh my God, I'm not going to survive. Rather, it's, I am madly in love with the biosphere.

I am allured. I am not just worldcentric at this point. My heartbreak has exploded just like my joy has exploded, and my heartbreak embraces the whole thing—because my heartbreak is my aliveness, longing, and yearning.

THE EVOLUTION OF HEARTBREAK IS THE EVOLUTION OF DESIRE

At each one of these levels, **my heartbreak allows me to recognize the depth of my desire:**

- My *personal* desire.
- My desire for *my circle of egocentric intimacy*, which means my egocentric heartbreak and my egocentric joy, and my personal circle.
- My *ethnocentric*, tribal heartbreak and my tribal joy.
- My *worldcentric*—meaning every human being—heartbreak and joy.

- My *cosmocentric* heartbreak and joy—meaning every animal, every living being, the inherent aliveness of the self-organizing Universe. Even at the level of matter, which is filled with will and moves from mud to Mozart, from bacteria to Bach, and from dirt to the most devastatingly beautiful sonnets of Shakespeare.

Once I *feel*, I feel *the need*, the evolution of need.

I first feel my need, then I feel the need of the tribe, then I feel the need of the world, every human being, and then I feel the need of the Cosmos, and I experience the *dignity* of need—that need is a *value*.

It's not just the need of all of planet Earth. It's the need of all of the galaxies, because otherwise planet Earth is going to become ethnocentric as life appears in Cosmos in other places (it will and already has). **When we begin to make contact and live in an intergalactic world, we have to realize that value is not grounded in planet Earth. It's grounded in Cosmos itself, and we are all children of the Cosmos, and value is cosmic value.** When I feel the need of the Cosmos, then I become intimate with the Cosmos.

We become intimate through our shared needs.

We become intimate through our shared desires.

What are intimate relations at the sexual level? This titillating, alive, living desire to touch each other. As we feel each other's desire, we become intimate. As we feel the primal-ness of each other's needs, we become intimate.

But the sexual *models* the erotic. We become intimate not just by feeling the beauty of each other's gorgeous and stunning sensual needs. We become intimate by feeling each other's primal needs:

- For food and nourishment
- For being held
- For creativity

- To be recognized
- To be desired
- To be needed
- To be chosen
- To be held

In other words, when we meet and feel each other's needs, we become intimate. **When we meet and feel each other's desires, we become intimate with each other.**

By being willing to expand the circle of our heartbreak, the evolution of heartbreak is the evolution of need, which is the evolution of intimacy, which is the evolution of desire, which is where we began.

- That's what it means to wake up.
- That's what it means to open up.
- That's what it means to become an enlightened or enlightening being.

An enlightened being means, I embrace it all, and even when I fall out, I fall back in; and I am constantly turning towards, and I am constantly wanting to be face-to-face, and I am willing to feel.

I am willing to feel.

I AM WILLING TO FEEL EVEN WHAT I CANNOT ENTIRELY HEAL

Now I want to go the last step and say: I am willing to *feel* even what I cannot entirely *heal.*

We close our hearts to heartbreak when we experience the gap between our ability to *feel* the pain of it all and to *heal* the pain of it all.

The first step is, as we have said many times, I realize I cannot heal the pain of it all, so I turn to my unique circle of intimacy and influence and say, *What unique Outrageous Acts of Love are mine to do?* **I go from being powerless to powerful again because I realize that I can turn to my unique circle of intimacy and influence, and I can heal.** I close the gap between my ability to feel and heal.

That's so deep, and we've gone so deep into this over the last decade.

But let's go even deeper now: I also have to be willing to stay in the heartbreak when I'm at the edge of the mystery, and I don't know how to heal it.

Even when I don't know how to heal it, even when there's this inconsolable longing, when there's a yearning I don't know how to fulfill, when there's a need that I can't meet—I don't close myself down to the need. **I'm willing to *stay* in the need.**

I am willing to feel.

I am willing to feel the pain even of God/Goddess.

I am willing to feel the infinity of the divine tears.

I am willing to feel so deep and so wide.

Even though I don't know exactly which way is forward sometimes.

Even though I feel paralyzed.

Even though I feel sometimes impotent and helpless.

I don't abandon the potency of my feeling. I don't shut my heart. **I'm willing to feel my longing, my heartbreak, even when it's inconsolable**. I stay in that heartbreak; I stay in that feeling.

I don't feel it through to *completion*—I cannot feel it through to completion because sometimes the heartbreak is nearly infinite.

> There is no completing the heartbreak of the Rwandan mothers who saw their children destroyed before them.

> There is no completing the heartbreak of the gas chambers.

There is no completing the heartbreak of the deaths of child soldiers in the Congo.

But I don't turn away. I participate in the pain of Reality because I can't *not*, because I feel it all. Because it's all part of who I am.

In holding that pain, something is broken open in me—because heartbreak doesn't close my heart. It breaks my heart open. And when my heart breaks open, my heart breaks open not to ordinary love—ordinary love can't touch any of this.

I break open to Outrageous Love, to the Eros that moves Reality itself.

That Eros is creative—and in that creative Eros, a new possibility emerges. The entire energy of evolution moves through me. New emergence becomes possible, new visions become possible, and I begin to imagine a new reality. But I don't turn away. I never turn away from feeling, from feeling as much joy and as much heartbreak as my heart can hold.

Now, friends, I cannot feel that all day. I cannot feel it every second. I wouldn't be able to function. I'd be paralyzed. But I need to **set aside some time every day, at least once a day, where I'm willing to feel the pain of the Goddess in exile, of the broken hearts and the broken vessels.** Part of my daily practice is:

I feel all of the joy, and I celebrate.

I feel all the pain and all the heartbreak.

And I never close. I never close. Can you feel that?

Wow. The Master from the town of Vitebsk, Menachem Mendel, who was my teacher's teacher, said: *The baby cries, and the old wise master cries. But they are completely different—their tears are completely different.* This is because **life is the evolution of tears.**

164

It's the willingness to open my heart, in tears of joy and tears of heartbreak.

It's the willingness to open my heart to more and more, to feel more and more.

Part of the Intimate Universe is heartbreak:

- Atoms come together—and then they can be tragically split, and unimaginable destruction emerges.
- There's allurement in all its beauty—and then there's the fusion of totalitarianism.
- There's holy autonomy, and there's the alienation of the reductive materialist marketplace lost in a narrow and pathetic success story.

We've got to go deeper. We have to become the feeling of Reality itself—because that's who we already are. It's the only place we feel whole. We have the capacity, at least for a few minutes a day, to feel it all, all of the joy and all the heartbreak. In that, we participate in the true nature of who we are—and from there, we can do anything. There, everything's possible.

We ourselves become, literally, the Possibility of Possibility.

PART TWO: FROM HEARTBREAK TO DESIRE TO NEED TO VALUE

We need to move from the first innocence to the second innocence.

I want to do a deep dive, to try to pick up a couple of things that we didn't fully get to today, while still talking about *heartbreak*.

We talked about this realization that one of the qualities of a baby is that a baby knows *how to cry*. A baby knows how to cry because a baby is connected to her own needs. Early on, the baby doesn't have any sense of their *needs being shamed*.

There's an original relationship to need that is sacred:

The baby experiences a need.

That need is a desire, and that desire is then not met.

There is a sense of desire not met, and the baby cries.

There's a *direct movement* between need, desire, the desire not being met, and tears. That's the original wholeness of the baby.

But of course, you cannot really look at the baby as a *complete* wholeness, or a *full* wholeness—a wholeness that's a model for us because the baby is essentially merged with the mother. **The baby doesn't have a fully (or even vaguely) articulated deep sense of empathy for the other.** It's just a proto-sense of the mother.

The baby doesn't have a fully developed consciousness.

The baby doesn't have an individuated ego self.

The baby is not torn between conflicting desires, at least not rational conflicting desires or conscious clashes between right and wrong.

The baby does not have a sense of compassion.

I wouldn't associate the word *compassion* with the baby. We wouldn't even really associate a highly developed sense of *love*. The baby has an allurement to, an attraction towards, a proto-sense of love—obviously more developed than an atom, but still very elemental, very primary.

People always hold the baby up as the model of enlightenment, but the baby is not the model of enlightenment. That's very important. The baby is cute, beautiful, primal, original, but not *good*. The baby hasn't yet *gotten* to goodness.

The Hasidic story of what we learn from a baby—that as soon as they need, they cry—is a very beautiful, poetic image, and it's even *more*: the baby is holding out a vision of possibility.

The idea is to get back to that innocence of the baby as *the second innocence*. The baby is a *pre-tragic first innocence*, a first simplicity.

You then have to go through the guilt.

You have to go through the complexity.

You have to go through *the tragic*.

Then you have to get to second innocence. You have to get to *post-tragic*. You have to get to *second simplicity*.

That's where we want to go. I want to come back and have that original capacity to cry when my need isn't met and my desire isn't met, but in a way that's post-tragic, so that I don't lose access to the essential goodness of my need, and I'm able to cry—not tears of depression, but I'm able to experience a heartbreak when my need isn't met.

What happens in the tragic when the baby doesn't experience their needs as being met? The Hasidic story paints this idyllic idealized image of the baby, but the actual experience of the baby is that the baby very quickly moves through the tragedy of disorganized attachment, of insecure attachment, of this alienation from the mother, of not feeling attuned, of not feeling their needs are being met.

That's the experience of the tragic. And, of course, that remains with the baby.

Now, I'm talking about the baby not as an actual *baby*, but as the baby grows up and becomes a toddler, a preschooler, a young child, and a little older, they start to experience the tragic—my needs are alienated, I split my needs off. **My needs are *shamed*—this is where shame comes in. I experienced shame in trying to get my needs met.**

The vision is to reclaim second innocence, to enter the post-tragic.

BY EMBRACING THE HEARTBREAK, I FIND MY ALIVENESS

If I reclaim, at second innocence, the innocence of the baby, and restore a fundamental relationship to the dignity and goodness of my need, then I can *embrace* my heartbreak.

I don't need to *deny* my heartbreak.

I don't need to *refuse* to suffer heartbreak.

I can actually *suffer* heartbreak. I can suffer the heartbreak of a need not being met, and I can suffer my heartbreak in a way that's somewhat clean.

I am heartbroken, but I'm not splitting off the heartbreak. I'm not denying the heartbreak but *embracing* the heartbreak.

There's something very beautiful in the embrace of the heartbreak.

When I embrace my heartbreak, I'm able to cry. I'm embracing the dignity of my needs—or even the *divinity* of my needs. This then allows me to begin to get the needs met. I can begin to meet those needs in a profound, beautiful, and potent way. That's only one dimension.

There's a second dimension: I embrace the need, the dignity of the need, the divinity of the need, and the longing, even though I know it *cannot* be met. **Even though I know it cannot be met, I still don't turn away from it, and I can be in the heartbreak of it—but I can somehow turn the heartbreak into aliveness.**

I've got to find just *the right level* of heartbreak.

If I allow the heartbreak to break me, paralyze me, and shut me off from aliveness, then the heartbreak is destructive, then it's breaking me.

But if I allow the heartbreak to break my heart open, I can be fully alive in that desire. Even if I live in the palace of imagination most of the time, in the fullness of my yearning and my longing, I can allow my yearning and longing to *Fuck* me open, to love me open, to make me more sensitive, more kind, more alive, more filled with Eros.

In other words, if I shut the heartbreak down because I feel like I cannot realize it, then I become deadened to the nerve endings of my own heart—and the nerve endings of my alive heart are needed. My alive Eros is *needed* because my alive heart is unique. It's unlike any other. Therefore, my heartbreak is unique—and **I offer my heartbreak as an erotic mystic on the altar of *She*, for the sake of healing all the broken vessels and all the broken hearts.**

I stay open. The point is that I stay *open as love*. I don't close. It's the decision, the commitment to stay open as love, to be *lived as love*, to stay open as love.

What usually happens is this: if our need is not met, we shut down the need, and we shut down the tears. The tears themselves are the temple. Tears are *bechi* in Hebrew, a word which shares etymology with the word *m'vukhah*, confusion. Tears can clarify my confusion, where I ask:

- Is life worthwhile?
- Is it even worth being here?
- What am I doing?

Tears give me the experience of my own Eros and aliveness and my unique aliveness, and I realize my life is self-evidently worthwhile. My yearning, the uniqueness of my yearning, the uniqueness of my desire, and the unique pattern of my Eros make life *self-evidently* worth living in a fundamental way. It's beautiful.

CLARIFIED DESIRE EQUALS DIGNIFIED NEED EQUALS VALUE

In one dimension of life, by reclaiming the dignity and divinity of my need, and therefore being able to practice the great art of crying again, **I am able**

to *see* the need, which goes from its hidden place to its revealed place, so now, I see the need and I can meet the need.

But in the second dimension, I live in the yearning; I live in the longing.

That's why the third face of Eros is yearning, longing.

In the four major faces of Eros, the third is *tshuka*, desire itself, because when I lose access to my desire, I lose access to my aliveness:

- My creative desire
- My desire to help a little old lady across the street
- My desire to feel the pulsing of Eros in my body
- My desire to be kind
- My desire for food
- My desire for goodness
- My desire for truth

It's all part of the same Field of Desire. Desire means there's something that I value that I want. And that's very important.

What is value? **Value is clarified desire.**

That's a huge sentence: clarified desire equals value. That's what value is. No one knows what value is. It's clarified desire.

Let's formulate it even more clearly:

Clarified desire = dignified need = value

This is huge.

My clarified desire—my true desire, my deepest heart's desire—is the desire of *She*.

Why? Because *She* is the Eros of evolution. The Eros of evolution pulses in me. It's not just that I live in the world, I live in a world that's *evolving*—the evolving world evolves through me. Evolution quite literally lives in me, in all of us, both interiors and exteriors.

Evolutionary desire lives uniquely in me. To clarify the unique evolutionary desire that lives in me is to know who I am. That's who I am: I *am* that unique evolutionary desire.

That clarified evolutionary desire discloses my authentic need, and my authentic need is a value.

That's why we said that the purpose of prayer is *pallal*. *Pallal* means a reality consideration, and it's to consider the nature of my need. When I consider the nature of my need, I disclose value in Cosmos. That's the dignity of a human being. Clarified need is value—what you truly need. Not just *valuable* but *value*—so, clarified desire equals dignified need equals value.

Once we can recognize need and value, we are allured to *meet* that value because **value generates allurement.** We are allured to meet value. Since we are allowed to meet value, we *feel* this arousal in us because we are moved by this allurement.

If we begin to generate a *shared* Field of Allurement, then we're all part of the same field. We are all Unique Selves, so there's a unique expression of allurement in all of us. **Our Unique Self is our unique set of allurements**.

We also share a common experience. That's why we can talk to each other. If we didn't have a common experience, language wouldn't work. There is a common Field of Allurement, a common Field of Need that we can clarify—and that common Field of Need and Desire is what generates value.

Once we generate value, once we have now entered a shared Field of Value, we can generate the energy of action, the energy of transformation. That's what we mean when we say evolution equals love in action. Evolution is love in action.

Evolutionary desire generates the movement to create greater wholeness, which is the action of evolution itself.

171

It's very beautiful, and we're just beginning to realize that the ability to stay in the desire, to stay in the longing, to stay in the yearning—even when we cannot see its fulfillment—is what makes us alive.

It's what makes us human.

It's what makes us noble; it's what makes us sacred.

And then, paradoxically, as we gradually stay in the desire, we are more and more alive, more and more Divine, so more and more possibility opens up because divinity is the Possibility of Possibility—and what seemed completely impossible begins to disclose itself in the glimmer of new possibility.

PART THREE: HEARTBREAK IS A STRUCTURE OF THE INTIMATE UNIVERSE

Heartbreak is a structure of the Intimate Universe.

Heartbreak means that the force of allurement that draws us together is interrupted.

Heartbreak means that the allurement that was there is broken—the connection, the mutuality of recognition, the mutuality of feeling, the mutuality of value, or the mutuality of purpose, all of which are the dimensions of the intimacy equation. Expressions of a sense of shared identity are broken. That's at least one expression of heartbreak.

- You don't have mutuality of recognition. That's heartbreaking.
- You don't have mutuality of pathos anymore. That's heartbreaking.
- You don't have mutuality of value; there's no longer a shared Field of Value, at least in your experience. That's heartbreaking.
- You lose mutuality of purpose. Again, that's heartbreaking.

That's one expression of heartbreak.

And the other expression of heartbreak is when all those mutualities are still there, the intimacy of shared identity is still there, and at the same time, the person disappears because they are sick, or they died, or they changed in some way.

Another expression of heartbreak is when mutuality shifts for one person but not for the other person.

This structure of heartbreak is an expression of the evolution of love:

- The more love evolves…
- The more love becomes self-conscious…
- The more the will becomes self-conscious…
- The more sense of choice seems to appear…

…the more the quality of separation or the quality of intimacies rupture, and this generates heartbreak.

Heartbreak is an expression of a core quality, and the quality is the breaking of allurement.

A beautiful question, a beautiful inquiry is how far down the evolutionary chain does heartbreak go? **We know that heartbreak does not only exist at the human level; it also exists at the animal level in very deep and profound ways.** Is there a quality of heartbreak that goes all the way down to matter? We don't know the interiority of matter. We don't know that protons, neutrons, and electrons experience heartbreak.

There is a text which describes the relationship between the Sun and the Moon in terms of heartbreak, in terms of the pain of intimacy's alienation. This is already in the realm of interior science and not yet understood or validated by the exterior sciences, but for now, suffice it to say that **heartbreak is intimately bound up with the play between allurement and autonomy,** or said slightly differently, autonomy and communion, or said slightly differently, attraction and repulsion, which are core qualities of the Intimate Universe.

There is a critical text about the nature of a broken heart, which appears in the third-century mystery texts of the Solomon tradition in one of the Jerusalem interior science texts by Said R. Alexanderi:

> A human artisan—if his tools are broken, it is an offense to him, and he cannot do his fixing. The Divine Artisan—*She*—all of her tools are broken, as it is written—*She* is intimate with all the broken hearts, and *She* does all of her fixing with broken tools.

Now, let's go even deeper. The word used in this Hebrew text to describe the Divine tools is *klei tashmisho* (*klei*, "tool" plus *tashmisho*, "that are used")—the tools that we use.

But the word *klei* is a two-letter root *chaf, lamed*, which means, *kallah*, bride, which means, more deeply, the yearning passion for full rapturous erotic union. *Tashmish* means the vessel that's used, but it also means sexual coupling, erotic union.

The word in the text that describes the Divine artisan's tools expresses the passionate yearning of God's erotic partner, which is the human being. **The passionate yearning of God's erotic partner, the human being, is broken**. It is out of this lineage, directly from these texts, that Leonard Cohen intuitively drew the notion of *the holy and the broken Hallelujah*—

> *There's a blaze of light in every word.*
> *It doesn't matter what you heard,*
> *the holy or the broken Hallelujah.*

We are the broken *Hallelujahs*. Our hearts do break. Heartbreak is part of our nature.

THERE IS EROS TO THE BROKEN HEART

There are two kinds of heartbreak.

One is *unnecessary heartbreak*—heartbreak that shouldn't be. Heartbreak that comes from human sloppiness, from turning away, from human ignorance, from human beings not transforming to the highest and deepest nature that we are. It comes from all manner of degraded, lowest-common-denominator, egoic, grasping human action, which creates unimaginable suffering.

Those heartbreaks need to be healed. That's the work of *tikkun*—the work of social transformation; it's the work of creating new structures of governance, new structures of economics, and new structures of power that emerge out of a new Story of Value.

That's a heartbreak that we need to say *no* to.

But there is a second form of heartbreak. The second form of heartbreak is inseparable from love itself. **You cannot love without being willing to have your heart broken a thousand times a day.**

Our hearts open, and then our hearts are hurt for a second, then we find each other more deeply.

There is no love without a heartbreak because, as we said earlier, the nature of the human being is that right after that one moment of pure attunement between the baby and the mother, from that moment on, for the rest of the baby's life as the baby grows up into life, there's actually a lack of attunement, because:

> We are both *allured* to each other, moving towards attunement.

> And yet we are also *distinct* and *individuated* and *unique*, and so there is a lack of attunement, there is *autonomy*, there is the sense of independence, and even repulsion. We need to actually stand in our own space.

There's both allurement and autonomy, and in that dance between allurement and autonomy, there is heartbreak. But we don't resist that heartbreak. We embrace that heartbreak—and there is a joy in it. It's part of our aliveness. It's part of our Eros.

There's a text that says that God is *harofe li'sh'vurei lev*, "God heals the broken hearts," *u'mechabesh le'atz'votam*, "and bandages the sadness."

As Simcha Bunim of Peshischa says, *Don't we know that the broken heart is holy?* Isn't it true that there's nothing more whole than a broken heart? If there's nothing more whole than a broken heart, why does it need a bandage?

He says—elliptically, subtly, and so beautifully—we are not putting a bandage on the broken heart. We're putting a bandage on the *atsvut*, which is a certain kind of sadness that turns into depression. In other words, if I don't resist the heartbreak, and I embrace the broken heart, then there is actually joy.

By embracing the heartbreak, there is joy—not a superficial happiness but an aliveness.

There is an Eros to the broken heart. I know I'm alive. I'm in love. I'm in the aliveness of Reality.

We don't want to lose our capacity to have our hearts broken, but we want to bandage the sadness that turns to paralysis, depression, futility, self-loathing, or helplessness. Rather, we hold the mystery, and we allow our beloveds to go on their way.

We allow our hearts to be broken, we hold joy in the broken heart, and we hold its aliveness and its divinity.

We feel that broken heart, and Goddess feels broken hearts like we feel broken hearts. That's what it means when we say that God is the Infinite Intimate.

It means God is saying: *I am willing to have my heart broken with you.*

CHAPTER EIGHT

WHAT WE NEED FOR THE ATTENTION REBELLION TO SUCCEED

Episode 382 — February 4, 2024

A NEW STORY GENERATES NEW REALITY

We are here in this time between worlds, in this time between stories, responding to the meta-crisis, and knowing:

- That crisis is an evolutionary driver
- That our crisis is a birth
- That as things fall apart, they also can fall together
- That emergency can generate emergence
- That when the vessels *break*, in the language of the lineage of Solomon, there is a new possibility

The original Hebrew word for breaking is *shever*. It means breaking, and it means nourishment: there is promise, there is nourishment, there is possibility. When the breaking happens—it's either going to be a *breakdown*, or something will open in our hearts, and we'll be able to see more clearly than we ever have before, and it will become not a breakdown, but a *breakthrough*.

That's the feeling of *ein shalem m'lev shivura*. **There is nothing more whole than a broken heart**.

In this moment of meta-crisis:

- We don't move to denial
- We don't move to a doomer position
- We move instead to *respond*—by telling a new Story of Value

We tell a new Story of Value because we know that a new story allows us to generate a new reality.

The meta-crisis emerges from the broken plotlines, the broken structures of the old reality. To the precise extent that the story told in modernity was accurate and beautiful, it birthed the dignities of modernity. But there were plotlines missing or broken—for example, the plotline of value.

The plotline of value got lost. We lost the thread of the Story of Value. **We thought we could *assume* value even as we *denied* it.** We thought we could make intrinsic value—the Good, the True and the Beautiful—an axiom even if we would undercut their roots and claim (*wink-wink*) that they're really just made up.

We thought we'd get away with that. And we did, in modernity. But postmodernity called the lie out and said, *No, no, no, you are making these stories up. There is no story of value.*

And once there is no story of value, then all that's left are separate selves lost in rivalrous conflict governed by win/lose metrics, generating fragile, complicated systems without inherent allurement between the parts—because there *is* no inherent allurement between parts:

- It's all contrived.
- It's all random.
- It's all a reductive, materialist, random cosmos without *telos*, without purpose, without direction.

Of course, that's not the case. That defies the inherent nature of science, but that became the dogma. That dogma was invested in the apparatuses of power and generated all the fragilities of modernity, and all the fifteen vectors of the meta-crisis that threaten us with either the death of humanity or the death of our humanity.

So, what do we need to do?

- We need to reweave the plotline.
- We need to retell the story.
- We need to reclaim the thread.
- We need to revalue value itself.

What I want to do today, my friends, is something which I think is wildly important.

It's a change that actually does, quite literally, change everything. It adds a new dimension to the Story of Value that really opens everything up in a new way.

Our topic today is going to be *attention*.

Evolutionary Love Code:

Eros is the placing of attention.

The placing of attention generates Reality.

The placing of attention is the ultimate creative act.

The placing of attention is the ultimate moral act.

Reality emerges from the Infinite placing attention on finitude.

Attention and devotion are joined at the hip. To be the receiver of well-placed attention, and to place attention well, makes life self-evidently good, true, and beautiful.

Placing attention is a First Principle and First Value of Cosmos.

Evolution evolves through differentiation and integration, which is the placing of attention.

Evolution is the evolution of attention, which is the evolution of love.

THE INTERNET IS DESIGNED TO SCATTER ATTENTION

We are at this new moment in society, in which **the act of attention hijacking is the primary movement of the new robber barons**—of the new oligarchs, of the new techno-totalitarians.

The theft of attention—stolen attention, *stolen focus* as Johann Hari calls it in his book by that name—is the basic movement of the mainstream structures of society. It has enfolded, enwrapped, engulfed society. Not by providing it with *tools*—the internet is not a set of tools. That's a mistake. The internet is an *immersive environment*, in which the next generation is being raised, which is based on the radical *scattering of attention*, to borrow a term from Nicholas Carr in his 2011 book, *The Shallows*.

There has been this entire leading-edge literature, and Nicholas Carr began the conversation in his book *The Shallows*. And then he wrote another book called *The Glass Cage*. Then he wrote another book, which is a collection of his blog posts. His blog is called *Rough Type*. He collected his blog posts, and he put them in a book called *Utopia Is Creepy*. He is describing, essentially, the hijacking of attention.

Our colleagues, Tristan and Aza, at the Center for Humane Technology, have placed their attention on the robbing of attention. Much has been written about B.J. Fogg and his Persuasive Technology Laboratory, which has taught generations of app designers how to hijack attention. The words used are *how to maximize engagement*, but engagement is a euphemism (euphemism is one of the core strategies of techno-totalitarianism).

Engagement is a euphemism for addiction.

Addiction is the consistent and obsessive hijacking of attention from the discomfort or the emptiness of ordinary life. One doesn't have—or loses—the capacity to sit through it until it gets to *fullness*.

We can't hold our attention on the actual experience of life in order to access its depth, and its pleasure, and its potency, and its potentiality, and its possibility.

We get discomfited by its pain, and so we *turn away* our attention. And the consistent turning away of attention is called addiction.

> *The internet is designed to scatter attention. It is designed to interrupt plotlines.*

It is designed with multiple links in every sentence that don't allow you to enter into the placing of attention, and the depth that emerges from the artistic act of *true* engagement.

That disruption of attention generates the shallows. *The shallows* is the opposite of depth.

Carr has written about it. And Shoshana Zuboff's book, *The Age of Surveillance Capitalism*, addresses it in a different way. A book by Brett Frischmann, *Re-Engineering Humanity* (2018), addresses the same issue. Doug Rushkoff has talked about it in multiple ways. There is a veritable literature on this distraction of attention.

But if you notice, the tech plex is not paying any attention to the literature accusing it of hijacking attention. Why? Because **the literature that accuses the tech plex of hijacking attention has not given any compelling reason *why* attention shouldn't be hijacked**.

It is not against the law. Advertisers have always sought to attract attention. True, this is an immersive environment, and true, it's micro-targeting—as opposed to the old broadband advertising of television, and that which emerged from the printing press, which is generalized writing. When writing becomes advertising, it is generalized broadband advertising.

That is different from the micro-targeted advertising that emerges out of the tech plex, which uses machine intelligence to develop a personality profile, a voodoo doll of you. It crafts and sculpts this voodoo doll by mining your data. It turns your *dark data*—all the ways that you unconsciously place your attention—into a personality profile in order to micro-target you.

It is true that it's not the same as the old advertising, but essentially the tech plex says, *So what? Technology advances, and ways of attracting attention advance, and it's a free market.*

Nir Eyal, a favorite son of the tech plex, a student of B.J. Fogg at the Persuasive Technology Laboratory wrote a book called *Hooked*. *Hooked* means that the purpose of the technology is to addict you. He wrote another book called something like *Indistractable*, meaning, *just turn it off.*

Eyal says, *What's the problem? We're trying to hook you and attract your attention. You have free autonomy as an end user, so turn it off. What's the problem*, says the tech plex, *with stealing attention?* They shrug it off.

Writers like Hari say, *We have to value attention.* But why? You see, neither Zuboff, nor Hari, nor Rushkoff, nor Carr, nor Harari—and I could go through the list of people who discuss this issue—none of them assert what needs to be asserted in order to be morally outraged and astonished by the hijacking of attention.

And what is that? **We have to actually affirm that attention is a First Principle and First Value.** Before anything else, attention is a First Principle and First Value of Cosmos.

If attention is *not* a First Principle and First Value—not a part of the very value proposition that suffuses all of Cosmos—then the hijacking of attention is not a problem.

A BRIEF HISTORY OF ATTENTION

Let's start with attention at the human level, in the premodern world.

There is a writer named Kreiner who just wrote a book called *The Wandering Mind*, which is one of those books that critiques the modern loss of attention and compares it to the medieval period where the monks, for example, were very careful to guard their attention. But why were the monks careful to guard their attention? What were they using their attention *for*?

Why did the monks, and the priests, and the imams, and the different religious practitioners—why did everyone basically take attention to be a great value? **The religious practitioners took attention to be a great value because it was through attention that you placed your mind on the mind of God.** It was through attention that you discerned the will of God.

It was the elite who were tasked with merging with the Divine, with disclosing the will of the Divine, and with sharing that will with the masses. What they were supposed to do was to practice, to meditate, to pray, to fast, to dance, to whirling dervish, to place their full attention on the Divine in order to access the nature of Reality.

Premodernity was all about attention. It was that placing attention on the Divine:

- In order to be obedient
- In order to appropriately surrender
- In order to know the Divine will
- In order to hear the Divine voice
- In order to interpret sacred texts
- In order to achieve *unio mystica*, mystical union, with the Divine

What happens then? Then we go to modernity. Attention turns away from God. **In modernity, God is still invited to the party, but there's a turning of attention from heaven to earth, from God to the human being.**

When you look at Michelangelo's creation scene, and you see the image of God, and you see the hands meeting—Adam is not *surrendering*:

- Adam is filled with Eros.
- He is filled with aliveness.
- He is filled with dignity.
- He is gorgeously formed.

We naturally place attention on his beauty, on his power, and his potential.

There is a turning of attention to nature, to the natural world, to the third-person perspective—in art and in science and in moral philosophy. We begin to look from the third-person perspective, and we generate universal human rights, and we generate the scientific method. We generate new forms of measurement (Kepler and Galileo), which are new forms of *paying attention*.

It's an active attention, which generates new gnosis.

That's the movement of attention in modernity. **The importance of attention is taken as a given because it generates science.**

We turn to the human being, and we move to psychology. We look at our own inner workings and how they operate. Freud begins to dissect the human being much as one would a steam engine.

But something gets lost because as modernity progresses and as science progresses, and as the exterior placings of attention and methodologies for placing of attention get ever more sophisticated, interior technologies begin to break down.

In modernity, value gets lost as a plotline in Cosmos. Attention becomes but a methodology. And along comes postmodernity and says:

> Actually, all of these stories, including the story of science, including the stories of the Western enlightenment, including the stories of universal human rights, are really just stories. They are really just contrived. Even facts are really contrived values.

Actually, the world is without a plotline. There are no First Values and First Principles, which means there is no *telos*, which means there is no plotline, which means there is no thread to follow.

In essence, what postmodernity is saying is that there's really nothing to pay attention to.

WHEN THERE IS NOTHING TO PAY ATTENTION TO

That incipient sense of *there is nothing to pay attention* to is exactly what Camus talks about in that famous first line in his existentialist novel, *The Stranger*, which I often point out. (*Forget about psychology. Strangers are we, errants at the gates of our own psyche*, writes George Steiner.) Camus' opening line is: *Mother died today, or was it yesterday?*

Mother dying *should* grab my attention. It should *arrest* my attention. Mother died, but that can't arrest my attention because it doesn't ultimately matter. **You pay attention only when it *matters*.** And when the world is said to no longer be constructed from *what matters*—it is reduced to *matter*—then nothing matters. Then there's nothing to pay attention to. Wow!

And so, the internet emerges—the first iterations in the '70s, and in the '80s, the '90s, it really begins to emerge. It literally *parallels* postmodernity.

The internet is the exteriorization, the exterior expression of the postmodern mind. The postmodern mind says, *There is no plotline.*

The postmodern mind would never do what Hawthorne describes in *Sleepy Hollow*. You'd never lean back against a tree and get lost in the depth of a plotline while reading:

+ Lost in the inward space of meaning
+ Creating flow states of attention in order to disclose the depths of Reality

This is because there's no depth of Reality to be disclosed. Plotlines don't matter, and authors don't matter, and unique forms of attention don't matter, which is why Kelly writes that we don't need *authorship* anymore. Let's just have all the *information*. It's all exterior information.

The internet is about the scattering of attention. It's about the interrupting of attention because there is nothing to place attention on.

The conceivers of the internet are the techno-totalitarians who speak in liberal slogans, but who are actually techno-authoritarian. That is to say, they are imposing a reductionist materialist dogma. Without having been elected, without actually having been *chosen* to teach, they are *encoding* the immersive environment with the premise that there are no plotlines, and that your attention can be stolen in every second.

Your iPhone is built to steal your attention. Have you ever noticed that if someone is texting you, the little three dots come up? When you're on WhatsApp, you see someone's texting you. Why? To steal your attention. And it shows up as red or not red, lights up in blue or not blue, whether it's your text message or whether it's WhatsApp—in order to *demand* that you return the message.

When you get on LinkedIn, it tells you what your circle of following is. We have *likes* and we have *views*. The entire internet is constructed to appeal not to the *depth* placing of attention, but to the *surface* vying for pseudo-erotic attention—because there is no genuine experience of the depth of attention.

Eros, or the erotic Universe, is the genuine placing of attention.

The pornographic universe is the hijacking of attention, and social media is an expression of the pornographic universe.

The reason the TechnoFeudalists governing the attention economy ignore the objections of this new cadre of writers (those who are screaming, *You are attention thieves!*) is because they don't see anything wrong with stealing attention. You can arouse moral astonishment and outrage only if there's been a violation of value.

When we see value violated, when we see George Floyd killed, we're outraged at the violation of value, and we storm into the street. If there hasn't been an actual violation of value, we're not moved.

For example, Johann Hari calls for an attention rebellion, and everyone yawns because nowhere in his entire book about the stealing of attention, does he ever tell us what *value*—what intrinsic value of Cosmos expressed at the human level—is being violated by the stealing of attention. He *does* say we have to value attention. He says it time and time again, but he refuses to declare attention *as a value*.

Unless I actually affirm that attention is a First Principle and First Value of Cosmos, there is no conversation. The conversation doesn't get off the ground.

TO BE IN LOVE IS TO PLACE ATTENTION

Let's do it right now, together.

Let's now affirm, in this moment, that attention is a First Principle and First Value of Cosmos.

That's what it is. The god you don't believe in doesn't exist. God is mystery. God can't be named. But we actually try to *name* the force *that's beyond and that moves through you*, upon which, as Henry Miller said, you have to place all of your energy—and only that is the real business of living.

Those forces beyond that move within, that larger movement that lives in us—that's where we have to place our attention.

> *That quality of placing attention actually is the quality of the Infinite turning to finitude.*

It's what William Blake meant when he said, *Eternity is in love with the productions of time.*

See, to be in love is to place attention. That's what it means to be in love. It's so beautiful. **To be in love means I'm willing to bracket myself and place attention on you.** When I place attention on you, I'm in devotion. My attention expresses itself as devotion:

- I am turning towards you.
- I am bracketing the self.
- I am powerful.
- I am not turning towards you because I have a utilitarian need, or an instrumental *telos*, or a superficial goal.
- **I am turning towards you in love.**

Isaac Luria, the interior scientist who incepted the Renaissance through the Lurianic mystery schools that live on the periphery of the Renaissance, talks about this Divine act. (And read Moshe Idel's book *Kabbalah in Italy*, which alludes to this, although it doesn't name it specifically.)

I'm going to call the divine "the Infinite Intimate." The name of God in CosmoErotic Humanism, our new Story of Value, is the Infinite Intimate. The Infinite Intimate steps back and brackets Herself in order to turn towards finitude.

That's what love means.

The parent brackets herself to turn towards her child.

The lover brackets himself/herself to turn towards his friend, her friend, his beloved, her beloved.

The bracketing of self to place attention on other is the primary act of Eros.

It's only when you place attention that *gnosis*—knowing—emerges. Every form of knowing comes from the placing of attention.

SEEING WITH NEW EYES IS THE ESSENTIAL QUALITY OF THE EROTIC UNIVERSE

I was reading last night this book, *Sketches of Etruscan Places and other Italian Essays*. It's a collection of essays by D. H. Lawrence. He writes here, "Everything depends on the amount of true, sincere religious concentration you can bring to bear."

D. H. Lawrence is not known for his religion—and yet he says, *An act of pure attention, if you are capable of it, will bring its own answer.* **Everything is about the placing of attention.**

Attention is the realization that something other than me is real and is worthy of my concentrated attention, of the placing of my heart.

The original Hebrew word for attention is *sim lev*—the placing of the heart, which is the placing of attention.

When we say the sexual models the erotic (which is a core principle in one of the core works of CosmoErotic Humanism, *A Return to Eros*), what we mean is that sex *discloses* the nature of Eros. But of course, there have been twelve billion years of Eros before there was any sex. **Sex encapsulates, models, incarnates Eros, but we want to live erotically in every dimension of life—and to live erotically is to place attention.**

To live pornographically is to have attention hijacked. The pornographic universe is about the *hijacking* of attention, while the erotic Universe is about the *placing* of attention. When we say the sexual models the erotic— what *is* sex if not the placing of attention? That's what it is.

Now, the pseudo-erotic placing of attention is when my attention is stolen by newness—by novelty. Novelty attracts my attention. That's the beginning. That's an original erotic moment.

But then Eros deepens; Eros discloses her true face.

When I bring my attention to bear, it's not the new breast, or the new belly, or the new posterior, or the new shoulder, or the new bare legs that capture my attention because I've never seen them before (and so it's a shiny new object)—that is the pseudo-eros of novelty.

No, no, no.

Erotic attention is when I can see with new eyes, not when I see new things.

To see something new and to constantly have that newness replaced by something else new is the demarcating characteristic of the pornographic universe. But to see with new eyes, that's the essential quality of the erotic Universe: *I see you for the very first time, even though I've seen you a thousand times.* And each time I place my attention on you, you are different. You're physiologically different. You are neurologically different. But you're also different from the perspective of your depth interior.

You are new. You are emergent.

When I see you, I allow myself to fall into the rapture of radical amazement again and again, and I fall in love with you, again and again. That's how the sexual models the erotic.

Sex is a model, not of pornography, as in the pornographic universe, but of the erotic Universe.

If in-depth reading is erotic, social media is pornographic.

To liberate attention is to liberate the quality of Eros, which moves towards intimacy—which is my nature.

THE ATTENTION OF THE INFINITE DIFFERENTIATES UNIQUELY THROUGH ME

Attention is not generic. **Attention is always unique.**

In the new book, *First Principles and First Values* (written by David J. Temple, who's a pseudo-anonymous author), there is a set of interior science equations. These interior science equations took me about twenty years. There are eighteen interior science equations, which express the evolving First Principles and First Values of Cosmos. One of the equations is about uniqueness. I am not going to read you the entire equation, but **uniqueness is the unique capacity to *allure* attention and the unique capacity to *place* attention**. In other words, I am a unique quality of attention.

I am a unique capacity of attention, which means that Infinity sees uniquely through me.

> *To be a Unique Self means that the attention of the Infinite differentiates uniquely through me.*

That's what it means to be a Unique Self.

I am Divinity's unique prism of attention, which means that Infinity, the Infinite Intimate, can see a dimension of Reality only through me.

There is all this discussion about loving God. Who loves God? Let's get real. Why would you love God? What does it mean to love God?

To love God means to let God see through your eyes.

And to be a lover is to clarify your own attention, which is to clarify your Eros, to clarify your desire, because desire is where I place my attention. Desire is the focus. That's what desire is. Desire equals that which I value, upon which I place my attention. When I clarify my desire, I clarify my attention. To be a lover is to see with God's eyes, meaning with clarified attention.

It's even more. Let's go deeper. One last step.

When I love you, for example, when I place my attention on you, a unique dimension of me shows up to you and to me that doesn't show up with anyone else.

When I am in love with my friend, with my beloved of any kind, it's because I see you, I placed my attention on you. Love is a perception. *I see you*, number one.

But number two, **I'm in love with you because you evoke—through the quality of attention you evoke for me—a dimension of me that doesn't appear in any other way**.

Isn't that gorgeous? Infinity generates the multiplicities of finitude, which are multiplicities of uniquenesses—meaning billions of Unique Selves—because Infinity, Divinity, Infinite Divinity experiences shocking self-recognition *through you*.

When Infinity feels your placing of attention on Him/Her, Infinity appears in a new way that She doesn't appear in any other way. **Reality is the Infinite placing attention on finitude, and finitude placing attention on Infinity—and both mutually generate each other.**

Wow! Both create each other. It's not *a creator creates creation*. Creator creates creation and creation creates creator, which is why the *Zohar*, the thirteenth-century *Book of Radiance*, begins by saying *bereshit bara Elohim*. In the beginning God created—but the *Zohar* rereads that as *bereshit bara Elohim, in the beginning we create God*.

We generate—through our attention—the disclosure, the revelation of the Infinite that appears in a way it couldn't appear in any other way. That's attention.

WE NEED TO RECLAIM ATTENTION AS A VALUE

Attention begins with subatomic particles placing attention on each other, and it goes all through the world of matter. Attention goes through the intra-attention mechanisms of the biosphere until attention breaks out at the human level.

> *Evolution is the evolution of attention, and the evolution of attention is the evolution of love.*

We go through all the stages of human experience until we get to postmodernity, in which we lose the thread of the plotline. We lose the thread of the evolution of attention because of the exterior technologies with their ability to place artificial attention, surveillance, tracking, eyes on you all the time: superficial attention, which is the opposite of a loving providence. The actual storyline of the inherent value of Reality breaks down, and the win/lose metrics take over, and attention is stolen and hijacked.

Writers call vainly for an attention rebellion. They say we should value attention, and they scream till they're hoarse. We should value attention, but they refuse to proclaim attention as a First Value and First Principle.

We are here to articulate the new Story of Value.

We are here to pay attention to attention, to place our attention on attention, which means to love attention, which means to affirm that attention is an expression of my Unique Self, which is an expression of my desire. **Attention is the natural incarnation of my Eros.** Attention is my right. It can't be stolen. Wow!

We are reclaiming attention.

We are placing our heart.

CHAPTER NINE

ALEXEI NAVALNY: TO LIVE IS TO RISK IT ALL, THE UNIQUE RISK OF THE HERO

Episode 384 — February 18, 2024

THE EULOGY OF A HERO

We have all heard the heartbreaking news that Alexei Navalny died.

Alexei Navalny was, first and foremost, a figure who stood for laughter and good cheer. The day before he died, he was videoed in court. He was making fun of the guards, with good cheer and laughter, telling them to put some money in his account because he was a little short.

Although I don't know exactly how to pronounce Navalny's name, **I do know that my heart is, and has been for several years, blown away by Navalny's courage, by his goodness, by his fearlessness, and perhaps most importantly, by his being literally *an incarnation of value*.**

He *became* value.

He became value itself.

If you were to listen to his younger colleagues and supporters these days, that is what you would hear in their eulogies, again and again: for them, growing up

in the postmodern cultural context, he became a revelation of value. Not (just) in what he said, but in *who he was*, they saw, without a shadow of a doubt, that value *matters*, and that changed them irrevocably.

He has been murdered. He was murdered—quite clearly—by Putin. He had been very alive a day before a blood clot was claimed by the prison authorities to go to his brain. It's clear that he was murdered.

I'll share with you just a little bit of his life. In case anyone wants to point out his imperfection—he *was* imperfect. In his early years, he was too closely associated with very problematic, ultra-nationalist, xenophobic, Russian patriotic movements that spoke in ways that were wrong. And he regretted it. He was imperfect. He went through many stages of development.

He wasn't a philosopher. He wasn't a moralist.

He was a leader of the Russian opposition, a political leader with enormous moral courage, with wild and beautiful imagination—with love in his eyes, a song in his heart, and courage in his blood, and fire in his veins, and fierce goodness in waging a campaign against corruption in Russia. Corruption which—in his experience, and he was right—had eaten at the very heart of the Russia that he loved. The Russia that he loved was the Russia that was filled with literature. He loved literature.

The Russia that he loved was a Russia filled with depth and nuance and a beauty that the world needed to hear. A Russia that participated in the global Story of Value.

I don't want to debate his life.

I want to eulogize.

To eulogize a person's life is to try to capture something of their essence, which both honors them in the next stage of their journey and allows them to impact us.

By their impacting us, they are fully alive.

By being fully alive, they are able to take the next stage of the journey.

By hearing them, by feeling them, the hope that they incarnated becomes a flame. That hope becomes alive.

This is not a moment to be silent. We have to eulogize. We have to feel the pain of the loss, and we have to celebrate. We have to celebrate Alexei Navalny's life as a life which is hope itself, a life which is itself a memory of a possible future, which must become true.

The way I want to do this is to let Alexei Navalny speak in his own words, and just to add a few thoughts. I'm going to pull up an interview from the website of Boris Akunin, probably Russia's most famous exiled writer. Akunin sent a 13-point questionnaire to an entire community of dissidents and political prisoners around Russia.

THE RESPONSE TO CORRUPTION IS LAUGHTER

Before I read the questions and Navalny's responses, it's enough to know that he spent five or six intense years between 2005 and 2011, realizing profoundly the core corruption in the system. He realized that:

- Corruption wasn't a side hustle in Russia.
- It had hijacked, in his experience, the soul of Mother Russia.
- Corruption was the essence of what Russia became.
- Putin posed a danger to the very heart of the Russia that he loved, the Russia that lives in its stunning literature.
- Fear and greed drove corruption.

Therefore, **the response to corruption had to be to expose and mock greed, and to laugh at fear.** And that's what he did. He laughed at fear, and he mocked and exposed greed. He ran for mayor of Moscow in 2011. Got some 27 percent of the vote, even in the election blatantly rigged against him. He was understood to be a profound challenge to Putin.

He was *an organizer* (think about the union organizers in the United States). Both on the internet and in real life, he organized a network of offices and anti-corruption websites, which became the core of his political machine. He would have run for president in 2018, but the Kremlin, of course, devised a law which prevented him from running for president.

But he became the symbol of holy laughter.

Laughter that was courage itself.

Laughter that mocked corruption.

Laughter that laughed at fear and exposed and mocked greed.

In the end, nine years later, on a plane, in the middle of a political campaign, he was poisoned and he almost died. He was miraculously airlifted to Berlin, and it took five months for him to recover. After he recovered, he could have spent his life leading Russia as a dissident in exile, but he made an insanely courageous decision to go back, to return to Russia. It was quite clear he would be arrested. He was.

He said at his trial:

> He (Putin) will enter history as a poisoner. We in Russia have had Yaroslav the Wise, Alexander the Liberator, and Vladimir the Poisoner of Underpants.

He said this because the toxin that was used to kill him was placed in his underpants. He had the last word at that moment. He mocked Putin. He laughed.

Laughter undermines evil. **Laughter undermines the pomposities of power.** Not immediately. It takes time. But laughter is the language of courage.

There was a particular moment when Navalny learned the identity of the key person who was involved in planning his assassination, the poisoning. And so, he actually calls that person, pretending to be someone else. And he says, *What happened? What went wrong with the Navalny thing? Why didn't we get him?* And the person is taken in and they start discussing, *Why didn't we succeed in killing Navalny?*

He's laughing. He's laughing with unimaginable audacity and unimaginable courage.

After he is put in prison in 2021, when he returns to Russia, he remains a potent, courageous, and shockingly beautiful voice. Putin wants to cut him off from all communication, so he is moved to Siberia. I know something about Siberia indirectly. Much of my family died in Siberia. My father was in Siberia during World War II with his father, and he described Siberia in detail. Descriptions of Siberia were part of my earliest youth. He is sent to Siberia, cut off from everyone, and essentially starved in isolation.

Yet somehow, he holds the mood. He holds his laughter. He says, *I can only be in prison if I decide to be in prison. Prison exists in my mind. I'm not in prison. I'm on a space voyage.*

NAVALNY LIVED AND DIED FOR VALUE

On February 16th, 2024, one leg of that space voyage, that voyage in the space-time continuum that is our world, ended. He went on to the next world, murdered and martyred. And his voyage has only just begun.

Alexei Navalny has only just begun to fight.

Alexei Navalny has only just begun to love.

I want to read to you his responses to the thirteen questions in the interview that I described earlier, which is posted on Boris Akunin's website. It was translated from Russian into English by Nikolai Formozov, edited by Joanne Turnbull.

The reason I'm going to read these questions and answers is because what I think you're about to see, and hear, and feel is this: what allowed, what caused, what empowered, what potentiated Navalny's courage was First

Values and First Principles, embedded in a Story of Value, which is the core of the revolution that we are standing for here in writing the Great Library of CosmoErotic Humanism, in this time between worlds.

He doesn't have the language for it exactly, but he understands it deep in his body, deep in his heart, deep, if you will, in his Russian soul, that a human being has to stand for value, or we are not really alive.

He was asked many times, *Why did you return?* And he said:

> I love my country madly and I have strong beliefs. And I've got to stand for them. I've got to stand for them even if that means sacrifice. Otherwise, they are not beliefs, just random thoughts in my head.

He understood that this might mean the ultimate sacrifice. He understood that if there is nothing that is a true value, an authentic value, a clarified value, nothing that I am willing to die for, then I am not alive.

Now, to be clear. It's easy to die for false values. People do it all the time. For example, there are fundamentalist Islamic versions of jihad, of the kind that perpetrated the October 7th massacre, which was premeditated and preordained, in which women were tortured—nails driven into their bodies while their breasts were cut off as they were being raped; eyes gouged out—all ignored by virtually the entire world. The people that perpetrated those actions, who were jacked up on amphetamines, were willing to die for those false values.

We have to be willing to die for values that are real. The idea is not to *die* for them; the idea is to *live* for them. But first, I've got to identify what I am willing to die for? What matters?

And if you want to know the spark of the sacred in the fallen forms of jihad, it is the realization that there is something worth dying for. That staying alive forever as the absolute value—*let me live as long and comfortably as I can, and I will give up anything just to stay alive a little longer*—is *The Picture of Dorian Gray*, by Oscar Wilde. It's the source of all corruption.

But I need to be able to clarify my values, to know what is actually worth dying for.

Not all values, the way they are presented, are true. Values can be distorted and degraded.

But we actually can get beneath the degradations. We can get beneath distortions. We can articulate a shared set of First Principles and First Values, a universal grammar of value as a context for our diversity, and a Story of Value in which we know that we stand together. That which unites us is so much greater than that which divides us, and we stand for value.

Value inspires us, and it ennobles us, and it makes us cry, and it makes us laugh. Those clarified values are good, and they're true, and they're beautiful.

And we live or die by them. I want to try to clarify this through Navalny's words.

A LIFE ALIGNED WITH VALUE IS A LIFE OF JOY

Question one: *Who are you?*

He answers,

> From the prison authorities, I constantly hear this disgruntled phrase: *Hmm. You seem to be in a good mood today.*

Meaning the prison authorities are like, *Why are you in a good mood? You're like in the middle of Siberia. You're never getting out of here. Why would you be in a good mood?*

Navalny says,

> So I guess it's like this. I'm a political prisoner who very much misses his family, work, and colleagues, but who keeps some good spirits. I'm also, of course, a reader. I spend most of my day with a book in my hands.

And that's how it begins.

So, the first thing he says is, *Mood is everything*. Heidegger got that right. Mood is the central category of reality, and I am responsible for my mood. My mood can be good if I am living a purpose-driven life, a life aligned with value.

A life aligned with value is a life of joy.

Not the values of some far-right xenophobic position—but the value which is the air we breathe. Value is the air we breathe. Just like there is space and time in the manifest world, there is value.

Value is not hard to find. Value is impossible to avoid. And if I live in value, then my spirits can be good no matter what. Wow!

He is asked, *What do you believe in?*

> In God and science. I believe we live in a non-deterministic Universe and have free will.

So, there are laws of science, and yet, there is freedom. In other words, freedom itself is a First Principle and First Value. Our choices matter.

> I believe we're not alone in the Universe.

That's what we would call, in CosmoErotic Humanism, the "Intimate Universe."

So, one: freedom is a First Principle and First Value. There is a new possibility. Reality is the possibility of possibility. It's not a deterministic universe. There are railroad tracks, there are constraints, but there are places where the tracks fork. New possibilities live in the system itself. And we're not alone in the Universe, meaning, in the language of CosmoErotic Humanism, we live in an Intimate Universe.

> I believe that our deeds and actions will be evaluated.

Evaluation is only possible when we realize that we live in a Field of Value. We are accountable. Not in a fire and brimstone way. We tremble before

202

evolution with joy, and we know that we count. **If I am accountable, I count.**

If I incarnate value, then it is appropriate, and a mad joy, to be evaluated. Not an evaluation that causes a free-floating, irrational, sick anxiety—an evaluation that arouses the sense of joy, the joy that I am *worthy* of being evaluated.

He says,

> And I believe in true love.

We call that *Eros*. The Eros that lives between human beings, and the Eros that drives and animates all of evolution.

And he says,

> I believe that Russia will be happy and free.

And as I believe in the future possibility, I believe that the status quo doesn't rule. That is the teaching of the Exodus and the Bible, which Navalny read well, just like he read Kant. The story of the Exodus is: Pharaoh will fall. And so too will Putin fall.

There will be a moment, Navalny would say, when we will look back, and Putin will be a bad memory. And that is true. **Putin will fall as pharaoh fell, because Eros is on the move, because love is on the move.**

And then he says,

> And I do not believe in death.

When he says I don't believe in death, he means I don't believe that death is the end of the story.

We know death is not the end of the story. We know that death is a night between two days:

- We know that because there is deep realization, deep knowing that lives in us, as us, and through us.

- ◆ We know that because there is empirical information.
- ◆ We know that because philosophically neither materialism—the reduction of the world to matter that doesn't matter—nor dualism makes any sense. Dualism means that God's over there, out there at the top half of the circle, and the bottom half of the circle is purely material, and they are two separate worlds. That doesn't make any sense.

We know that Reality is interiors and exteriors, all the way up and all the way down.

We know that Reality is interiority. Every exterior has an interior. **We know that the raw and real essence of Reality—the Eros, the consciousness, the value—is not bound by a particular material predicament.** We know that.

Again, we know it empirically through mounds of evidence collected in the last 140 years, we know it philosophically, but we also know it anthro-ontologically.

I remember being at my dear friend Barbara Marx Hubbard's deathbed. It was clear that the Barbara I had just spoken to two days before, who said, *Marc*, as the doctor put her on the phone—she hadn't disappeared. Barbara was here. Barbara *is* here.

When I feel my beloved friend, Sally Kempton, especially in the last ten days, speak to me, speak to me in the sense that I feel her presence, I feel her reality. I feel her living presence. It is a direct experience. There are actually twelve gateways which are direct experiences that live inside of us, in which we have direct access to the continuity of consciousness.

Navalny is filled with courage because he lives in a Field of Value. Because he knows of the continuity of consciousness. Because he is delighted. Delighted to be alive, because he is in love with love. He knows that love is real.

And he knows that everything always changes. He knows that dictators fall. He knows that Putin is going to be known as the Poisoner of Underpants. Wow!

He is asked: *What's the main thing in life?*

He responds: *To be useful to society and to remain a good person.*

And I would add, to be *uniquely* good. *To be good* is not *generically* good. It is unique for each of us: to be the good person that only I can be, and to be of service, to play my instrument in the Unique Self Symphony.

What brings you the most joy?

Remember the scene that we played two years ago in the movie *Don't Look Up*? They've got just a few minutes left to live, and they gather, and have dinner together, and talk, and drink wine.

Alexei answers:

> What brings me the most joy are simple family moments. Like going somewhere together in the car. One of us starts goofing around and singing and the rest join in. And we can't stop until we've sung a bunch of songs. And the love and happiness overflow.

WE HAVE TO TAKE A STAND FOR EACH OTHER

What most saddens you?

> The unwillingness of many people to think, their incomprehension of basic cause-and-effect relationships. Every time someone says to me something like, *Corruption doesn't affect my life* or *The people in power have done all their stealing, but if the new people come to power, the stealing will start all over again*, so they give up. I think: How is it that hundreds of millions of years of evolution have given this person the most amazing brain and they don't use it?

How can they not realize that their actions matter? That standing for a cause matters?

What brings the greatest evil to man and mankind?

> *All it takes for evil to triumph is the inaction of good people*—a phrase attributed to many, though no one knows exactly who said it (I checked). It is amazingly accurate. The hypocrisy of neutrality, *apoliticism*, and recusal, concealing laziness, cowardice, and meanness, is the principal reason why a bunch of well-organized villains have ruled over millions throughout human history.

This is one of the tragedies of the integral movement, which is an important and beautiful movement, animated by its leading philosopher, my dear friend, Ken Wilber. Too many of the people in the integral world—Ken and I have talked about this many times—manage to find all sides of an issue. They take all perspectives, which is beautiful. That's a good step.

But then, after you take all perspectives, you've got to get brave. You've got to get courageous. You've got to take a stand.

And in the integral world, way too many of its core personae hide in perspective-taking and lack the genuine courage to take a stand. Rather, they get involved in the corruption of clicks, and the corruption of popularity, and the corruption of commodified intellect sold to prop up the fragile ego. And they lose contact with basic decency, basic honesty, basic integrity.

The hypocrisy of apoliticism, says Navalny, *which conceals laziness, cowardice, and meanness.*

It's a big deal. It's very tragic.

We have to move to the post-tragic. **The move to the post-tragic is the claiming of courage.** The claiming of courage says: *I am willing to take a stand. I am willing to transcend my obeisance, my kneeling, my bowing to various forms of McCarthyism, my bowing to the rule of a broken information ecology that reigns on the internet.*

I've got to actually take a stand. I take a stand in small acts of courage, which are large acts of integrity. I don't negotiate: *Well, I'm going to betray this person. I'm going to let this person be run over. I'm not going to take a stand on the truth here. I won't have courage there because I am protecting my legacy; I am protecting my good works.*

That's bullshit. Take a stand. **We all have to take a stand for each other.** All of us. And there are a thousand reasons to justify the politics of neutrality.

Navalny says:

> The hypocrisy of neutrality conceals laziness, cowardice, and meanness. And it's the principal reason why a bunch of well-organized villains can rule over millions.

What's the great act of being alive?

And Navalny answers beautifully. He says,

> Engaging in the battle of the good versus the neutral.

It's not even the good versus *evil*. It's good versus *the neutral*.

The reason people are able to stay neutral is not just laziness, not just cowardice, not just meanness. They actually step out of the Field of Value, and when you step out of the Field of Value, you're not going to take a stand. You only take a stand when you are in the Field of Value.

What art has the strongest effect on you?

> I love literature, and I consider that I know something about it.

And me too. Beautiful.

I like movies.

By the way, Navalny loved *Star Wars*.

> Music and architecture. But I don't know much about them. As for the rest of the arts, I will diplomatically say I treat them with respect.

> Literature has the strongest effect of any art form. After all, it works through your own imagination. What could be stronger than that?

Do you have a favorite maxim?

He has two (a maxim is a saying of wisdom).

One he quotes from Kant:

> Act in such a way that the maxim of your action may become a rule of universal behavior.

Meaning, the value that you stand for is a value which is universal. It's part of the intrinsic structure of Reality, so you standing for it points to it as a universal value.

And finally:

> Do unto others as you'd have them do unto you.

Wow!

VALUE IS MORE POWERFUL THAN ANY OTHER FORCE

Why was Putin so afraid of Navalny? Why did Putin kill him? Why did he need to be killed?

From Putin's perspective, he needed to be killed because value stands against fear, and value stands against corruption.

This is precisely why, at this moment of meta-crisis, as we literally stand poised between utopia and dystopia, we have to speak the truth.

This is not just an issue of Russia, or of Israel, or of the battle against the value that Hamas stands for, which is a form of anti-value, a form of anti-truth. It has nothing to do with Gaza and Israel. It has nothing to do with Jewish-Arab coexistence, which should be a given. **Hamas stands for anti-value at its very core.** It's got nothing to do with the particular context of Israel. Hamas stands for jihad in its most corrupt form. And jihad takes place in Iraq and Libya where there is no Israel. We are afraid to say that.

Don't say that, Marc! Don't say that! That's going to be unpopular. You'll lose a couple of people.

Fuck that. We have to speak truth. When we are afraid to speak the truth because we'll lose some people on our channel, because we'll lose some popularity, it doesn't work.

We stand against any kind of ethnocentrism, which says that my people are more important than value. Value lives in all of us.

> *We stand for value, and value is more powerful than any other force in the world.*

See, it's value that makes a hero, and Alexei Navalny is a hero.

He loved Hollywood movies in which heroes won, because he understood, in his very bones, that the next stage of human history—the emergence of the new human and the new humanity—is going to be a new human and a new humanity who stand for value. *Heroes.*

This is why a hero is filled with valor. A hero is valiant. When I grew up, we would read about a particular knight named Prince Valiant. And *valor* and *valiant* derive from the same Latin root, which is *valere*. Be strong in your worth and your value. *Valentia*, the intrinsic worth that lives in reality and that lives in you and Valentine. Valentine, love, Eros.

Alexei Navalny sent a message just a few days ago, on Valentine's Day, to his wife. He said, *I love you madly. I love you so much. And although you're so far away, you're so close right next to me by my side.* They're madly in love with each other.

He says, *I believe in true love.*

Our love lists are too short. Love is real. And the hero stands for *valentia*, for Eros which is value, which creates the hero, who is valor, who is valiant, who is value, who is the unique valence of Cosmos, the unique incarnation of value moving through him.

And Putin is not a hero. Putin is a coward. Putin is the poisoner of underpants. Vladimir the Poisoner of Underpants.

Alexei Navalny, a hero, says, *It's time for a new world. It's time for the democratization of the hero.*

WE STAND FOR THE DEMOCRATIZATION OF THE HERO

The hero is imperfect. The hero is flawed, but the hero is a hero.

The hero is a hero because he or she stands in Eros, or value. **We live or die for value, for goodness, truth and beauty.** It lives beyond death. Value transcends—it ends the trance—of death. We step into the next journey of value.

That's why Marvel movies, in the middle of the postmodern collapse of value, have been so popular for the last ten years. Because the hero is the early adopter of *Homo amor*, the new human, the new humanity, in which every human being knows:

- I'm a unique hero.

- I've got a unique risk to take and a unique life to live in it.
- A unique gift to give, a unique quality of Eros to shine into reality.
- A unique song to sing and a unique poem to write.
- And a unique way of laughing, living, and loving that's irreducibly mine, that the world desperately needs.
- It's my value. It's my gorgeousness. It's my Eros. It's my intimacy. It's my aliveness. It's my art. That is me.
- I am literature. I am great literature. There is no truly lived life that is not great literature.

Alexei Navalny—friend, brother, father, husband, beloved hero, valiant man, man of valor, man of value, man of Valentine, valence of Reality—go in peace. And may your flame burn bright, and free Mother Russia, and participate in the birth out of this crisis—our crisis is a birth—of the new human and the new humanity, and the emergence of the most good, true, and beautiful world that we've always known is the true nature of the Real.

Go in peace, brother.

I want to just add two more things.

First, this is not just about one man. We are talking here about the democratization of the hero, the democratization of unique risk.

There is an entire world of Russia—of heroes who gave up their lives to oppose Stalin, to oppose later versions of Stalinism, and then to oppose Putin, at the cost of their lives. I am just going to mention a couple of names. In some sense, the father of someone very close to us who's here today, might well be on this list of names. But let me just give you four names, so that you can, through them, get a sense of so many, so many names, and all of them are inscribed in the very fabric of reality.

All of them are inscribed in the Book of Life.

All of them are inscribed on the divine throne.

All of them are inscribed in the continuity of consciousness:

- **Anna Politkovskaya**, journalist and author of *Putin's Russia*, who was shot dead on October 7th, 2006, Putin's birthday, in the elevator of her apartment in Moscow. She was 48 years old.
- **Alexander Litvinenko**, was hospitalized for Polonium-210 poisoning and died 22 days later on November 23rd 2006. His chief crime was saying out loud what everyone suspected—that Russian intelligence had killed the oligarch Boris Berezovsky.
- **Sergei Magnitsky**, responsible for exposing corruption by Russian government officials, served a 358-day sentence in a Moscow prison. He died in 2009, on November 16th, at 37 years old.
- **Boris Nemtsov** was assassinated in 2015 on February 27th, on a bridge near the Kremlin in Moscow, where he was organizing a rally against Russia's invasion of Ukraine. And Boris once wrote:

There's always been a surplus of servitude and a deficit of freedom in Russia. We value those who grovel, which is why Russia remains a nation of slaves and princes to this day.

I don't know what Russia remains. That's not for me to say. But it is for me to say that we hold and remember every person.

No one died in vain. There are no forgotten deaths. Everything is recorded. Everything is inscribed. **What allows Navalny to be fearless is that he understands, in his body, that it's beyond death.**

That it doesn't end when it ends.

That death is not the last act. It is a transitional act. It is when the play really starts. Integrity comes only from that knowing.

WE ALL HAVE A UNIQUE RISK TO TAKE

I want to end with a funny, serious, beautiful, poignant, painful note.

In 2021, when Navalny was going back to Russia, five months after being poisoned, he was sitting next to his wife. On the plane, they watched *Rick and Morty*, an animated series involving a mad scientist. A month later, he is on trial. And he quotes *Rick and Morty*. The simple quote is:

> To live is to risk all. Otherwise, you're just an inert chunk of randomly assembled molecules drifting wherever the Universe blows you.

That's what we mean by unique risk.

I want to close just by asking you a question.

Why did Navalny go back to Russia?

He could have stayed in Germany. He could have been a leader in exile. I don't know if he was wrong or right. I don't know if there is a wrong or right here. I'm certainly not going to second-guess Navalny after he gave up his life.

But he decided to go back. He decided that there was a unique risk that was his to take. Even if it cost him his life, he was willing to stake his life on it.

Is there a place *for each of us* where we need to *go back to Russia*? Is there a flight we need to get on?

For 99.9 percent of us here, that's not going to mean imprisonment in Siberia. That's not what it's going to mean. For 99.9 percent of us, it's not going to mean death, but it might mean dying to a part of ourselves. It might mean being born in a new way.

It might mean being willing to step into my greatness.

> *To step into my greatness, I need two things. To live with being afraid, and to be fearless—and to do them together.*

But the question is: *Do I have a flight to catch? Is there a flight back to Russia that's mine to take?*

Can I look Alexei Navalny in the eyes right now and say, *Thank you?*

Thank you for inspiring me to get on my flight, to take my unique risk, to be Homo amor, to be Unique Self, and to play my instrument in the Unique Self Symphony.

Navalny, shalom, shalom. Go in peace. Until next time.

CHAPTER TEN

TOWARDS THE
POST-TRAGIC HERO

Episode 388 — March 17, 2024

I CANNOT BE WELCOME IN THE UNIVERSE UNLESS I AM A HERO

This is a very important week—in this time between worlds, this time between stories. We are going to talk about the hero today (we are using the word *hero* to refer to both male and female hero, in the same way as we use the word *poet*). It's one of our most important weeks. We're going to talk about the hero, and *be* the hero, and *become* the hero—because there's no way to respond to the meta-crisis without the emergence of a new Story of Value.

A new Story of Value answers three questions:

- *Where?* Where am I?
- *Who?* Who am I?
- *What?* What ought to be done?

We call these *the three great questions of CosmoErotic Humanism*, the new Story of Value in response to the meta-crisis. We are here to be heroes for Her Majesty, the Queen of the Universe.

Do you remember the Three Musketeers? *One for all, and all for one, and all for France.* To be a hero for Her Majesty Queen of the Universe—*Malchut.* An old friend of mine likes to talk about being *secret agents* for Her Majesty, the Queen of the Universe. It's beautiful.

To do that, we need to begin to understand what it means *to be the hero*—because to be the hero means something new. It's not the old version of the hero. To be a hero for Her Majesty Queen of the Universe—along with the King of the Universe, in *hieros gamos*, with line and circle together—we need to *participate* in royalty.

We are not only the hero *for the sake* of royalty—for the sake of the vision. We become the vision. We *become* the royalty. I actually become the queen; I become the king.

We want to talk about how to evolve the source code and elicit the new hero.

I cannot be welcome in the Universe unless I am a hero.

It's okay—and sometimes beautiful and necessary—to critique each other. But we can never critique each other in a way that undermines our ability to evoke the hero in you. I want you to get this distinction. It's so precise and so beautiful.

There's a certain kind of critique that we can hold: *You are giving me an important critique to help me become better.*

But there is another critique that has a withering effect. It's the silent assassin of the anti-hero: *There are no heroes. You're not a hero. I'm not a hero. There's no Her Majesty. There's no Field of Eros, and I critique you in a way that undermines your capacity to be a hero.* Sometimes friends do that to each other. Sometimes parents do that to their children. Sometimes children

216

do it to their parents. Sometimes a teacher does it to their students, or students do it to their teacher. All of that is off-limits. *None* of that is okay.

All critique has to be in the context of *welcome*—and I can welcome you only if I can *see* you, if I can love you madly.

To love is to see with God's eyes.

To be a lover is to see with God's eyes.

To see with God's eyes is to see that my significant other—whoever that significant other is—as a hero. My beloved—whoever that beloved is in my circle of intimacy—is a hero. When someone sees me as a hero—and not in a bypass-y way, not in a superficial way—I am actually being seen with God's eyes.

You are a hero.

HERO IS A FUNDAMENTAL CATEGORY OF REALITY

Very few people know how to see us as a hero.

I took a New Age seminar, and I studied Joseph Campbell, and I'm on the hero's journey. This kind of language has been a bit overused. It's stopped meaning anything. But in fact: **Hero is the fundamental category of Reality itself. I am not I, unless I am a hero.**

Does that make sense? There's no *I* without being a hero. Who I am, in the most fundamental way, is a hero. The emergence of the new human and the new humanity, which emerges in this new Story of Value as a response to the meta-crisis—that's *Homo amor*:

- The human being who incarnates uniquely the Eros of the Universe
- The human being who is giving their unique gifts and living their unique presence, which itself becomes a gift as an expression—an irreducibly unique expression—of the Field of ErosValue

That's a hero.

Homo amor **is about the democratization of the hero.**

It used to be that there were only a few heroes in service of Her Majesty Queen of the Universe, a mixture of public and private heroes: A few 007s, private heroes, and some Walter Scott public heroes and some Musketeers (from Dumas's novel). But in order to respond to the meta-crisis, we have to do the only thing that ever changes history—we have to tell a new Story of Value, in which *each one of us is a hero*, and we all have different roles. We have different instruments to play in the Unique Self Symphony—and we are *all* heroes, and then together, we form the Unique Self Symphony, which is the ultimate hero.

We have a name for the Unique Self Symphony. We have named the hero. **We have named the hero David J. Temple.** It's a pseudo-anonymous name, and it's the Unique Self Symphony itself—the hero.

I am welcome in the Universe only if I am a hero.

I love feedback. Feedback is important. One of the things I've actually said in the Unique Self Symphony is that—and I function in many roles, but one of them is a teacher role—I want feedback always. But there is a distinction between two different kinds of feedback. I give feedback and sometimes sharp feedback. And I always want to hold that distinction on my side as well, which is I always want to give feedback that makes you *more* of a hero.

We recognize each other as heroes.

THE CROSSING: TO EXPERIENCE MYSELF AS A HERO

Let me share with you how you can be more of a hero.

I cannot be welcome in the Universe unless I experience Reality profoundly *needing* me. I am needed to save the day.

Sometimes, I'm actually a secret agent. 007 never gets disclosed. 007 is always operating behind the scenes. Sometimes, I'm in the 007 mode. James Bond or Jane Bond—James's sister. She doesn't just have to be James's love interest. She can be Jane Bond. We like her.

And sometimes my job is to be the Three Musketeers, to be a public hero. It depends on what part of the incarnation and which incarnation. But it's all about being a hero.

Fundamentally, the people who love me know that I'm a hero. Now I've got to actually *be* that. That's what it means to become *Homo amor*.

We're going to be doing an event in a few weeks called *The Crossing*. I named it The Crossing after a hero named Ibrahim, Abraham. Abraham crosses over to the other side. He becomes the ultimate antecedent founder of Islam, Christianity, and Hebrew wisdom. He moves to the East as well. **Abraham is a hero *because* he crosses to the other side.**

So let's cross to the other side.

The way I cross the other side is that I begin to *experience myself* as a hero. Can we hold that? It's so crazy deep. Let's go deep into the hero. The beginning is a re-visioning of the self, but not an intellectual, cognitive restructuring. It is about how I actually, literally experience myself as a hero.

I want you to notice the reaction to that. Our first reaction to that—even if we love each other, and I'm home, and I hope you love me, and I love you, and we love each other—nonetheless, our first reaction to that is psychological. *Huh! I wish he could do some psychological work to deal with that grandiosity.* Otto Rank, one of the inner players in Freud's inner circle, talks about this. No! Wrong! You cannot reduce the grandness of the hero to a superficial, reductive materialist grandiosity.

The artist experiences himself or herself as a hero: *I've got to paint this canvas; I've got to write this verse*—wherever the tapestry of my artistry might be and whatever form it might take. **When I experience myself as an artist, I experience myself as a hero.**

I experience the urgency of my creativity.

I experience that it's ultimately valuable, that it matters, that I stand for it with everything that I have, that I lay down my heart, body, and soul for it—and I have this sense of ecstatic urgency.

The artist is the hero. The hero is the foreshadowing of *Homo amor*. It's one of the reasons why, in modernity and late modernity—and then in postmodernity—when human beings thought they were stepping out of the Field of Value, they continued to revere art. And not just love art, but *revere* art—because the artist is still the hero.

Or we revere sports figures as heroes. And then there were comic book heroes. It started with a bunch of kids creating *Superman* in Cleveland, Ohio, in the 1930s. That was still the era of modernity, but then even as postmodernity exploded in the mid-1990s, it's still there. There is this glimmering of the hero.

But when you step out of the Field of Value, you go to *destroy* the hero. That's why postmodernity said there are no heroes. Postmodernity is the great destruction of the hero. Postmodernity problematized—in many ways correctly—the premodern and modern hero and then said there are no heroes, that heroism is a problem, that it is fundamentalists blowing themselves up as suicide bombers. Yes, yes, of course, there is a problematized hero. Of course, we need to move from the pre-tragic hero to the tragic and recognize the potential tragic in the hero, but then we move to the post-tragic and reclaim the hero.

That's *Homo amor*.

That's the democratization of the hero. And literally the first spiritual practice before any other spiritual practice, number one—not two, not three, not four, but number one—the very first and primary spiritual practice is: **I have to experience myself, accurately, as a hero.**

I commit to being a hero. That's the *Crossing*. That's the crossing to the other side. I'm a hero. Not a *grandiose* hero but a hero, a *grand* hero.

It's only in the true grandness, which is the truest index of my real situation, that I begin to feel welcome in the Universe.

BARAYE: FOR THE SAKE OF THE WHOLE

Evolutionary Love Code:

> There is no way to be filled with joy unless you are a hero. Heroes are real.
>
> Postmodernity problematized the hero. Postmodernity mocked the hero. Postmodernity said the hero is dangerous; let's do away with the hero.
>
> Postmodernity was not entirely wrong. Heroes were dying for the wrong things. Heroes were covering up their vulnerability, which was far greater than mere kryptonite.
>
> We *needed* to complexify the hero. But now that we've complexified the hero, we have to *reclaim* the hero. In CosmoErotic Humanism, we call this *the post-tragic hero*.
>
> *Homo amor* is the post-tragic hero.

Shervin wrote a very beautiful song called *Baraye*. He was sentenced to several years in prison for this song. It was in response to the terrible murder of a wonderful young woman, Mahsa Amini, in Iran, which set off this explosion of brutality, in which young boys and many young girls (meaning high-school age) were taken out, beaten, killed, abused for opposing the fundamentalist version of the hero, the premodern hero:

- Who was the hero who had to deny their essential nature
- Who had to deny their participation in the Field of Value
- Who was the hero because they submitted to a larger field that wasn't *truly* a larger field

It was a larger field that contradicted the language of their body, the language of the heart, and the language of their soul. But in submission to that, they were thought to be a hero. It's a desecration of the hero.

And so, Shervin writes a song. We are going to play the original version of the song with his words. He is going to prison. I want to really just honor him and be with him. And I want to find a way to actually make contact with him. He is a gorgeous man, and he is a hero. He's going to prison for standing against the old version of the hero. He actually incarnates the hero.

I want to just take a moment to honor the hero together and just hear that song. And see the words. And feel it together.

He's going to jail for several years for that song. May he'll be able to leave jail alive, whole, and healthy—which is not obvious.

We are here not in wisdo-tainment, not in entertainment. We are coming together as a Unique Self Symphony. In order to bring down this next chapter in the Story of Value, we want to become the hero.

I want to invite you to actually, in this moment—not later, not tomorrow, not in twenty minutes from now, but literally now—to make the transition. The transition is: *I am a hero.*

WHEN I AM AROUSED, I AM THE HERO: REALITY IS MAKING LOVE

Imagine what that means, to actually *be* a hero—then everything changes, doesn't it?

Everything changes—how I hold my anxiety and how I hold my pain. Isn't that true? This is the Crossing. The Crossing is right now. We are crossing to the other side. I am going to change the fundamental experience of who

I am—not to a diluted grandiosity, but to an accurate grandeur, to knowing my true nature.

My true nature is that I'm *not* merely separate from the whole. The experience of being separate from the whole is an *optical delusion of consciousness.* Albert Einstein got that one right. I am actually inseparable from the field. The Field of the Whole is seamless. Everything is connected to everything. There is no separate self. There is nothing that's separate.

But that field is not merely a Field of *Awareness.* It's a Field of *Wholeness.* Can you feel that? Read David Bohm's later writings on the wholeness that Reality moves towards. One of the core qualities of Eros is the yearning for wholeness. The field is not merely a Field of Awareness. Awareness is but one predicate of the field—the field is actually a Field of Wholeness. It's a Field of Eros.

One of the four core qualities of Eros, its primary quality, is wholeness—nothing is separate from anything. But it's a quivering, trembling, infinite, tender wholeness of which I am an irreducibly unique, gorgeous expression:

- I am a part of the whole that makes the whole more whole.
- I am a whole emergent from the whole that makes the whole more whole.
- I am a whole who is part of the larger whole.
- I participate in a larger whole.
- In realizing my own irreducibly unique wholeness, the Field of the Whole becomes more whole.

That's a hero. That's *Homo amor*!

Baraye means *for the sake of.* Isn't that gorgeous? *For the sake of.* I am a hero. I experience myself as the hero—and then my wholeness makes it all more whole.

The original lineage word for hero is *gibbor.* It has two meanings: it means *hero,* and it also means *arousal.* It's a particular quality. It's the line quality of arousal that lives in all men and all women. This line quality of arousal—because **when I am aroused, I am the hero**.

It's why lovemaking means arousal—whether you're kissing your partner's shoulder or just looking into their eyes across the room. Or it's with a friend or beloved… There are many ways to make love. We've exiled lovemaking to a very narrow field.

Reality is making love.

When I am making love, I am aroused—and when I am aroused, I am a hero. I actually get that what I'm doing is ultimately significant. I could be making love as I paint, as I write, as I search for a document, as I organize a piece, or as I'm writing an outrageously beautiful note to the milkman—I'm telling them I'm going to be away for a few days, so don't leave any milk. But then I add something to that note that makes it an Outrageous Love Letter—and the person feels recognized and seen. It is an Outrageous Love Letter.

It's the experience of being aroused. And **when I am aroused, I am in the field.**

See, there is no local arousal.

There is no local desire. It doesn't exist. All desire is non-local. I'm participating in the Field of Desire.

Even if it's completely unconscious, I am experiencing the whole moving through me. And I experience the ultimate significance of my actions, of my engagement.

Do you know why people kill and destroy each other—for the sake of passion, for the sake of relationships made and relationships broken?

Because they are disconnected and alienated from the Field of the Whole.

Because they don't feel like heroes at any place in their lives.

The only place where they feel a glimmering of the aliveness of being a hero is in that one relationship:

> And if you don't relate to me in the way I want to relate to you forever, and then I feel that I've lost access to the field and to being a hero, I am going to kill you to cover up the emptiness. I am going to explode murderously to murder your Eros because I've lost access to mine.

No, no, no. The word *hero* and the word *arousal* are the same because the hero is omni-considerate for the sake of the whole. The whole lives in the hero. *Baraye*—for the sake of the whole.

Play the song again, Shervin's song. Let's just be in it.

We are in practice. We are in mad, holy practice around the world.

We are the hero. We are coming together. We are linking hands. Heroes for Her Majesty. Shervin is a hero for Her Majesty Queen of the Universe.

Baraye means, *for the sake of*. It changes everything. It is not a psychological strategy. It's *dharma*. *Dharma* means the nature of Reality, the best integration of First Principles and First Values.

YOU KNOW AND I KNOW THAT YOU ARE A HERO

We just did the Academy Awards in the United States, in the year 2024, in the month of March. And Ryan Gosling did a rendition of "I'm Just Ken," which was the great Ken song in *Barbie*, which brought the house down at the Oscars. What a tragic moment! The entire point of the song is: *I'm just Ken; I'm not really a hero.*

When you read the text of the song, you realize that Ken is actually looking for the hero. He looks to his arousal, which is dismissed. He looks to his desire to love, which is dismissed. And then he just falls back into singing "I'm Just Ken," which is understood as a silly song. Why did this bring the house down? It was of course a beautiful moment. It was done well, aesthetically, artistically, at least from a performance perspective. It was actually a tragic moment because everyone got together around the silliness of it all. *I'm Just Ken.*

But I'm not just Ken. I'm a fucking hero—Ken is a hero, and Barbie is a hero.

The Universe desperately needs my service.

I am the unique hero of Her Majesty Queen of the Universe.

It's one for all and all for one.

I feel the Whole pulsing in me, trembling in my body, I hear the voices of the trillions of unborn who look to our generation to be heroes.

That's why we're doing *The Crossing* in Europe. That's why we're doing the Mystery School. That's why there's a Center. That's why there's *One Mountain*—to be heroes. We are the heroes of the future.

And my friends—Romans, countrymen—lend me your ears just for a moment. We have to get over the fear of our grandiosity in order to be grand. This is the secret. It's the furtive secret that lurks deep within.

> You know and I know that you are a hero. You know and I know that that's actually your true nature.
>
> You know and I know that your life *matters* insanely.
>
> You know and I know that you were intended. You didn't just appear; you were intended by All-That-Is. You are completely a radical surprise, and yet you were intended by All-That-Is.
>
> You know and I know that you are the chosen one, that you are the one—that you are Paul Atreides, that you are Messiah, that you are the hero.

You know and I know that you are recognized by All-That-Is—recognized, seen. All of Reality is a stage and you are center stage. You are the hero.

You know and I know that you are madly adored. You're not just loved. You're adored by All-That-Is.

You know and I know that only a series of explosions of desire could have brought you into existence—unique meetings of desire. You know and I know that you're both contingent, radical surprise and an expression of the deepest, most stunning design. You are desired by All-That-Is.

And finally, you know and I know that you are needed by All-That-Is.

What are you needed for? You are needed to be your unique transformation. Your transformation, my transformation. When I speak to you, I'm speaking to *me* and to *we*. A mirror in front of me, speaking out loud to you. **Your trajectory of transformation is heroic and unique—and from that place, you give your unique gift, which is desperately needed by All-That-Is.**

Sometimes you'll do it as a secret agent of Her Majesty Queen of the Universe. You're going to be her hero. Sometimes you'll do it publicly, but sometimes you'll do it as one of the Three Musketeers. But that's who you are. It's who I am. It's who we all are. We are a league of superheroes.

That's who we are but not fancifully, not as an interesting motivational talk. No.

It's the true nature of who we are.

CHAPTER ELEVEN

MAD LOVE: WHEN MADNESS BECOMES SANITY

Episode 413 — September 8, 2024

TO LOVE MADLY IS TO BE IN THE FIELD OF OUTRAGEOUS LOVE

There is so much we want to touch, and do, and feel today. We are at this incredible moment, filled with portent and with possibility, with promise and with peril. We want to find our way and potentiate this moment. We want to find our own potency, which will allow us to potentiate the moment—to love the moment open, and to allow the moment to love us open.

In this path that diverges in the woods, we can take the path less traveled, and we can make the difference that desperately needs to be made. The last six weeks were a time of enormous beauty on so many levels, and enormous heartbreak on so many levels. Part of the heartbreak was cataclysmic, and apocalyptic, and horrific.

For example, the execution of the six Israelis in Gaza was horrific. It was a terrible, and tragic, and senseless insanity—apocalyptic death that stands against a culture of life—against Eros.

There were also beautiful turnings of the wheel—death which is part of life, death which is a kiss, death which is a night between two days, which opens us up into the new world, and the next possibility, and the next stage of the journey. Our beloved Becca passed. She passed onto the next stage of her journey, and we miss her dearly and deeply.

What does it mean to be a mad lover?

That's what we want to talk about today. We want to talk about the experience of mad love:

- Mad love in politics and economics
- Mad love in the way we wake up in the morning
- Mad love in relationship
- Mad love in art
- Mad love even in war; even in war, there is mad love

What does it mean to love madly?

I began talking about Outrageous Love somewhere back in 2011. And then, when I started studying with Kristina Kincaid, my partner, she sent me a song, which became *our* song—about this quality of Outrageous Love, which Rumi called *mad love*. She evoked the term *mad love* as one of the ways to talk about this quality I was trying to share—this quality of Outrageous Love, which is core to existence itself.

What does it mean to love madly? What does that speak to?

- We don't want to be mad. Don't we want to be sane? Why would we want to be mad? Who would want to be mad?
- What is this quality of Divine madness, of human madness? The place where the human being and God meet is in this madness.
- Why is this quality of mad love the only way we can respond to this moment of meta-crisis, which is itself a moment of madness?

It is, as one author called it, a Molochian moment. In many circles today, the ancient Canaanite deity of Moloch is invoked to describe the systemic underpinnings of the meta-crisis. It's not one person. It's not one event. It's a Molochian system.

The response to *Moloch*—who is madness in its shadow form, madness in its anti-value form—is actually madness in its light form:

- Madness as an ultimate value
- Madness as an ultimate achievement
- Madness as the summit of our spirituality
- Madness as the summit of our depth

Rumi wrote a lot about mad love, and my lineage master in the Solomon lineage, Leiner, also talks about madness. There is a beautiful text, which says *greater is light than darkness*. It is a Solomon text, from the book of Ecclesiastes: *Greater is light than darkness. Greater is wisdom than madness.*

That is a binary split: light—dark, wisdom—madness.

Then the Zohar, the Book of Radiance, comes along in the twelfth or thirteenth century and says, not *greater is light* than *darkness*, but *greater is light that* comes from *the darkness.*

Greater is wisdom that comes from the madness.

There is wisdom that emerges from the madness, and Solomon says, that's the moon in her fullness. By *the moon*, he means Eros, *She*, the full possibility of a new form of governance, and a new form of economics, and a new form of relationship between nations, and new forms of religion—all of what Solomon was looking for. That's called the Wisdom of Solomon, and it's a hidden crosscurrent of world history.

There is a wisdom of Solomon's strata, a quality of that wisdom. You could also call it a *tantric quality*, but *tantra* not as a particularly Eastern tradition, not as a particularly Hebrew tradition, but as a particular way of thinking, a quality of consciousness, a phenomenology, a way of being. **It is a new way of being—because our current way of being generates the meta-crisis**. Our current way of being is the Molochian systemic rivalrous conflict governed by win/lose metrics that generates fragile systems that optimize for efficiency and short-term profit instead of depth, and holding, and love, and resiliency, which is the core source of the meta-crisis.

At its very core, we saw a very tiny, minuscule dress rehearsal in Covid, when the entire world shut down because the world had optimized for efficiency and short-term profit—not resiliency.

The response to the madness of meta-crisis—to the madness of *Moloch*— is the madness of a mad love, of Outrageous Love.

We are going to talk about what that means. I want to make that real.

Are we ready to participate as mad lovers in the evolution of love in a way that is so grounded, so responsible, so rigorous that it avoids all ruptures, but also so rapturous, so filled with celebration, so filled with joy that every step we take, we tremble with joy, and we tremble with potency, and we tremble with possibility, and we tremble with potentiation, and we tremble with poignancy?

That's the quality of mad love.

REALITY IS CONSTITUTED BY MAD LOVE

The single best recapitulation of the interior sciences and the contemporary exterior sciences is: Reality is constituted by mad love. Mad love is the true Real, and the true Real is mad love. Mad love is Outrageous Love.

Run from what is comfortable. Forget safety.

Rumi writes:

Your life has been a mad gamble.

Make it more so.

You have lost now a hundred times running.

Roll the dice a hundred and one.

It's a beautiful text. The one who is in mad devotion to the whole—to the Divine—is in devotion *a hundred and one times.* The one who is in devotion *a hundred times*—that's someone trying to be sane; it doesn't work.

You can't actually serve, you can't be a devotee, you can't be an artist at a hundred times. Anyone who serves in devotion at the level of a hundred does *not* serve, and is *not* devoted, and does *not* create art. **The move between a hundred and a hundred and one is not one extra. It's the place of madness.**

Your life has been a mad gamble, says Rumi. *Make it more so. You have lost now a hundred times running. Roll the dice a hundred and one.*

I am so mad with love, says this mad Sufi love prophet, *that mad men say to me, be still.*

The reason I'm sharing Rumi is not because he's a good poet, although he is, but because Rumi was a profound realizer of the interior sciences. He headed one of the most important formal schools of Sufism. Sufism is under attack today by Islamic fundamentalism the world over: the Shiite attack on Sufism within Iran tries to undo the deep ground of Sufism in Iran; but even within Sunni Islam, which is in part Sufism, there is a deep attack on Sufism. Sufism is hated by Hamas, hated by ISIS, hated by Hezbollah.

Sufism's spirit is alive and well in the world, and Rumi is not one person. Rumi was part of a school that has existed for several hundred years. Hafiz was also in that group of thousands of Sufi realizers who spoke, breathed, and felt this mad love. *Run from what's comfortable,* writes Rumi. *Forget safety.* When we say *forget safety,* we don't mean be unsafe in some absurd way—but today, we have created an idolatry of comfort.

We never get to mad love, because you have to reach an optimum point of discomfort to experience mad love.

Mad love is maddening. It is not comfortable. People say, *the opposite of pain is pleasure*, and we always say, *no, the opposite of pain is comfort*.

Comfort is comfortably numb (Pink Floyd). There is no place for mad love.

We have this idolatry: to get as safe as you can possibly be, to be completely safe, no risk of any kind, to live as long as you can live, as comfortably as you can live. Safety, longevity, and comfort are the new holy trinity—but of course, in the end, you die. Because life is unsafe; no one gets out of life alive.

It's not the end of the story. Life as we know it here is but one dimension of Reality, that's true, but it ends. When I am not willing to recognize death as my close friend, then I become corrupt, as in Oscar Wilde's *The Picture of Dorian Gray*.

That's what Rumi is writing. He is talking about this idolatry of safety. Of course, there were ways that we weren't safe before. In previous generations, we needed to create safety on multiple levels. Of course, that's sacred and good. But within that construct of safety—of protecting your family, and the stable structures of your life in all the ways they should be protected— *Run from what's comfortable*, says Rumi, *forget safety. Live where you fear to live. Destroy your reputation. Be notorious. I have tried prudent planning long enough. From now on, I will be mad.*

Finally—last piece—Rumi again:

> *The intellectual is always showing off;*
> *the lover is always getting lost.*
> *The intellectual runs away, afraid of drowning;*

the whole business of love is to drown in the sea.
Intellectuals plan their repose;
lovers are ashamed to rest.
The lover is always alone,
even surrounded with people;
like water and oil, he remains apart.
The man who goes to the trouble
of giving advice to a lover
gets nothing. He's mocked by passion.

What Rumi is pointing to is this sense of living life out loud and in love, madly.

OUR LOVE LISTS ARE TOO SHORT

Couples often have a song. KK and I have a song, "Truly Madly Deeply" by Savage Garden. This is our song. It's a mad love song. We are going to do something with the song. We are going to turn it on its head in the most mad possible way.

It's a gorgeous song that we love. And—in all of its stunning beauty—the song itself is making a mistake. What's the mistake of the song? It's about just *the two of them.*

It's gorgeous. It's beautiful. It's stunning.

But our love lists are too short. That's the first quality of mad love: our love lists are too short. The song personifies the contemporary move in culture. That song should live between beloveds. That's beautiful. We include that stunning, unimaginable beauty.

But mad love is *not* mere human sentiment, as gorgeous as human sentiment is; it participates in the Field of ErosValue. It participates in the Field of Existence.

Mad love is not something that emerges at a particular poetic moment in human culture:

- Whether that's in the *Epic of Gilgamesh*, in the wild love scene there at the very beginning
- Whether that's in the Arthurian tales of the medieval period
- Whether that's Jacob madly in love with Rachel in the canonical text
- Whether that's Magdalene and Jesus

No, no, no! Mad love doesn't appear as industrialization sweeps through Europe, and individuation appears, and social mobility becomes a possibility, so being in love becomes a new commodity.

No, no, no, mad love is not mere human sentiment.

Mad love is the heart of existence itself.

What that song is describing is not that couple, but Reality itself.

Reality itself is about the quality of allurement of mad love that demarcates and animates Cosmos, all the way up and all the way down.

We've talked so many times about the love dance of Cosmos that incepts Cosmos and plays in the first nanoseconds after the Big Bang, when—if you do your physics well—you see that there is autonomy and communion, coming close and holding my individuation, which is what love is.

Love is not merging, and love is not fusion. Love is the dance of union.

Love is:

- We come close, and we step apart; and we come close again, and we step apart.

- We come close and we step apart, but we never look away.

That's the Song of Songs of Solomon.

That gorgeous and beautiful song, "Truly Madly Deeply," is a Song of Songs. The lovers are looking for each other; it literally plays with the same movement as the Song of Solomon—but the lovers can't quite find each other. Just like as the author of the Song of Songs, or Canticle of Canticles, tells the story, there is a duo, these two gorgeous men in this little band of two called *Savage Garden*. The *garden* is the garden of Eden, and *savage* is: it's hard, it's complicated, it's paradox, it rips your heart apart. They are the bards, they are the minstrels of the song, and they are looking for each other, and they find each other at the end, but then they are going to lose each other again, and then they find each other—but they never look away.

But that's not just them. That's the story of Cosmos itself.

THE MITOCHONDRIAL DANCE OF EROS IN OUR CELLS

Science has dogmatically overreached its bounds and moved to hide that story.

For example, has anyone here ever heard of mitochondria?

Mitochondria are constantly converting energy; they are essentially the activating force of all cells, whether it's nerve cells, or bone cells, or skin cells. **What mitochondria are doing is, essentially, accessing the flow of Eros—the flow of love between electrons and protons and neutrons**. They are accessing that proton flow. They are actually accessing the currents of Eros and allurement which emerge from particular configurations of Eros, of union, of intimacy. They access that movement, that yearning, that energy of allurement, that energy of radical aliveness, that energy of Eros, and, through a very complex process, they distribute it.

Essentially, science has lied to us.

Here is how science describes mitochondria:

> The machinery that the mitochondria use to convert energy is called the electron transport chain.

Do you get what a lie that is? First off, it's called *machinery*. It's *an electron transport chain*, meaning it's this mechanical device, like a forklift in the Amazon warehouse or something like that.

> Mitochondria convert chemical energy in the form of a chemical called adenosine triphosphate (ATP for short). ATP is an energy currency that every cell in our body can use. The electron transport chain is made up of four complexes, which are groups of proteins.

Do you get what's going on here? A protein is a configuration of Eros. It's a particular, gorgeous configuration, a stunning allurement, a new erotic whole. And then, there are five different patterns of protein groups. There are these different configurations of intimacy, and five broad groups that are dancing with each other in this unimaginably sophisticated, dazzling dance of Eros and allurement.

They are madly at play. They are madly in love, and they are filled with value. There is a value, and the value is life.

And the value is depth.

And the value is feeling.

And the value is, ultimately, cognition.

And the value is uniqueness.

And the value is transformation.

In other words, the movement of mitochondria is to support all of the First Principles and First Values that we have outlined in CosmoErotic Humanism.

In the book, *First Principles and First Values*, we talk about the value structures of Cosmos. Those are ErosValue structures.

Mitochondria access the flow of Eros that takes place in the electron chain and then actually draw that Eros, absorb that Eros and distribute it through a very complex dance of Eros, which has nothing to do with machinery.

This is not *machinery*; this is *music*. It's not *an electron transport chain*—it's literally *a mad love dance*, which is unimaginably precise and unimaginably passionate. All of the Universe is constituted by that play of Eros—the play of Eros that happens in the world of matter. That which happens in the world of matter is driven by value; it is driven by *what matters*.

Matter itself is driven by value—by what matters. **This entire subatomic world is driven to create more value, more of what matters—which is more depth, and more uniqueness, and more possibility, and, ultimately, more care, and more cognition—all the way up the evolutionary chain.** There is obviously discontinuity (there are not a lot of therapeutic issues in the electron community); that's absolutely true. There are new emergences of love and Eros all the way up the evolutionary chain; that's absolutely true.

But it's not *just* discontinuity. It's not *just* new emergences.

The flow of allurement, Eros, and love in the world of subatomic particles (the *physiosphere*), and in the world of living organisms (the *biosphere*), and then in the world of humanity (the *noosphere*) are inter-included. You and I are now in the middle of this mitochondrial dance of wild mad LoveEros—in this very second, every single one of us.

That is not mysticism. That's the reality of our lives.

That mitochondrial structure is participating in the subatomic structure. The flow of Eros that lives in the world of matter is accessed and then intensified in its participation in the mitochondrial unfolding. **The jump from matter to life is an intensification of intimacies.** Stuart Kauffman got this, in a couple of little passages (I thought I had made it up in my own meditative dreaming, and then I saw a bunch of very important scientific footnotes, both in Levin and in Kauffman, which validated this reading).

We, human beings, are constituted by all of the subatomic world and its flows of Eros and mad love, and all of the biological world. Just one small dimension of the biological world, but a crucial one, is the mitochondrial dance of Eros in every one of our cells. That's what we are.

That's literally our very identity; and then Eros intensifies; intimacies deepen.

There is an evolution of love. We participate in the evolution of love, and then it emerges *in us*. We can become—if we actually grow up, if we actually wake up, and we begin to show up in our lives—**we actually *become* mad love, awake, alive in person.**

The weakness of the song is that it suggests that the quality of searching, that quality of yearning, that quality of longing exists only in that couple. But they are actually mad love awake and alive, and their mad love itself can't survive if they're only looking deeply in each other's eyes, because mad love is the quality of Cosmos itself.

Mad love is the heart of existence.

If I hijack mad love, and I make that a quality that's only mine, that's only between the two of us—but I don't madly love the cab driver, and I don't madly love the people across the world or down the street who have nothing to eat, and I don't madly love the gardener, and I don't madly love the clerk at the bank who is harried and busy and tired—I am not a mad lover.

MY MAD LOVE PARTICIPATES IN THE WHOLE

The first quality of a mad lover is: I have an experience of my mad love being part of the whole. My mad love is not separate from the whole.

The beginning of mad love is that I have a direct and clear experience that my experience of mad love is an experience which is the quality of all of Reality, all the way up and all the way down.

I am participating in this Field of Mad Love. The Field of Mad Love is awake and alive in me.

Therefore, even when I'm having a bad day, even when I'm feeling depressed and sad and devastated and hurt and harmed or irritated, it's okay. I'll work on that, and I'll stay safe; I'll do the best I can to take care of myself. But that's not who I am.

- Who I am is mad love come awake.
- Who I am is mad love in person.

Homo amor—the word that we've used in CosmoErotic Humanism to describe the new human and the new humanity—is a mad lover.

The first characteristic of mad love is:
I am in relationship to the whole.

I don't exile mad love to a white-picket-fence particular relationship that looks a particular way, and is socially acceptable in a particular way, and is conventionally appropriate in a particular way. We love who we love, and we want to love wide, and we want to love deep, and we want to love big.

We want to be radically committed to our closest relationships, gorgeously—so, we love that couple. KK and I love that song, and we love each other. We have our exclusive mad love.

And then, we open up, and we open up, and I can actually say to my friend, *Oh my God, I love you madly. I love you madly* doesn't mean romantic love. It means something else. **I love you madly means this quality of aliveness, this quality of depth, this quality of care, this quality of commitment.** It's so deep.

We've exiled love. The exile of love is threefold.

One, we claim that love is purely human. That's the first exile.

Two is, it's only between particular groups of humans. It's only particular configurations of humans: heterosexual married couples—that's where mad love lives.

But then, since it doesn't work there all too often, we say, oh it works, but between heterosexual married couples at the very beginning of a relationship, when they meet and fall in love. That's the third exile.

So, we exile mad love:

- Into the human world,
- Then into a very narrow sector of the human world,
- Then to the very beginning of the relational structure in that particular vector in the human world.

It's a triple exile.

No, no, no! **Mad love is everywhere**. It's always there. It's always already present. It's actually my true nature. I am a mad lover. And my mad love participates in the whole; it's the quality of the whole. That's the first characteristic.

MY MAD LOVE IS WILDLY POWERFUL

The second quality of mad love is: I have a capacity, a feeling that I want to influence the whole, that I want to impact the whole, that I want to give to the whole. I want to have a direct realization:

- That my loving, my aliveness, my being, my mad love loves the whole
- That my mad love impacts the whole
- That my mad love changes the trajectory of the whole
- That my mad love is wildly powerful

The second quality of mad love is that it's unimaginably powerful and has a power to transform the whole, to lift the whole, to create this Field of Radiance and this Field of Possibility.

When I am madly in love with the whole, then the whole opens up to me.

In the mystery schools that animated the Renaissance of Italy in the sixteenth century, there was a strong set of sources drawn from a great thinker named Isaac Luria. At the core of those sources was the second quality of being a mad lover. It is articulated by Luria as the invocation that one makes in every movement of one's life, often dozens of times during the day: *LeShem Yichud, for the sake of intimate communion.* I do this action for the sake of intimate communion.

I do this action:

- Whether it's to say hello to my cab driver
- Whether it's to edit an episode on *One Mountain*
- Whether it's to turn to my child and put them to bed in the most beautiful way
- Whether it's to help my sister get to a critical meeting or through a pregnancy class
- Whether it's to help my sister find her way in transforming her life
- Whether it's my brother, whether it's my friend, whether it's my dear Beloved, whether it's some new person I just met and I realize that I need to help this person, I need to stand forth

and be there
- Whether it's the way I distribute my funds
- Whether it's my willingness to take my resources and pour them where they should be in a way that's mad

I do all of this for the sake of the whole.

I step out of the exile of the song, where I speak the *language* of mad love, but really it's about me and my family; I'm really egocentric. I say this because it makes me feel better, but the way I spend my resources, my time, my energy, my funds, is about me and my small group of people. No, be a mad lover for the sake of the whole!

Luria says that **in every action I do, I can pour the resource of my energy into the fabric of the whole**. I do it for the sake of the whole. And I say, *LeShem Yichud, for the sake of intimate communion.*

The intimate communion of what?

Of all the broken people, of all the broken parts, of all the split-off parts, of all the broken hearts, of all the shattered minds, of all the twisted scripts, of all the distorted yearnings, of all the sadnesses, of all the breakings. It's all holy and broken. When I say *Hallelujah*, when I say, *LeShem Yichud*, then:

- Something becomes more coherent in Reality.
- Something becomes more whole.
- Something becomes more alive.
- Something becomes more filled with joy.

I have unimaginable power.

The second quality of mad love is that it's powerful. I have the capacity well beyond the capacity of any of the presidential candidates in the United States and any of the high office candidates anywhere in the world. I don't need to be a senator or a prime minister or a king or a queen or a president or a vice president. I am royalty. I am king or queen.

MY MADNESS IS MY PROTEST

But here's the thing: I need to be actually (not figuratively) mad.

To be mad means I have the capacity to see beneath the surface:

- I can access depth.
- I have the capacity to be mad.
- I have to be mad in some sense, in order to realize that my action truly affects the whole, my transformation actually *is* the transformation of the whole.

The small action that I do as I paint is transforming the whole.

The small action I do as I create a blog post in order to open up space.

The small action that I do as I collect clips and I edit them.

The small action that I do as I buy a couch so me and my wife (or me and my partner, or me and my guests whom I entertain at my house) have a nicer place to sit, so we can actually find each other's eyes—**if I do that for the sake of the whole, then something actually changes in the whole**.

For a mad lover, the relationship to Reality changes. A mad lover has *omni-pathos*, they are *omni-considerate*, they are *omni-feeling* with the whole. That very experience, to know that that's true—it's madness, but it's divine madness.

In other words, if I'm very normal, if I'm a reductive materialist rationalist, it's *insane* to know that what I do affects the whole. Yes, it's insane—that's the point. **Mad love means to be out of your mind, but *out of your mind* means out of your *materialist* mind**.

That's this third quality of mad love—the madness part. That's the third quality.

Let's get this madness.

Level one, you have classical sanity and insanity. That's good. We should be sane. There is developmental psychology. There are stages of development. There is knowing that this is my arm and it's not your arm, that there are appropriate boundaries between people. We want to be sane, right? And if I feel like I have some condition, I might want to work with that condition. I need to be sane.

Sanity means the right proportion: I don't make myself bigger or smaller than I am. I take responsibility; I show up; my word is good. I'm reliable. I'm steady. I don't get hijacked.

There is a way that mad love can have shadows. I can lose proportion. Murders and crimes of passion happen when mad love gets dissociated from ordinary grounded-ness, from ordinary sanity. I need to be sane, not mad—of course. Insanity is not an excuse; pleas of insanity are overplayed these days. I am responsible for being sane. **I've got to take responsibility for my sanity**. That's beautiful. That's level one.

But then there's level two. At level two, we realize that we've been confusing appropriate sanity for resignation to the status quo, and often for corruption. **What we're calling *sane* was actually *corrupt*.** There was a fabulous movie, I think in the mid-sixties, called *King of Hearts*, where everyone was involved in slaughters and wars. There was one person, the King of Hearts, who was insane. It was clear that he was insane. But of course, his insanity was a protest against the slaughtering sanity, the cruelty of the sanity, the senselessness of the sanity, the barbarity of the sanity, the brutality of the sanity:

- Is it sane to have factory farms in which we torture animals for three months in order to eat them, to have our lamb chop be a little more succulent? Is that sane?
- Is it sane to have ten million dollars in the bank, and make sure to distribute it well, when that money would be much better spent in other places in the world, where I could save

200 lives or change the course of the evolution of the source code? Is that sane?

♦ Is it sane to spend my entire life trying to be safe and comfortable and live as long as I can when, in the end, I'm going to die?

♦ Is it sane to be lost in my narcissistic bubble?

Sanity can become an excuse for corruption, an excuse for betrayal of my deepest self, an excuse for an abandonment of my true nature, for an abandonment of mad love.

What I need is a level two of protest.

The sacred text of the Solomon lineage says that in our day-to-day life, prophecy is with the madmen and the fools. That's what Rumi was talking about. **I need to be responsible and safe in all the appropriate ways, but then, I need to protest, and my madness is my protest.** My level two insanity protests against this level one dichotomy between sanity and insanity, this very respectable conventional appropriate dichotomy.

CLARIFYING THE SPLIT BETWEEN SANE AND INSANE

One of my closest friends died two years ago, and I actually didn't know. We didn't talk often. When we did, we went deep in all the way, and we both had intense lives, and he wrote a book called, *The Tyranny of Malice*. His name was Joseph Berke, and he was the key student of R.D. Laing. Laing wrote a book called *The Divided Self* in 1960, and another book called *Wisdom, Madness and Folly*. They're beautiful.

What he basically said was: we can't make that easy split between the sane ones and the insane ones; some of those who are insane are actually mad lovers. They're actually protesting. They are the King of Hearts from that sixties movie; they are saying, it's not okay. They are saying the status quo which claims to be sane is actually insanity:

- A status quo in the twentieth century which allowed for 100 million non-combatants to be killed is insanity.
- A status quo in which the entire world doesn't rush to the aid of Ukraine today is insanity.
- A status quo which cannot distinguish between a culture of death and a pluralistic democracy with all of its flaws is insanity.
- A world in which two billion people don't have drinking water.

Why is that sane? Laing said that there's a continuum between sanity and insanity; there's no sharp divide. **Sometimes we move into insanity for a moment, as in a shamanic journey.** There's a descent, but it's a descent for the sake of ascent. There's a moment of protest. I need to let myself go mad.

Now, I don't mean to go mad in a clinical way. I don't mean if you're taking appropriate balancing medication, you should stop because we said to go mad. That's not what I mean, obviously. That needs to be checked individually in every case, to see where you are. This is not about that.

It's about something deeper: we can't use sanity as our defense plea when we're held at the bar of cosmic joy and justice, and we're asked why we didn't live our lives.

We have this huge life of unlived love, and unlived life, and unlived commitment, and unlived integrity. Why did we betray ourselves? We were being sane.

R.D. Laing points out that there's a mad lover inside of us that's protesting. The mad lover understands that, yes, I do affect the whole world. **The mad lover says, Oh my God, I'm the king of the world.**

And we say, Oh my God, you're mad. You're not the king of the world. Why are you saying you're the king? You're crazy mad.

And of course, he or she *might be* mad. That might be an actual state of madness that needs to be addressed, but in many cases they're seeing something. They are understanding this quality of Luria's *LeShem Yichud*:

- I am actually powerful.
- I actually *am* royalty.
- I actually *can* affect the whole thing.

A gesture, a flutter of my eye, a caress of my heart, an opening of my deepest interior, a flutter of my soul, a moment of my purity, the moving of my lips in sincerity, the opening of a space that I was never able to open before, the digging deeper, the unearthing, which creates an authenticity that I thought could never happen. When I offer that, and pour that into the source code, I am affecting—quite literally, ontologically, for real—I'm changing the whole.

TRUE SANITY IS MAD LOVE

The truth of Reality is that Reality is my canvas. I have a relationship to the whole.

The mad man, the mad woman, understands that for a second. We call them mad, but actually they're on a shamanic journey, trying to bring back an important message: **True sanity is mad love.**

Enlightenment at its core is sanity, but what sanity means is knowing my true nature.

My true nature is not a desiccated separate self who uses love as a social convention in order to get sufficient comfort and sufficient status to get by, to live as comfortably and as long and as safe as possible. No, that's not sanity. Sanity is to know my true identity, and my true identity is: I am a mad lover; I am an Outrageous Lover.

That's actually who I am. That's actually my true nature.

Enlightenment means that I am intimate with everything. Enlightenment is intimacy with all things, wrote Master Dōgen—but I am not just intimate, I am *uniquely* intimate, and my intimacy, and the quality of my intimacy, and the quality of my gifting, and the quality of my laughter, and the nature of my poetry, and the movement of my sincere and pure and devoted heart changes the whole.

I am royalty.

My mood changes the mood of Cosmos.

It *matters* to find my deepest mood, and to pour that expanded gorgeous deep profound self into the source code of Reality—because I *do* change the whole thing. That is actually sanity.

The ultimate sanity is when the knowing of madness is disclosed to be true. That's the ultimate sanity—where we go mad, we think, *Oh my God, I am superman; I can save the whole thing.* Actually yes, in fact you can.

And then, I become sane *for real*, not sane *as a disguise*—a thin veneer for a desiccated separate self for the hollow men and the stuffed men—sane as a mad lover.

That's the third quality. The third quality is: I am mad; I've broken the boundaries of the narrow separate self. **I am deeply grounded. I am sane in all the good ways, and then I go insane as a protest. I go mad as a shamanic journey.**

Why does a person do a medicine journey? A medicine journey is a descent into madness, but it's not a descent into clinical insanity. It's a descent into a world in which I can see more clearly. In which I realize that that stunning and beautiful song, "Truly Madly Deeply," is about the whole world. Mitochondria are truly madly deeply.

I'll be your dream.

I'll be your wish.

I'll be your fantasy.

I'll be your hope.

I'll be your love.

I'll be everything that you need.

That's what we are all saying to each other.

We are a band of Outrageous Lovers. We are unique incarnations and discretions of the field. That's what we mean when we say *we live in a world of outrageous pain, and the only response to outrageous pain is Outrageous Love.* The only response is to love madly.

LET'S REACH FOR A WORLD BEYOND BETRAYAL

The opposite of loving madly is betrayal. Judas loves Jesus madly, and then he can't hold the mad love, and the mad love becomes sane and ordinary. The only sane thing to do is to be with Rome, to betray Jesus. **Betrayal is a violation of mad love.**

There are a thousand ways we get to be committed to each other.

There are a thousand ways we get to be madly devoted to each other.

We forgive the betrayals that have happened, but let us commit fully. Let us commit not to the cynical notion that betrayal is just part and parcel of human life—**let's reach for a world beyond betrayal!** Let's reach for a world in which we are madly loyal to each other. There is a loyalty in mad love. There's a seeing. We see each other. We know what matters.

It's not what *appears* to matter. It's something so much deeper.

Do you know Nachman's story of the mad king that Kafka loved so much?

The king's country is starving, and they eat the grain, and when they eat the grain, the grain makes them mad.

We are starving. We need some sort of nourishment, but we are fed a fare that is not nourishing. We are fed a fare of insanity, which makes us mad, and not in a good way. They eat the grain, and they go mad—not a holy madness, but a level-one madness, when they don't remember who they are.

- There is a madness which causes us to remember our true nature. That's **holy madness**.
- And then, there is a **fallen madness**, which causes us to forget our true nature, but not only to forget our true nature, but to forget that we've forgotten.

There is a madness which invokes a memory of who we really are, and there's a madness that causes us to forget.

The grain that they ate in this story made them mad in the bad way; it was a fallen madness. The people were starving, and so they became consumers, and they consumed and consumed the grain, until they were all mad. Just the king and his advisor were left:

> *King:* What do I do? All of my people are mad, and I love them madly, and I want to be with them, but they are mad. How can I be mad?
>
> *Advisor:* Well, you can't be their king if you're sane and they're mad. You've gotta eat the grain, but you can't be a mad king, unless it's holy madness, says the advisor.
>
> *King:* Well, how am I going to find my way to holy madness?
>
> *Advisor:* You know what? I'm going to eat the grain with you. But before we eat the grain, let's make a mark on each other's forehead. And after we eat the grain, we are going to be mad, but then if we look at each other, we are going to see the mark on our

forehead, and we're going to remember. It's going to become holy madness. We're going to remember who we really are.

Beloveds, we all have marks on our foreheads.

- ♦ It's the spark in us, which is un-betrayed and unbowed.
- ♦ It's the love in us that flames and refuses to be quenched.
- ♦ It's the hope that refuses to be extinguished.
- ♦ It's the Possibility of Possibility.

It's the feeling that I actually matter so immensely that the whole world was worth creating just for me—not as a narcissistic predicament, but as the truest indication of my true nature. I'm mad with love—and the whole world is mad with me, but it becomes a holy madness.

I want to drink with you.

L'chaim! Let's become holy mad drunkards, what Hafiz calls the *rogues* and the drunkards and the madmen. We don't want our place around just the civilized.

We want to be so civilized, and yet we want to be rogues and madmen and holy thieves and holy beggars.

There are three kinds of drunkards. There are drunkards who just feel the pain of their own lives, so they just drink a little bit. But if you feel the pain of all of your people, you can't just drink a little, you've got to drink a few good glasses. But now, in the mystical realm in the palace of imagination, let's drink bottles and bottles—for all the people in the world that ever were, that ever will be.

Let's be holy drunkards, holy madmen for the whole thing, because that's the only sanity.

Mad love, everyone. Mad love, mad love.

CHAPTER TWELVE

THE UNIQUE OBLIGATION
TO TAKE YOUR UNIQUE RISK

Episode 423 — November 17, 2024

WE'RE IN A TIME BETWEEN WORLDS, A TIME BETWEEN STORIES

We're in a time between worlds. We're in a time between stories. We haven't been at this time actually ever in history before. It has never happened. The only kind of time that's relatively similar to it in the last few hundred years, that we have a kind of obvious access to, if we actually understand what was happening there, was the Renaissance.

The Renaissance was also a time between worlds, a time between stories, in which the old world was breaking down, In this world, there were medieval or premodern understandings of:

- Science
- Sexuality
- The Divine
- Value
- Meaning itself
- Relationships between human beings
- Touch

255

- ◆ Medicine
- ◆ Universality or particularity

Everything. It all lived in a certain context, what C.S. Lewis calls *the discarded image of the premodern*. And it all began breaking down.

That breakdown exploded in the form of a plague. The plague was called the Black Death, which swept across Europe, and there was no known approach to fighting it. There was a huge conflict of major proportions that rocked Europe in terms of how to understand the plague.

Shortly after this, when a quarter to half of Europe lay dying, there was this small group of people in Florence, and they stepped out of the politics of the papal state, and the different cities and the wars between different cities— and they actually realized that this was a pivoting point in humanity. That it's a time between worlds in which the old world is breaking down, but the new world hasn't yet emerged. They can't get to every place of suffering in Europe or Asia. They realize that the future hasn't yet been born and that the future needs to be birthed. We need to access a memory of the future. **The Renaissance was the articulation of the memory of a future, a new story, a new possible story for humanity that emerges**. That story is what we call modernity.

MODERNITY GOT THE PLOTLINES HALF RIGHT AND HALF WRONG

As we've said here many times, the strength of the new story depends on the extent that we understood that there *is* a new story and the extent to which we got the plotlines right. The accurate plotlines were laid out by Marsilio Ficino, and da Vinci, and Pico della Mirandola—the whole gang that da Vinci gathered, funded by Cosimo de' Medici and Lorenzo de' Medici.

They have this moment in which they come together and they tell this new story. **And to the extent that they got the plotlines right, they birthed what we've called here many times *the dignities of modernity*.**

Whether that was the emergence of universal human rights, or the scientific method, or third-person perspective, or new forms of realism and depth in art, new kinds of music, new understandings of the relationship of the sexes—what it means to be a man and a woman—and sexuality itself and Eros, natural law, modern medicine at its best, antibiotics at their best—all of that emerges out of getting the plotlines right.

To the precise extent that they get the plotlines wrong:

- Reality goes off.
- Reality moves in a direction, not of value, but of anti-value.
- The storyline gets lost.
- A success story steps in and becomes a plotline.

So, in the vacuum of full plotline—meaning in the place where modernity didn't get it right and the stuff they skipped in the directional movements of Cosmos, that they ignored and thought would take care of themselves—in that vacuum, what's born is what we call the success story.

Modernity's success story is *rivalrous conflict governed by win/lose metrics.*

That's one of the core generator functions from modernity that in turn produces fragile systems. Fragile systems are systems that optimize for efficiency, not for resiliency. **Fragility, or what are called by Dave Snowden,** *complicated systems,* **means systems where the parts don't know each other, and are therefore prone to collapse.**

For example, there's a plague that comes out of Wuhan, China, probably a lab leak, and it shuts down airports all over the world. And everyone stays at home.

People don't even know how to manufacture masks, let alone to understand where the virus came from, how to respond to the virus, find accurate feeds of information that would actually create coherence in the public trust and the ability to respond. All that is not possible.

There's this phenomenal breakdown in the information ecology and we see this dress rehearsal of catastrophic risk, where the system that seemed to be completely coherent and completely resilient actually turns out to be fragile.

Literally out of nowhere, you're not allowed to leave your house, and you don't even know whether the science is accurate in telling you not to leave your house because you're getting contradictory vectors of information.

That's because the system itself is fragile, because the plotline at the center of the system or at least one dimension of the plotline has become a success story.

VALUE GOT EXILED TO DOING EVALUATION

Still, there are all these plotlines from modernity that are actually successful. They introduce the scientific method, and a sense of universal human rights that people take seriously, and democracy, and new forms of governance. All of that comes from the best plotlines.

Modernity got that we need to talk about how we gather information and how we analyze information.

Modernity got that we move from relying on my own first-person experience to also having a third-person method of verification. And that produces notions of peer review and it produces *the scientific method*. All that stuff is great.

But there's a breakdown at the center in one part of the plotline, which is, *where are we going?* It's a breakdown in meaning. There's actually a fundamental meaning crisis.

At the core of the meaning crisis is a failure to actually chart a vision of inherent value.

Where's the Cosmos going? *Telos* (direction) gets thrown out of science. How *telos* gets thrown out is actually a fascinating story—which we'll tell in one of the upcoming books in the Great Library. *Telos* gets thrown out of science; it finally happens in the mid-nineteenth century.

Reality is not going anywhere, according to science. The notion that you would claim that Reality has an inherent *telos*, that it's going somewhere, is viewed as fundamentalist and religious. So, *telos*, the notion of direction, becomes religious and wrong.

There's a sense that we live in a world that *becomes*. In modernity, there's an intense and beautiful sense that we can rest in all goodness, and all fulfillment, and all wonder, and all beauty in this world, but we're going to actually forget about the larger issues. We're going to say that we reject this larger view *of becoming* because in this larger view of the world, there are many dimensions beneath the world we see.

That larger view of the world was hijacked by different religious systems in order to create domination. This is the view of the world that says there are multiple incarnations, multiple dimensions, multiple vectors, and that what you see in this world is not the whole story.

That view of the world got hijacked big-time, by ethnocentric fundamentalist dogmatic systems. And so, modernity said, *Take that out of the picture.*

It's a big deal to get that. Modernity said, take that out of the picture. *We're not interested in those.* So modernity threw those plotlines out—plotlines essential to the ancient and premodern world—because they got hijacked.

Modernity says, *Okay, in our plotlines, we're going to skip value. We're just going to assume value.*

We wrote about that in the book *First Principles and First Values*. There's an entire section on how modernity just assumes what we might call *common sense sacred axioms of value*, but skips the actual discussion about *how do we know they're true* and *where are they from?*

So, modernity said, *Oh, we hold these truths to be self-evident.* Huh! The most important truths of value, you hold to be self-evident? But where are they from? Where's that self-evidence from? They would ascribe it to old versions of natural law and it doesn't work. It doesn't work. Like the idea that there's no value without the other, invisible dimensions. Not true.

What is value? Value means:

- There's something that's beyond the immediate.
- There's something that's beyond the rational calculus.
- There's a Field of Value, which is the ground in which everything arises.

It's what Plato calls, *from the invisible comes the visible, sensible God.* But the visible, sensible God, means the Field of Value.

There is no value without being sourced in that which is beneath. **So, if all of the manifest world would disappear, there would still be value.**

Value evolves, shifts, discloses new faces in response to this manifest world.

Value itself is the ground of all being.

It's critical that I find value in speech. Language expresses value.

But language emerges from the silence. As language is not merely an agreement, language is, as the interior scientists pointed out, *a coded expression of an inherent Field of Value.* Wow!

And in silence, I have a direct experience, an unmediated experience with value itself.

All practice is about is opening the Eye of Value. **And the Eye of Value is, itself, the invisible made visible.** For example, when I dance, or in any practice, when I actually feel, in my body, the entire Field of Value at play. Okay, wow!

So, value is not the evaluation I do. It's not a commodification; it's not an evaluation. Although that's a later usage of it.

Value itself got exiled to doing evaluation.

But value is not that. Value is immeasurable; it's not commodifiable:

- You feel it and you know it inherently and intrinsically.
- It's the source of all life.
- It's why I'm often willing to lay my life down for it, for this invisible order, which is about the inherent rightness of Cosmos.
- There's a rightness to Cosmos. There's a direction, a *telos*, an inherent fairness that *should* be.
- We know that fairness, that justice should be, that goodness should be, that kindness should be.

It's not because of a rational calculus. It's not reducible to a rational calculus. It's not *Homo economicus*; it's not the rational actor.

The rational actor can *align* with *a value*, but value is underneath. It's deeper.

EXISTENTIAL RISK DEMANDS A NEW STORY OF VALUE

So, the intention, what are we doing here? We're actually here in this time between worlds, in this time between stories, which is a moment like the Renaissance.

We're just like the Renaissance, except we have exponential technologies. We have existential risk. We have technologies that can actually destroy the planet, which have developed exponentially more sophisticated forms than they had in World War II when the first mushroom clouds explode over Hiroshima and Nagasaki.

There are exponential technologies that are available to rogue non-state actors. That's one form of existential risk, *and there are about ten other forms.*

So, now we're at this moment, this time between worlds, this time between stories, with massively distributed existential risk technologies. **These existential risk technologies can actually either *end humanity*—that possibility never existed before—or they can cause the death of *our* humanity.**

That's the structure we're in. We're in this time between worlds, this time between stories. So, what do we need to do?

We need to make the da Vinci move. The da Vinci move is to not deny existential risk.

We're not going to take a *doomer* position. We're going to actually talk about this and experience this as the *dawn*. **Not denial, not doomer. It's the dawn of a new age, and that new age is a da Vinci age.**

By da Vinci, we mean, as artists, as social artists, as spiritual artists, as world philosophers, as those who are willing to take responsibility for the whole and bear that unbearable burden with unbearable love.

We have to respond by telling a new Story of Value.

We have to tell a new story of meaning, but not made-up meaning.

Viktor Frankl made that paradoxical postmodern move. He writes this book that was originally called *Death Camps and Existentialism*. That didn't sell well. So, he changed it to *Man's Search for Meaning*.

After he survived the Holocaust, he called this school of thought *logotherapy*, in which he talks about this fundamental human drive searching for meaning. But he was so caught up in the ethos of his day, he basically says:

- All this meaning is made up. None of it is real.
- And all meaning is a survival mechanism.

So, as dramatic and as beautiful as his book, *Man's Search for Meaning*, is, his larger *logotherapy* essentially says that this is some human survival drive and meaning is ultimately not real. He couldn't move beyond that moment in his day.

For Frankl, it didn't matter that he was one of those people who *philosophically* said meaning is not ultimately real. He lived it in a way that was so real that his philosophy didn't matter.

So, Viktor Frankl writes right after World War II. He's writing out of Europe when existentialism has swept Europe, but no one really believes it. **Everyone really experiences in their life that value is actually real, even if you deny it philosophically.**

It's funny, you read Sartre's book, *Being and Nothingness*, and it's an utter poem to meaninglessness. And yet paradoxically, when you finish reading him, you're filled with the sense of meaning and purpose. In other words, the existentialists themselves are so close to meaning that in their rebellion against it, meaning is still completely evident and suffuses everything they say.

It's kind of like the generation of secular Jewish people who utterly rejected the validity of the lineage and the texts and the beauty of the texts. They said, *We don't need any of this, or we certainly don't need any authority from it. And we certainly don't need to be guided by it.* They were furious with the whole 2,000-year-old tradition, and yet they studied it all the time and argued with it and spent all of their lives engaging it. They assumed that they could throw it out, and yet it would always still be there with them. Does that make sense?

POSTMODERNITY TOOK OUT A LOAN FROM PREMODERNITY

So, existentialism assumes we can throw out meaning; but *who* is throwing out meaning? There's a group of men and women who are spending all day and night writing about *meaning*. Then along comes postmodernity, which actually breaks the contract and says, *No, no, no, you actually can't assume meaning.*

Modernity and postmodernity took a loan out from premodernity, *assuming* **meaning, assuming value, while at the same time saying,** *value is not real.*

And this postmodern chill begins to chill humanity.

It appears in movies like *Barbie*. It appears in tragic stories, like Mike Tyson's, who just fought Jake Paul. Beautiful Jake. And then Mike does an interview[2] right after this insane, crazy, and staged fight.

And there's a whole conversation we can have about what that is in the modern moment. What is an influencer—like boxers Mike Tyson and Jake Paul—and how does all of that work and not work. What's beautiful about it and what's tragic about it—but that's not our conversation now.

But in any case, this fight takes place in the United States that gets an insane amount of viewership. And then a 14-year-old girl interviews Mike Tyson after the fight and says, *How does this affect your legacy?*

And Tyson says, *Legacy?*

And I'm not quoting him directly, but he basically says:

Fuck legacy.

Legacy is when I'm dead.

When I'm dead, there's nothing.

2 See "Mike Tyson talks about his childhood, happiness, legacy, & his fight with Jake Paul" (https://www.youtube.com/watch?v=0jA3fKMiKMs)

There's nothing when I'm dead.

Nothing matters. I have no legacy.

I don't give a fuck how it expresses and affects my legacy.

That's just nonsense.

It's like, wow. It's heartbreaking, actually.

So, Mike Tyson is one of a thousand sources I could cite and we've talked about a more, kind of formal, popular source like Yuval Harari. And Yuval's not saying something different than Mike Tyson.

Yuval's saying something like,

We've got to do everything we can to make a better world, but ultimately you die.

It's over.

There's no intrinsic meaning.

There's no inherent meaning.

End game.

We lost the plotline. Does everyone get what I'm saying? We lost the plotline.

When you lose the plotline, when you basically declare that value's not real, then the only thing you can see in front of you is the world of the visible. You only see the material visible and you can't actually open what we're calling the Eye of Value, which is as empirical as the material visible.

We stake our lives on the Eye of Value, or the Eye of the Heart, or the Eye of Consciousness, or the Eye of the Spirit, or the Eye of Transfiguration to be real. It's the eye that feels *the Reality of dimensions*. There's also an enormous amount of empirical research to show that they are true. But we lost the thread.

And so, what we're here to do in *One Mountain* is a big deal.

> *We are here to literally re-weave the source code of Reality in the way that they began to do in the Renaissance but stopped.*

They did part of it. They reset. They began to tell a new story, but they left out the most important plotlines. They thought they could get away with it because everyone would just assume that meaning is real. And they would just assume that value is real. But they were wrong. We can't make that assumption.

You can't begin to understand neoliberal politics—which are infused with postmodernity—nor populist strongman politics, which is breaking out around the world everywhere, without understanding this breakdown in the Field of Value.

When there's a Field of Value, we trust each other because we each understand that we're incarnations of this inherent Field of Value. So, there's a sense of trust. When there's a Field of Value, we can have a conversation in which we trust legacy institutions, in which we trust scientific process, in which we trust each other in some deep way. There's a deep conversation at the center.

But when trust explodes because the assumption is that there's no Field of Value, what happens is the essential intimate communion at the center of culture breaks down. This postmodern moment begins to infuse, paradoxically, populism. And what populism says is *don't trust anyone except for perhaps me, the strong leader.* Just trust the strong leader.

The first move of totalitarianism is to trust only the strong leader because there's no Field of Value to actually trust. Does everyone get that? It's a big deal. We're basically one person or one tiny group of people, the elite, the Ministry of Love in George Orwell's *Nineteen Eighty-Four*. Trust who? *Trust just us,* because that's the only thing that's real. The only thing that's real is me, my little group, my party, the Ministry of Love. There's nothing else to trust.

This is the source of populism. It's the source of totalitarianism: The notion that there's not a Field of Value, out of which we create a common Story of Value, which can actually allow us to challenge injustice, to challenge the lie, to challenge the people of the lie, to challenge the failures of kindness, to challenge the failures of ethos, and to challenge the failures of goodness.

Without a Field of Value, the conversation can't happen.

And paradoxically, the neoliberal world that wants to challenge the strongman can't actually do it effectively because it's dislocated itself—in its own self-experience, in its own self-perception—from the Field of Value.

That's what we've been talking about here, one way or the other. It's one thread of ten threads that we've been talking about.

I've read the literature in the last years challenging populism, as well as the critique of artificial intelligence, the critique of potential digital dictatorships through the web, or the critique of any number of other populist positions in politics.

However, the critique falls flat because even though it says the right words and it invokes the right popular phrases—even God gets invoked—it's very clear that *no one really believes it.* There's a postmodern confusion which runs through the entire neoliberal world.

So, what do we need to do? What we need to do is actually crack value theory and understand why value theory collapsed. Why did it collapse? It collapsed for a whole bunch of reasons I'm not talking about right now, but it collapsed for some really good reasons.

THE UNIQUE RISK OF TAKING RESPONSIBILITY FOR THE WHOLE

But our topic for today is *unique risk*. And I want to share with you about unique risk. I want to argue that and suggest that our unique risk as human beings in this moment in time—and in particular our unique risk here in *One Mountain, Many Paths*, in the seat of revolution—**our unique risk is to actually be able to see the whole, to actually be able to see everything that we just outlined right now.**

The introductory essay to this volume, "Love or Die," articulates this fairly clearly. *Love or Die* is a crazy big deal. *Love or Die* means that we need to articulate a new vision of loving, but not a New Age vision, not a mythopoetic vision.

We can start with an artistic vision, but then it's got to become a cogent, coherent, philosophical vision that I can explain to any seventh grader, or a fourth grader, or third grader, and any graduate student, and any initiate practicing deeply in a tradition. We need to be able to explain it all over China, all over Russia, all over Poland, all over the Maldives, all over South America, and all through Africa.

We need a shared Grammar of Value as the context for our diversity.

We can't move without it.

We need a shared Story of Value.

We need to identify the plotlines.

To do that, we need to revivify the Field of Value and to revivify the Field of Eros—the Field of Eros Value. So what is our unique risk? There's lots of great things to do in the world. There's lots of projects to get involved with. It's very easy.

I know myself. I want to just say this tenderly. There are ten books that I'm dying to write, and none of them have to do with the meta-crisis, and none of them have to do with revivifying the Field of Value.

They're just topics that I'm madly, insanely interested in. And those topics have something to do with the interior experiences of beauty and of Eros and of silence and of laughter and of dance, and of understanding those in their deepest scientific context.

There's a whole library I want to write. I probably won't get to write a lot of it in this lifetime. Some of it maybe, but I have to actually take a unique risk, and I need to take it together with my best friends who are here—my evolutionary and biological family.

I've been with my son all weekend. And one of the things that we do when we're together, we just jump into the bed, and we kind of cuddle up, and we watch the series *Flash*. We watch these Marvel shows on superheroes. *Flash* is a Marvel show. And Flash is a superhero.

There's what's called Team Flash. Team Flash is this group of like seven to ten people who gather around to actually take responsibility for saving the world. So people are watching *Flash*; he's this kind of Marvel superhero. Saving the world means, not that I put on an actual cape, but it means *I put on a cape*, meaning I'm actually willing to see the whole; I actually trust myself to see the whole.

But do to so, we have to take responsibility for the whole. I actually study carefully. I look at the whole thing. I gather people, we gather together, in *One Mountain, Many Paths*, in the Center for World Philosophy and Religion. **We pretend to be a think tank, but really, we're a band of Outrageous Lovers taking responsibility for the whole.**

In Tolkien's terms we would call it *The Fellowship of the Ring*. That's what Tolkien was talking about, the Fellowship of the Ring. Or, in terms of heroes, we're Team Flash. And Team Flash means, *we're in.*

We're evolutionary family to each other. We care about each other, insanely. Every single person reading this is involved in this Team Flash, in this band of Outrageous Lovers, in this think tank, in this Unique Self Symphony— every single one of us is involved, or you wouldn't be reading this.

And I'm going to invite everyone to step in one step closer to Team Flash.

We're taking responsibility for the whole. And in order to do this, we have to take our unique risk. Because every one of us could be doing something else. And every one of us could be doing something else that's actually meaningful, that actually matters. There's lots that needs to be done.

There are local things that need to be done, local charities. There are books that need to be written. There's important social work that needs to be done, and kindergarten that needs to be taught, and spiritual communities to join, and practices to do, and psychological work to do, and family work to do. And that's all valuable. It's all beautiful.

But that's not Team Flash.

Let me give it another name. If Team Flash is kind of hard for you, let's go back to the Renaissance, when Cosimo Medici, together with Marsilio Ficino, starts the Florentine Platonic Academy. That was also a Team Flash. It was this small group of people.

Or let's go to the *Zohar*, written by Simon, son of Yochai. The *Zohar* is actually the major work that creates Lurianic Kabbalah. This book actually defined, in many ways, the Renaissance. It has enormous influence on Ficino's Platonic Academy, and on Medici, and many other figures of that time.

And the people that wrote it were Team Flash. They were the band of Outrageous Lovers.

They were a group, actually, of eight people at the core, and surrounding those eight people, there was another 50, and surrounding those 50, there was another 100, and surrounding those 100, there was another 1,000. Surrounding those 1,000, there was another 5,000.

But it was this small group of people that came together. Not to be spectators. No, we've got to be *in the ring*.

I love Jake, and I love Mike, but I don't want to be a spectacle like Jake and Mike, attracting attention in a particular way, and enacting a fight.

No, let's be in the *real* fight. We need to be in the ring.

- We're tag-teaming in the ring.
- We're in the ring together.
- We're Team Flash together.
- We're the Fellowship of the Ring.

And you can't be in the Fellowship of the Ring without taking your unique risk. Does that make sense? Okay, let me see if I can break this down.

There's a unique risk. **I can't play my instrument in the Unique Self Symphony without taking my unique risk.** We want to unpack this next level of understanding of what it means to take my unique risk.

UNIQUENESS IS A VALUE OF COSMOS

So we will get to unique risk. What is unique risk? First, we need to talk about the word *unique* and the word *risk*. *My unique risk*. So who is *my*? Who am I?

First of all, uniqueness is real.

Does everyone get that? Uniqueness is real. Uniqueness is a value of Cosmos. A little uniqueness is located in the first pressure waves in the inception of Cosmos. Uniqueness is real.

In one of the key books of the Great Library we're working on called *The Universe: A Love Story*, there's a section on uniqueness, a short history of uniqueness. We actually need to do a short history of all of the First

Principles and First Values. So, in this book we mentioned earlier, *First Principles and First Values*, there's a list of what we've established as First Principles and First Values that can be validated scientifically in the interior and the exterior sciences.

One of them is uniqueness. Uniqueness is a real value of Cosmos.

The goal is not to move *beyond* uniqueness. **The goal is to actually realize uniqueness and to understand that uniqueness is not separateness.** Uniqueness is not separateness; it is not to be separate. It's not to be alienated from; it's not to be dissociated from. Separation, alienation, and dissociation is the pathology of uniqueness. Just as, for example, *fusion* would be the pathology of *intimate union*. Instead of intimate union, *I fuse with you. I become codependent in a tragic way.* So, that's the pathology of intimate communion.

So, separation, or dissociation, is the pathology of appropriate autonomy. Does that make sense, everyone? I get separated; I get dissociated; I get alienated.

Uniqueness starts with the first pressure waves, and uniqueness goes all the way down the evolutionary chain. **Uniqueness evolves all the way through matter.**

Matter keeps differentiating. There is differentiation. You can read chapter fifteen of Herbert Spencer's book, *First Principles*, the chapter's called *Differentiation and Integration*. Reality differentiates to more and more uniqueness. **And then uniqueness itself, like a puzzle piece, becomes the currency of the Eros of integration.**

So when two people come together, we come together because we're differentiated uniquely, and then our uniqueness becomes the currency of our connection.

> *The movement of Reality, the plotline of Reality is differentiation and integration, which is another way of saying, the movement towards more uniqueness.*

It always has pathology, as we just pointed out.

So, for example, the diversity politics, or what we might call today identity politics, in their shadow form, are expressions of the pathology of uniqueness. In other words, on the one hand, I have identity politics, so I have a unique identity, but identity politics means that somehow some dimension of what seems to be my unique identity separates me from the whole.

I'm no longer part of the whole. I no longer recognize people by the content of their character. I'm actually paradoxically doing an identity politics, which means I start to identify people by the color of their skin—mistake.

I actually need to be, on the one hand, deeply resonant and respectful of the unique, intimate quality of every person and of every group, every communion, and yet, we are all *first* brothers and sisters in the Field of Value. We need to recognize each other in the Field of Value, and we need to actually be ultimately colorblind. Meaning colorblind in the sense that, **underneath color, underneath ethnicity, underneath nationality, underneath gender, I am an irreducible unique incarnation of value itself.**

So, that's uniqueness. It's deep. There's this quality of uniqueness.

UNIQUE SELF IS INDIVIDUATION BEYOND EGO

There's this quality of uniqueness in Cosmos. Matter is unique. Matter keeps differentiating towards more uniqueness, from quarks, to subatomic particles, to atoms, to molecules, to macromolecules, to unique cells, to unique multicellular structures, to neural nets and neural cords, all the way up until we get to human beings, we get to the depth of self-reflection in human beings.

And then we go through all the structural stages of human evolution, which is an evolution to ever more uniqueness until I move from unconscious uniqueness to conscious uniqueness. That's not just the emergence of separateness. It's not just the separate self that emerges in the Renaissance in a very clear way. **It's a realization that I'm not just separate; I'm actually a unique expression of the field—that's the emergence of uniqueness.**

At a certain point, early on, we realize, *Oh, I'm part of True Self.* That realization comes pretty early. A few thousand years ago, there's this deep realization that I'm part of the Field of True Self.

After the realization that *I'm not separate from the Field of the True Self; I'm part of the larger whole,* comes this realization that *I also have dignity as being a separate self. I'm also separate.*

But then we get stuck in separate self.

So, first, *wow, I'm part of the field.*

And then the Renaissance realized, *No, I'm not just part of the field; I actually have dignity as a separate self.* But then we forget that there's a larger field.

So, we have to actually get from the separate self, back to True Self and realize: *I'm a separate self, but my separate self is not my entire identity. I'm not alienated from the field. I'm part of the larger Field of ErosDesire, part of the larger Field of Consciousness.* It's called True Self.

And then I individuate. I have a higher individuation beyond True Self. I individuate as Unique Self. **Unique Self is a higher individuation beyond the ego self of separate self**. It's also a higher individuation, which emerges from the field, the artistic Field of Reality, the creative Field of Reality, which is the Field of True Self, the Field of ErosValue.

I individuate as a unique incarnation of value. That's my Unique Self. Now, all of Reality intends that Unique Self, my individual Unique Self.

It also intends a Reality in which I can't do anything myself.

Even though I'm a Unique Self, my uniqueness, my puzzle piece nature draws me to the puzzle.

- I need Team Flash.
- I need the band of Outrageous Lovers.
- I need the Florentine Platonic Academy with Ficino and the gang.
- I need the Fellowship of the Ring.
- I need what the Zoharic mystics in the thirteenth century called, *hevra kadisha*, the holy band.
- I need the intimate communion.

Now, the shadow of intimate communion would be a cult. Does everyone get that? In a cult, a bad cult—meaning *I don't know the dignity of my separate self*—I forget that and I'm certainly not in the dignity of Unique Self. I regress to the pre-personal because I'm afraid of the responsibility and the dignity of separate self. And I certainly can't even begin to imagine the dignity of Unique Self.

So, then I regress to a pre-personal cult—that's a mistake.

I've got to move beyond the pre-personal; I step into the personal. By the way, in some of the old versions of True Self—*I'm part of the whole*—in the way they expressed themselves socially and religiously are what we today we call a cult because there was no dignity given to the separate self.

- So, we first needed to move beyond the pre-personal cults of the medieval period in which there was no dignity to the separate self.
- I then move into the Renaissance. I move into this dignity where the separate self is the center of gravity and culture. It's

the center of gravity in culture. *I'm now separate self.*

- And then I realize, *No, no, no, I'm not just separate self. I'm part of this larger field.*

- And out of this realization, *I'm part of a larger field*, I then individuate as my Unique Self.

So, that individuation of Unique Self is literally happening in this generation.

TO ACTUALIZE A UNIQUE SELF SYMPHONY, WE EACH NEED TO TAKE OUR UNIQUE RISK

This is one of the primary intentions of this revolution, of this think tank, of this group of people. I founded it together early on with Ken Wilber, and Ken and I spent an enormous amount of time formulating this notion of Unique Self.

This is an Evolution of Love itself. It's an evolution of *She*. It's this new realization of *who am I?*

Who am I?

- I'm a Unique Self.
- I'm needed by All-That-Is.
- My Unique Self is not my separate self. I'm not separate from intimate communion.
- I'm in intimate communion with the larger field.
- I'm an irreducibly unique expression of the larger field.
- The larger field is the seamless coat of the Universe, seamless but not featureless—and I am its unique feature.
- Reality needs my unique gift.
- Reality needs my unique intimacy.
- Reality needs my unique quality of Eros.
- Reality needs my unique contribution to the Field of Value.
- Reality needs my unique value proposition.

- ◆ Reality needs my unique presence, which is value itself.
- ◆ Reality needs my unique story.
- ◆ Reality needs my unique love story because my love story is chapter and verse in *The Universe: A Love Story*.

TO TAKE OUR UNIQUE RISK MEANS TO LOVE OR DIE

So how do I live that story? The only way I can live that story is by taking my unique risk. So now we're going to get kind of insanely personal and intimate and close if we can. Let's get real intimate here.

In order to actually be my Unique Self, I have to take my unique risk. That's in the structure of Reality. **You cannot respond to existential risk without taking your unique risk.**

When there's a huge risk in Cosmos, existential risk, which is risk of the death of humanity and risk of the death of *our* humanity, you can't respond to existential risk by not taking a risk. You can't respond to existential risk without taking y/our unique risk, and your risk is *our* risk. There is no separateness.

I'm a unique expression of the whole. I'm in intimate communion. I have my instrument to play in the symphony, but there's a symphony, and it's a symphony of Unique Selves.

To play my instrument in the Unique Self Symphony, I need to take my unique risk.

Now, what does that mean? So my unique risk is the risk that if I don't take it, I die. And I have to risk death to take it.

I want to now add a whole dimension here. When I say you risk death to take it, sometimes you actually have to risk death. My children at this particular moment are literally risking death to protect democracy. It's intense. So, you have to sometimes risk death. That's a horror. And there's two insanely beautiful people I know, two doctors from Gaza who've risked death, a man and a woman, to save people in the last year. Wow!

But I want to talk about something which is even closer and immediate. You can kind of catch it immediately in your own life right now, which is: unique risk is love or die. **I either become my unique incarnation of Eros or I die.** But in order to become that unique incarnation of love, *I have to be willing to risk death.*

What does it mean to *risk death*?

- ◆ It means I've got to risk some loss.
- ◆ I've got to be willing to risk my safety.
- ◆ Or let me say it more clearly: I've got to be willing to risk my *pseudo*-aliveness, my *pseudo*-safety to find my deeper safety and my deeper aliveness.

In other words, I have to be willing, as the Zen masters would say, to *die on the cushion*, and to die on the cushion means to give up those separate-self patterns, those winning formulas that you've formulated or adopted early in life in order to feel safe, in order to feel like I have a place in the world.

So, for example, sometimes the way a person feels they have a place in the world is by always displacing themselves. It's a paradox.

So a person might say:

> Well, my integrity is, and the lineage of my family is, for example, that I challenge authority and I'm willing to die for it. My father, my mother, my grandfather may have died challenging authority. And so, the only way I can have a place in the world is to challenge authority.

That's good. That's good. *I'm actually challenging authority in a good way. I'm self-authored.*

But sometimes even that can become a pattern.

And then I don't feel at home in my life unless I throw myself out of every place. So then I'm going to keep challenging and challenging and challenging until I succeed in provoking the people that I want to be close to and getting them so mad at me that I hope they'll throw me out. Because if they throw me out, then I actually feel comfortable in the pattern of my life.

You see how subtle that is? It's very subtle.

My integrity is to challenge, but then my challenge itself becomes mixed with a kind of automatic pattern: I challenge because that's what I do. And even if my challenge is completely right, I can't actually identify what part of it is right and what part of it is the pattern that I've become accustomed to. So I'm audacious, but is my audacity rooted in courage, or have I just gotten used to being audacious? It's a good question.

My unique risk is always to give up my place of safety. But sometimes to give up my place of safety means to give up my need to provoke people to throw me out.

Does everyone get that? And I just made up one example. In other words, Unique Self always means I'm willing to give up my *pseudo-aliveness*. Does everyone get that? It's so subtle.

I'm willing to give up my pseudo-aliveness in order to get my real aliveness.

I'm willing to give up my pattern and my story, and my religious story, and my psychological story—which is well-honed; it's well-developed. I'm really good at telling that story. I'm willing to give that up in order to be in my *real* story. I'm willing to give up my pseudo-success to be in my real success.

And my real success is success which encompasses the whole:

- It's not success 1.0, where I'm listening to what God told me and I'm being obedient and I emasculate myself. Success 1.0

is kind of a premodern success.

- It's not success 2.0, where I'm being successful in the win/lose metrics. Success 2.0 is where I've succeeded in achieving status and gaining attention.

And by the way, success 2.0 used to be that I would succeed in getting attention for having done something worthwhile. I'm going to do something worthwhile, that will cause me to get attention. Now, the most dramatic form of success 2.0 is that the worthwhile act is getting attention. **Attention is no longer a corollary of having done something worthwhile; the achievement itself is attention**. Instead of attention being a reward for achievement, the achievement is attention. That's the tragedy of the social influencer world. The social influencer world has a lot of good to it, potentially; but it is dramatically unrealized, tragically so.

So the tragic form of success 2.0, which is what's more realized today, is that the achievement becomes attention. But attention is supposed to be a by-product of depth, right? Success 2.0 is that I succeed in putting myself forward and achieving status—this means I'm successful.

Success 3.0 is:

> I individuate as a Unique Self in the field of the larger whole.
>
> I'm uniquely individuated.
>
> I'm the artist of my own life.
>
> I'm the hero of my own life in relationship to the whole, and I'm contributing to the whole, and I'm playing my instrument in the Unique Self Symphony.

To do that:

- I first have to do **transformation**, meaning I've got to do the inner work of classical separate self transformation. That's the first T, *transformation.*
- Then I've got to do **transcendence.** I've got to transcend. I've

got to transcend my own personal story and be in the field and just live in the field. I've got to experience the sunset, be in the depth of art, be in the depth of the Eros, in the depth of the silence, and the depth of the beauty. That's *transcendence*.

♦ And then I've got to go from transcendence to the third level which is **transfiguration**. I transfigure. Transfiguration means *I've transfigured; I've actually taken my unique risk.*

I've done the work of transformation. I've then done the work of transcendence.

Transformation—separate self.

Transcendence—True Self.

Transfiguration—Unique Self.

And now, I'm in this Unique Self place, in which I've transfigured, and I've become *Homo amor*—the fulfilment of *Homo sapiens*.

I've become a unique incarnation of the Field of Outrageous Love. I'm an Outrageous Lover, and Outrageous Lovers take their unique risk in order to commit their Outrageous Acts of Love.

We do that as individuals, and we do that as a symphony.

As a Unique Self Symphony, we're going to say a thousand *no's*. I'm going to say a thousand no's in order to say one *Yes!*

Because there are a thousand places we can play. We can fill up our time with a thousand important things. They all really matter. **But to be *Homo amor*, to be a whole mate, is to be omni-considerate and omni-responsible for the whole.**

♦ I can feel the whole pulsing through me.
♦ I can feel the whole tumescent in me.
♦ I can feel the whole throbbing in me.
♦ I can feel it all happening through me.

- I feel the whole and I respond.
- I can feel the cries of the unborn.
- I feel trillions of unborn, and I feel them calling me and I hear them calling me.
- I feel all of the past wanting to be fulfilled.
- I feel all of the present lost in win/lose metrics, and I'm able to both be in it and transcend it, to *end the trance*, and transfigure, and become *Homo amor*.
- I'm willing to do my work to take my unique risk. I can't take my unique risk unless I know something about my unique wound.
- What's my unique wound?
- What's my unique shadow.
- What's my unique silliness?
- What's the unique art that's mine to do?
- What's my unique gift?

We're in this revolution. To be in this revolution, we have to take our unique risk. Paradoxically, for me, personally, the unique risk is to actually stay focused on enacting this Great Library of value with you, and I'm hoping that's your unique risk as well, because I can't do it alone. We're the Fellowship of the Ring. We can do it together. Right?

We're Team Flash.

We're family.

We're Team *She*.

We're Team Humanity.

We're doing this radical thing: We're taking responsibility for the whole thing.

I just want to thank everyone for taking our unique risk together. Unique risk is not simple. It's a big deal. It's a big deal. And it's risky. Here's the thing: If I don't take my unique risk, I die.

And last sentence: it's actually not everyone's unique risk to take responsibility for the whole. Most people don't even know what we're talking about, and they're beautiful people. They're doing other things. Great. But we're here because we're allured to this. Because we know, *we need to do this*. We're self-selected, and for us not to take our unique risk is actually to die. So, the only aliveness is in taking that unique risk with each other.

So, thank you. Mad love. Mad honor. Mad respect. Mad desire.

Desire for *She*, and for all of it.

CHAPTER THIRTEEN

THE VOID IS REAL, AND THERE IS A WAY HOME

Episode 427 — December 15, 2024

WE ARE FACING DARKNESS

We are here in this moment—a time between worlds and a time between stories. The nature of a time in between is that we are in this liminal space. It's a time between worlds. The old world is breaking down. The very existence of the world is threatened. Potential death of humanity has become a probability, if you check the vectors of existential risk—unless we step in and realize that:

- We're Conscious Evolution in person.
- We're *The Universe: A Love Story* in person.
- We can and need to become, at this moment in history, a new human and new humanity—who can stand on the abyss of darkness and say, *Let there be light*!

We're at the point where we understand that there is a threatening darkness.

Many of you are aware that I've been giving Yuval Harari a little bit of a hard time the last several months, but this is one of the things Yuval and I deeply agree on. He writes about this at the end of his book, *Nexus*. In the appendix,

all of a sudden the postmodern sheen drops away, and there is this heroic human who emerges in a very beautiful way, and says, *We're facing the darkness.*

For him, the potential death of humanity means there will be no consciousness left in the galaxy; from his perspective, consciousness emerges out of material, and it might exist only on planet Earth.

Although I think that perspective is deeply flawed, he gets the nature of this moment very beautifully. What we share is that **we actually *are* in this moment when the lights can go out**. It's very hard for people to see around the corner. When I started saying something like this in 2010–2011, people thought I was completely crazy—now, just partially crazy. People began to get it when, during the Covid crisis, everything all of a sudden just stood still. You couldn't get on a plane. You couldn't leave your house. People realized that *it's not too big to fail.* The lights *could* go out. We are faced with the potential death of humanity and the potential death of our humanity, the two forms of existential risk.

The old world order and the institutions we trusted, and the givens of understanding that we trusted, are breaking down. The only thing that never changes is that it always changes—and so it's going to change, and it's changing dramatically. The drama and speed of change is unimaginable.

All of a sudden, AI is on your iPhone. How did that happen? All of a sudden, AI is right there on your computer, asking if you'd like information. AI is no longer a search engine—it's an oracle. *Tell me what you want to know, and I will tell you. I will gather the information for you, and tell you the nature of what truth is.* There is so much that's happening, and we are in this moment in between, and we haven't yet articulated the new possibility.

What's the next evolutionary step? This is how evolution works. We are in this massive crisis. **Our crisis has to become a birth.** We have to be in a moment when crisis becomes an evolutionary driver; and it has to become an evolutionary driver for the evolution of love.

A TIME BETWEEN EMPTINESS AND FULLNESS

We are in a time between worlds, the time between stories.

The time in between is empty and, at the same time, there is a potentiating fullness, because the old structures are breaking down. It is this fullness *which responds to the emptiness.*

A third-century text in the Talmud describes the destruction of the temple in Jerusalem—the ancient temple of Solomon, the source and (in a sense) the matrix of Solomon's wisdom lineage, which is a deep context for this attempt we are making to respond to the meta-crisis by enacting a new Story of Value.

In the temple, the Ark of the Covenant is situated in what's called the Holy of Holies, or the *Sanctum Sanctorum* (it always sounds better when you say it in Latin, but it means the same thing). There are erotically entwined cherubs above the Arc of the Covenant. In the mystical iconography of the Temple:

- In moments of deep peace, deep wholeness, deep justice, deep harmony, the cherubs would turn towards each other face-to-face. They would be centrally entwined.
- At a time of collapse—when things had already collapsed, when there was a violation of any sense of harmony or wholeness or justice, the cherubs would turn away from each other. Their faces were facing back-to-back, they weren't face-to-face anymore.

This sacred text records that, at the time when the temple was being destroyed, the cherubs were actually turned *towards* each other. The masters say, *How could that be? Isn't it true that, at the time of destruction, of disharmony, the cherubs turn away?*

We are in these moments between life and death.

There's this deep understanding in the lineage that at the moment when the breakdown is imminent, the space between, in the space in between times, we either are in a headlong blind movement towards collapse—or something new will emerge.

That's why it's such a privilege to know about your death, because then you get the space in between. It's the actual structural reason, in the Cosmos, for old age. Sometimes people say, *I'd rather just go in a moment.* Sally Kempton's brother Michael and his wife had a head-on crash when he was 28, and they died instantly. They didn't get the privilege of that time in between. It's a tragedy.

When we have the time in between, it can actually birth something. **Knowing that we are in this time in between, facing the second shock of existence—the potential death of humanity—can birth something**. Paradoxically, sometimes it allows us to avert death, and sometimes it allows us to experience death in an entirely different way. But it's always about a new birth.

The knowing that it can collapse, the space in between, is about birthing something new.

In this time in between, we either fall through the cracks into the void and we get lost, or we somehow manage to find our way. We walk through the void.

What does it mean to walk through the void? That's what we want to talk about today.

What is the void? This time between worlds is a moment of immense void and yet, of immense potential; of peril beyond imagination, and yet, a promise beyond imagination.

This time in between, how do we walk through it?

We can't do a-void-dance. **We can't dance around the void**.

- ◆ When we turn away from existential risk, we pretend it's not there, we're just going to do business as usual—that's a-void-dance. That's the denial response to existential risk.
- ◆ There's also a whole group of people, a powerful group of serious thinkers, who've looked at the facts and said, we have to start the grieving process. There's nothing to do. We are doomed. That's the doomer response.

We are not taking the doomer response; we think that's wrong. It falls into the void and in the name of realism it loses access to the promise.

We are not taking the denial response, which denies the void.

No, no, there's a deeper reality we can find. We are going to meet the void today, and we want to walk through the void.

Here's the Evolutionary Love Code for this week:

> We always meet the void. A-void-dance, meaning *avoidance*, never works. There is no way around the void. The only way is through. There are three ways through the void: Eros, silence, and song. And the three ways are one.

THE POSTMODERN ZEITGEIST AND THE PATH OF THE VOID

We are in this time in between worlds; we are in this time between stories.

There is a figure who is, paradoxically, quite close to me in certain ways, even though he represents the zeitgeist of postmodernity, which has deconstructed value. My friend and colleague Yuval Harari (and we're all already friends in the deepest place, on the Inside of the Inside) writes as a given something like, *any meaning that people ascribe to their lives is mere delusion.* And *meaning* and *value*, for Harari, mean the same thing (correctly); if meaning is mere delusion, then there is no value. Value is not real, in any sense, shape, or form.

He represents this very strong movement in the zeitgeist. It's why 50 million of his books have been sold. I've tried to address the fundamental dogmatic flaws in this position because I think everything depends on it. **The capacity to establish that value is real is everything.**

The movie *Gladiator II* has one key line in it, *strength and honor.* The question in the movie is very simple: Is Rome simply about power?

Paradoxically, this is exactly the postmodern moment of today.

There is this key figure played by Denzel Washington. His name is Macrinus. He is an actual historical figure. They played with the history, of course, but there's a moment when he says, *There is no dream of Rome. There is no honor. There's only one thing: power.* The fundamental notion of Foucault (who was an early postmodernist influenced by Nietzsche) is that the only issue at stake, ever, is power. He assumes there's no value. Value becomes a fig leaf for power. And there are very significant and powerful critiques of value that we've talked about in multiple earlier conversations.

What we are saying is, *No, strength* and *honor.* But not in the Roman way, where strength and honor meant the particular Roman version of morality at that particular moment, in the beginning of the Common Era. Not a freezing of a particular system. **We are saying that there is the noble in Reality; there is the Good, there is the True, there is the Beautiful.** There is value, and value is real; everything depends on that. I am willing to give my life for it. Everything depends on that: value is real.

If value is real, then there's one way that we unfold.

If value is *not* real, there's another way we unfold.

In the U.S. election, which caused some consternation in liberal circles around the world around a particular candidate, this particular candidate is, on many levels, a side issue, almost a false flag, almost a distraction. What is far more significant is that a group of TechnoFeudalists who call themselves *effective accelerationists* came to power (the people associated with the *Techno-Optimist Manifesto* in 2023, and Marc Andreessen, Peter Thiel, the whole Palantir gang, and Elon Musk of course).

These people have a TechnoFeudalist vision of Reality—that Reality is going to be, ultimately, subject to a certain kind of technological control, and that human beings, in the end, are going to become inferior processing machines—essentially, ineffective AIs.

These people actually take as a given what Harari presents as a scientific given in *Homo Deus*—that an organism is an algorithm. For example, in *21 Lessons*, his later book, he takes it as a given that emotions will be completely manipulable, and they are ultimately reducible to biochemical causes. Once we understand the biochemistry of emotions, then the manipulation of emotions becomes possible ever more precisely, and any notion (or illusion) of free will disappears.

But we are not coming here to argue with the TechnoFeudalists (although that needs to be done); here, I don't want to approach the TechnoFeudalists in an adversarial way. I don't think, for example, that Elon Musk is wicked or evil. That's just not true. Elon is ruthless, but he is not evil. He actually wants to do good, and he's actually open to a new possibility—and it's a possibility that we, as culture, haven't provided.

Harari, as a populist and an extremely effective and insightful raconteur and cultural critic, ranges over a wide movement in history, in which he is not always the expert. But he's an effective and insightful person and, I think, a good person; and he's presenting this vision of collapse. He assumes that there is no value that's real, and therefore no Stories of Value that are real.

Where does this deconstruction of value come from?

Now, he is wrong. He is making any number of dogmatic assumptions. There's also a major set of flaws in value theory that haven't been solved (we've tried to crack through them in *First Principles and First Values*, which he is not aware of, particularly the relationship between eternal and evolving value). And there's a whole set of understandings of what we mean by *value is real* that he doesn't have available. It's not his field, but it's not really even available in philosophy. **Philosophy is stuck in a postmodern moment, which implicitly assumes moral relativism:** that value is ultimately not real. Even the moral realists say that you can make real moral statements based on evolutionary selection, but that there's no real quality of value in the Cosmos.

There are huge flaws in value theory itself, and in understandings of the Field of Ethos and the Field of Eros, and how Cosmos works, and there are flawed understandings of biology, and flawed understandings in chemistry and molecular chemistry. And Yuval, being a generalist reader, reads those conclusions and assumptions in the mainstream of the academy— its superficial reductionist assumptions. He can't (like any human being) go all the way deeply and transform all those fields, so he is stuck in collecting those reductive materialist assumptions, and doesn't know how to penetrate them.

It's my job—our job at the Center—to penetrate those fields and literally crack through values, re-understand biology, and re-understand molecular chemistry. Those are all the things we're trying to do—a major re-visioning of the world of life, and the world of matter, and the relationship between matter and life and the depth of mind. That's not Yuval's job. That's our job. And Yuval and I need to have a conversation about this in a deeper way.

But there is something that the postmodern zeitgeist gets right in its deconstruction of value. When I say *they are right*, I don't mean *ultimately* right. But what is it that resonates deeply in their souls, hearts, and bodies, that allows Yuval to come to these conclusions?

If we skip that, if I don't address that, then we're basically fundamentalists ourselves. If your interlocutor is serious and you can't understand how he got there, how he came to those insane conclusions—if I cannot feel what he feels—then we are not intimate.

I wrote a chapter about this in 2001 called "The Path of the Void" in a book called *Uncertainty*, written in Hebrew in 2001. The void has been a major theme in my own understanding of Reality and my own teaching over the last 20 to 25 years.

THE PERSONAL EXPERIENCE OF VOID BEGINS WITH BETRAYAL

There are two moments of the void: a personal void, and a collective void— and they're deeply related to each other. What do I do when I encounter the personal void? And what is the feeling of the personal void?

It's a place where I can't find my way. I am suffering beyond suffering. My spirit feels broken. I feel like I'm out of control. I"m spiraling down. I can't find my joy. It all seems too much. It all seems so radically unfair, so radically wrong, so radically unkind. I am exhausted beyond exhausted. I can't find my energy. I can't find my aliveness. I feel so unseen, so irrelevant, so profoundly lonely and unmet.

The void is anti-erotic.

According to our interior science equation, Eros is the experience of radical aliveness, reaching for ever deeper contact and ever greater wholeness.

That's the experience of Eros. The void is anti-erotic. **The void is the matrix of depression, and the internal animating structure of depression is futility**: I can't have an impact, and it doesn't matter. I have no power to change or to impact, and it's futile. The whole thing doesn't matter. That's the void.

We often cite Camus; his book, *The Stranger*, begins: *Mother died today, or was it yesterday?*

- ◆ Mother is Eros.
- ◆ Mother is the experience of presence.
- ◆ Mother is the experience that it matters.
- ◆ Mother is the experience of being held.
- ◆ Mother is the experience of being welcome in Cosmos.

In the experience of the void, there is no mother. *Mother died today, or was it yesterday?* But at some point, the Mother died, and I no longer felt welcome in Cosmos. What Camus is saying is, if I can cite Steiner, *Strangers are we, errants at the gates of our own psyche.*

Meursault, Camus' main character, is speaking personally (*My* mother died today, or was it yesterday?)—and he's speaking as the collective, as the culture. Mother died today or yesterday, but at some point, mother died.

At some point, we entered the void.

At some point, we couldn't find our way through.

The personal void and the collective void are deeply related to each other.

What triggers the experience of the void?

The personal void is triggered by betrayal, when I feel betrayed by the mother:

- ◆ The mother who's supposed to hold me
- ◆ The mother who's supposed to love me
- ◆ The mother who's supposed to protect me

Sometimes the mother is a biological mother, and sometimes the mother is a brother, and sometimes the mother is a husband, and sometimes the mother is a son or a daughter, or the mother is myself. Many people play the role of the mother. The mother is the place where I am welcome, where

I can rest, where I am held. **The mother is the realization that every place I fall, I fall into Her hands.** When the mother dies in my life, when I feel betrayed by the mother, the experience of betrayal triggers futility.

It could be that I've been in a community my entire life, and then something happens in the community, and somehow I'm thrown out of the community. The community that I poured into and I built in my blood, and my sweat, and my tears; the signature of my deepest soul essence, the signature of my deepest yearning, the signature of all of my holy and broken Hallelujahs is inscribed in the teachings of the blood that are supposed to be the core of this community. And then, all of a sudden I find myself on the outside.

In the experience of betrayal, even though it looks like I've dealt with it, and it looks like I've worked with it, and it looks like I've got it together—I don't. It throws me into the void. I am catapulted into different realities, and I can't find my way home. I had an image of what it's going to mean to have a son. I am going to pour my energy, I am going to educate the world, and I am going to give a transmission to the next generation, and my son or my daughter, they are going to carry on. And then my son doesn't understand me. My daughter doesn't understand me. They might betray me overtly, or they might take very good care of me, yet leaving me profoundly lonely and unseen by those I'm desperate to be seen by.

When trust is broken early on, that's what we call early childhood trauma. Early childhood trauma is the recognition of the betrayal by those that we trust most:

- To hold us in our aliveness
- To hold us in our goodness
- To hold us in the purity of our Eros

And yet, we are not held. We don't experience Reality being attuned to us.

We put our best self forward, our most vital energy—and it's rejected, denied, mocked, ridiculed. And this experience is repeated again and again and again through life. We are bullied. It's unfair. Where are the school authorities? Why did I get bullied?

And we are all betrayed. **There is no one who is not potentially Christ, and there is no one who doesn't meet Judas.** And there is no one who, at some moment in their life, was not Judas.

We've got to get over being Judas, and we've got to start being Christ, but we can do that only by realizing that the beginning of our *religio*, of our *religare,* and of our finding our way home—of our reconnecting into the gorgeousness of our lives—is to realize that we begin the act of *religio*, of finding our way home, in response to betrayal.

EVERYTHING EMERGES FROM THE ENCOUNTER WITH THE VOID

It always begins with betrayal.

The Garden of Eden is a story of betrayal. It's just not clear who betrayed who. Did Adam betray Eve by not standing with her? Did Eve betray Adam by giving him the apple, which was against the command? Did God betray Adam and Eve by putting them in a no-win garden with a snake? Who's betraying who? Was the snake betrayed, because man refused to talk to him and only Eve was willing to begin a conversation?

But the story of the Garden of Eden, however we tell that story, is a story of betrayal. This great journey of the Solomon lineage begins, in this great historical epic, this great mythology (but mythology in the sense of being more than history, not less than history), with the story of a betrayal, the story of a fall, the story of a murder, the story of a fratricide. Was it *sapiens* killing Neanderthals? One brother killing another brother?

And it begins in the void. Everything emerges from the encounter with the void.

Either I am lost in the void or I find my way through, but it's all about the void.

I either engage in a-void-dance—I dance around the void by denying it—or I dance around the void to the doomer response. The doomer response is really also a way to avoid the void. To engage the void means that I'm going *to become*, I'm going to step in, in the middle of the night—as Jacob does when he encounters the stranger, and he wrestles with the stranger. He's in the middle of the night; he's by himself. He's about to meet his brother, in chapter 32 of the *Book of Genesis*.

He sends all of the family away. He says, I need to be by myself in this night, in the depth of the void, before I meet my brother in the morning. In the depth of that night, a stranger comes. We don't know the stranger's name. The stranger wrestles with him and wounds his inner thigh. He limps the rest of his life. He is profoundly wounded. And yet, out of that wounding, out of the depth of that night, Jacob (the word Jacob, Yaakov, means *the crooked one*) becomes Israel, Yashar El, the one who is straight, who is throbbing and powerful.

He doesn't leave his crookedness behind. He's called Jacob again later. We always include and transcend our crookedness. **Our holy and our broken *Hallelujah* becomes holy *only* when it includes the broken.** When Moses breaks the tablets in the *Book of Exodus*, and then he goes up again on the mountain and receives a second pair of tablets, the sacred lineage says that *luchot v'shivrei luchot munachim ba'Aron, the tablets and the broken tablets are both in the Ark.*

What does it mean to move through the void?

There's always a void.

I'm always going to be broken.

I'm always going to be betrayed.

Mother is always going to die.

Mother is always going to die personally—and, at this moment in history, there's going to be a moment where mother dies collectively. Meaning, the old truths will be challenged. That's the void.

Many, many times, we've talked about this and I want to bring it to the table—because you can't understand postmodernity if you don't understand that postmodernity is experiencing the void in the deepest way.

Again, the void is real. **Before we fill up the void, before we find our way through the void, we need to take the void seriously.**

When Mother dies, I'm crushed:

- You cannot cheat grief.
- You cannot cheat the tears.
- You cannot shortchange the broken *Hallelujah*.

Hallelujah is *hallel, pristine praise*, and *Yah!*—the breath of the Divine, the perfect world.

And *Hallelujah* is also, in the same original Hebrew, *holelut, drunken intoxication*—because I've fallen into the void, and I can't find my way through. You cannot avoid the fullness of *Hallelujah*. I've got to be willing to embrace the void, to be in the void.

That's the first step. There's no a-void-dance. **You can't dance around the void; Mother died, and I need to be willing to experience the full pain of betrayal.**

And remember, you can be betrayed only by those people, or those institutions, or those knowings that you thought could never betray you. And then you are betrayed.

We are all betrayed, my friends. We are all betrayed. Not because the world is a dark and horrific place.

298

The world is filled with darkness and light.

The world is filled with *tremendum*—and with terror.

The world is filled with unimaginable dignity and divinity—and with devastation.

The world is filled with beauty—and the world is sometimes filled with the degraded beast, the *demon* that's gotten cut off from the *daemon*, the angel that becomes demon, who falls from heaven. The Lucifer that lives within; it is always: I'm cut off from heaven. I'm cut off from my roots. I'm in the void. And in the void, I go demonic. I go Luciferian.

Devils are real. But devils are not people with pitchforks. Devils are what Scott Peck called, in the *People of the Lie*, the dimensions of us that lose their ability to feel. We cannot feel anymore. We shut down. The void is too painful. We cannot access our aliveness. Moreover, we actually begin to think and feel:

- That there's no aliveness
- That there's no Eros
- That there's nothing to access
- That there's only *matter*—not *what* matters
- That it's a tale told by an idiot, full of sound and fury and signifying nothing
- That tomorrow is going nowhere, because there's no place to go

TZIMTZUM: THE SPACE OF THE VOID THAT IS SACRED CONVERSATION

In some sense, the depth realization of the Solomon lineage was the realization that you have to take the void seriously. The lineage of the erotic mystics whose mystery schools animated the Renaissance, the teachers of Pico della Mirandola and Ficino, were the erotic mystics of the Solomon lineage. They talk deeply about this realization that *leit atar panui mi'mei*, "there's no place devoid of presence."

No place devoid of presence.

There is no void—it's all filled with sacred conversation. The hills are alive.

All of matter is filled with what matters. *She* is everywhere. Look behind you, and *She* is there. Look inside you, and *She* is there. Look in front of you, and *She* is there. *She* is always there.

And yet, the erotic mystics tell the following story:

The world is filled with absolute *no-thingness*. The world is suffused, the world is full—absolute, radical divinity, infinite value, and radical aliveness. **And then, in order to allow for the possibility of transformation, for the possibility of gifting, for the possibility of a new emergent goodness, for the possibility of the possible human—Infinity, resting in itself, felt this desire to give this gift, and only in giving this gift could it actually feel full intimacy.**

It had the infinite desire to gift, and the infinite desire to be intimate, and the infinite desire to be more, and the infinite desire to somehow grow.

But how can the Infinite grow?

There are no complete sets of axioms in mathematics. This is what Gödel actually showed. There's always more to come. There's more possibility to come. But the only way I can have more possibility to come is—and this is the lineage's deep erotic realization—to step back, empty myself out. If I'm the Infinite Divine, I must make room for you, just like a parent has to step back and make room and make space for the child, even if the child chooses against the parent. The teacher has to be an artist, who steps back and lets the canvas breathe, and lets the canvas speak, and lets the art emerge, and doesn't just impose their will on the canvas.

There is something that wants to emerge, and we've got to step back.

Luria in the sixteenth century plays with this very deep realization dance, where he says something like:

> When I love madly, if I love madly enough, I am going to step back and make room for you. I love my child so much, I'm going to let her choose.

> And even if you choose against me, I love you so much that I'm going to honor your choice, even if that choice seems to be, for a moment, against me.

That's called *tzimtzum,* Divine contraction, withdrawal, *kenosis.*

I empty myself out because I love you so madly. I don't know how many of you have ever had an argument with a beloved. One of the hardest things to do in the heat of an argument is to bracket yourself. Stop. Bracket. Stop. Take myself out of my feeling tone, out of my early stuff, out of my defensiveness—and actually listen. It's insanely hard. But the only thing that allows us to do it is mad love.

Mad love allows me to bracket myself to make space for you. That's *tzimtzum.*

There is this emptying out. There is the space of the void.

All metaphysics lives inside of us. All theology is only logic that reflects Divinity (*theo*); by finding it, I can discern it in the story of my divine life. That's the "divine life" Aurobindo was writing about. It's in me. Here it isl it's in me. Now, if I bracket myself, if God withdraws, that means there's a space that's empty of the Divine, and then God penetrates that space, as it were—Divinity, Infinity, the Infinite Intimate. The Infinite penetrates that space with this shaft of intimacy, the shaft penetrates the circle, the circle rides the shaft—and this line and circle come together and explode into Reality, in which again, *Leit Atar Panuy Mimei, There's no place devoid of She.* That's the creative process.

POSTMODERNITY IS THE EXPERIENCE OF THE VOID

Now, is that void real? Is that real?

Is She really not there? Is She really absent? Did She really empty Herself out, or is She actually there, but hidden? The fancy way of saying it is: *Is this act of Divine emptying epistemological or ontological?* But you don't need fancy ways to say things. Ontological means *for realsies*, meaning it's real. This is a real emptying out. The space is really empty. Or is it epistemological, that is, it just looks like the space is empty, but it's not?

If you have kids in this lifetime, or you've seen someone else or you've talked to someone else who has, you know there's this moment when you are teaching your kid to walk. I can remember that moment. You stand behind your kid and you let go—and at that moment when you let go, you're more there than you've ever been before. Isn't that crazy?

You've stepped back. It looks like you're absent, but you're actually more present than you've ever been before. That's the way the erotic mystics of the Solomon lineage generally understand this Divine emptying out.

But did the void disappear?

Was the void absolutely filled up?

Or is there still a dimension of Reality that we encounter that is the void? Not an ultimate ontology, but an appearance, an experience of the ontology of the void, where I just can't find myself, where I just don't know how to get through, where I am overwhelmed, I am shut down, I can't find my voice, I can't find my energy, I can't find my goodness, I can't find my sweetness, I can't find decency—and I want to find it desperately, but I can't find it.

Is that just that I am pathological? And if we would just medicate that properly, we can *pharmacologize* the void. So we pathologize the void, and then we pharmacologize it.

But no! And that's what Krishnamurti meant when he said, *don't feel so good about being so sane, so normal, so healthy in a sick society.* It's not such a great achievement to be sane in an insane society, when I don't feel the insanity. I don't feel the void. **There's a moment where I've got to feel the void—and collectively, that's the moment of postmodernity**.

Postmodernity has this experience that Mother died. Mother died. Was it today or was it yesterday? But Mother died. Mother died. And where is she? Where is she?

Luria, the great erotic mystic of the sixteenth century, says, you have a flask and it was filled with wine, and it's now empty—and in that emptiness is the void.

Postmodernity has this experience that there were these great cathedrals of value. Notre Dame reopens in Europe, and everyone is excited that Notre Dame reopens. But no one goes to any of these cathedrals in Europe. Why is everybody so excited, a week and a half ago, that Notre Dame opened in France? Why are people excited about royalty in Great Britain, which has become a caricature of itself? Because royalty is the experience we were chosen by the Divine. Even though we don't believe the royal story, we have the sense that there *might be* royalty, even though the castles of Europe are empty, and the great cathedrals of Europe are empty. They are tourist attractions. There is no prayer in them, even if there are a couple of priests who are still doing prayer.

Notre Dame is corrupt and empty, and yet, we yearn for Notre Dame— and so, all the dignitaries of the world flocked to Paris to see: Oh wait, Notre Dame is here. Notre Dame has been rebuilt because we are reaching out for Notre Dame from the void—but we have to first recognize the void. Postmodernity is the experience of the void. That's how I tried to write about it in 2002—to say that we have to take the void seriously. There is a path of the void.

Postmodernity is not just an expression of "cultural materialism" (as Jordan Peterson thinks). That's sometimes true, but there's also something real. **Postmodernity wouldn't have ground if it wasn't saying something**

that didn't live inside of us. There is a moment where I can't find it. I am overwhelmed. I can't get there. The void is real.

Yuval Harari is holding that moment. Postmodernity is holding that moment. When it talks about there being no value, it relates it back to all sorts of cultural forces, or to evolutionary selection:

> The human being evolved in an accidental universe, in a particular way because accidentally there was a drive for life. And therefore, we, over millennia, develop these evolutionary intuitions, which are universal, that we call morality. But it's all made up. There is a universal morality, but it's made up.

> Either it's purely socially contrived—and it's not universal, it's subjective, everyone makes up their own—or there might even be a universal morality, but it's made up; it is contrived in its essence, because the whole thing is an accident. It's not reflective of any quality of the Cosmos.

This notion comes from this place where I confront the utter pain and absurdity of this dimension of existence.

This world is outrageously beautiful. It's also outrageously painful and outrageously unjust.

AN ENTIRE GENERATION IS THRUST INTO THE VOID

Sometimes, an entire generation is thrust into the void.

It used to be that I knew only about the suffering around my town, in my village. If I lived in Holland, I might have some neighbor who has a cousin, who has an uncle who works for the Dutch West Indies Company, which is one of the most brutal oppressors and destroyers of human beings that ever lived. But I am living in Amsterdam in the fifteenth, sixteenth century, and my neighborhood might be bad, and there might be some prostitutes that were killed because they had debts, and some terrible things may happen around me. But that's all I see. I see a very narrow band of suffering, and somehow I can deal with that. Somehow I can find my way through it, as horrible as it is.

But what if I'm in the twentieth century?

It's after World War I. The Darwinians are reigning, and the old dogmas of religion are getting exploded. It's clear that religion overreached and made claims that were incorrect. Penicillin is sweeping prayer away in people's understanding. There's this sense of this imminent progress, that human beings need to take it into their own hands. And then I'm wildly overwhelmed by a level of suffering that I have direct access to—which, before World War I, only God knew about. As the information technologies grew during the twentieth century, our staring in the face of brutal suffering began to get a God's level of omniscience. And we already have omni-benevolence in us. We already have God's love in us.

We love. We see. But we are not omnipotent. We have no potency. We have no power to affect it—and so we are just overwhelmed with images of suffering in the twentieth century, in a way that never was true before in human history.

Of course the postmodern moment is going to enter the story. It doesn't enter the story solely because of wrong interpretations of biology or physics. That's part of it—but there is this sense that we're actually confronting evil. It's in our faces, and we see it, and we are driven into the void.

At the same time, there is a dislocation of the human being, because I can't rest in the discarded image of the traditional world, as C.S. Lewis called it. I don't have an easy and obvious answer to the question of my place in the Cosmos. I realize the vastness of the Cosmos. I realize it's not just planet Earth. It's a hundred billion galaxies.

Side by side with the utter, unbearable intimacy of suffering, on the one hand, and the breakdown of the classical categories of self-understanding, on the other, I realize there are a hundred billion galaxies. There are billions of light years to the universe. **The vastness leads to this sense**

of insignificance, and the insignificance merges together with the breakdown of the old structures of knowing, together with the direct experience of radical suffering at a virtually divine level of omniscience.

All of those birth the re-experience of the void. That's ultimately the root of the postmodern moment.

There was a moment I was in an elevator in the Brown Palace in Denver, Colorado, where I first met a young gentleman, a very compact, short man who's done some beautiful work in the world. He's done some beautiful opening up of Reality, particularly Eastern Kashmir Shaivites structures. His name is Deepak Chopra.

We are in this elevator, and we happen to meet each other, and we start chatting. I happened to have a book that I'd written back then called *Soul Prints*. I gave him a copy, and we stayed in touch. At a certain point, he said, *I want to send you this book I just did with Leonard Mlodinow called War of the Worldviews.* Mlodinow is a physicist at Caltech, and Deepak had been doing a dialogue there on spirit versus science, and it didn't go well. Mlodinow was in the audience and publicly challenged Deepak's readings of physics, and Deepak was graceful, and creative, and beautiful. He said, *Well, teach me physics. Let's study physics together.* So they did. And they wrote this book, *War of the Worldviews*, where Mlodinow is presenting classical, materialist, reductionist physics, and Deepak is doing classical Kashmir Shaivism, and they don't impact each other at all (which is why they call the book *War of the Worldviews*).

Now, you would expect that conversation would've gone further, but it didn't go anywhere. It's very subtle; it's very beautiful. There is a place in the book where Mlodinow tells the story about his mother, who is in a death camp. It's a winter, freezing day. And the commandant of this Nazi death camp has ten people kneel in the snow, and he walks behind them with a revolver, and randomly kills five. You don't know if he's going to kill you or not; his mother was in that chain of ten.

Mlodinow writes in that passage (and it's a passing passage, just a story that obviously came to him as he was writing this particular point), *I have nothing to do with such a God. You're telling me about this good God? Like really? I want out of this conversation. I'm not interested.* And that's also Dostoevsky in *Brothers Karamazov*; in certain passages, he holds that position.

TAKING THE VOID SERIOUSLY

There are schools of erotic mystics in Sufism, and in Christianity, and in Vajrayana, and in Shingon Buddhism. Erotic mystics are always about taking the void seriously. That's one of their principles. **Paradoxically, they are *erotic* mystics because they're so committed to walking through the void—and they talk about how to find your way through the void.**

One of them is Nachman of Breslov, the Hasidic master, student of the Baal Shem Tov, son of Eliezer and Sarah, Master of the Good Name, the founder of the erotic, mystical Hasidic movement that swept throughout Europe in the latter half of the eighteenth century, one of Kafka's favorite writers. He wrote an essay on the "path of the void," where he says that you've got to take the divine emptying-out seriously.

You have to take the void seriously.

You can't find your way around it.

You have to walk through.

There's an experience of the void that's real. If you get the ontology of the human being, you know something about the Reality of the world. There are moments that I experience the void, and the void is real. In that void—in those hardest moments—I can't find *Her*. I'm exhausted, I'm devastated, I'm decimated, and I'm hurt. I am traumatized, and I can't find my way. That's the void.

Nachman is saying that as part of being a *Homo religiosus*, as part of being a human being who is *in* the Field of Value, I need to experience and take the void seriously.

Paradoxically, that's exactly what Harari does, but then that becomes his entire moment.

That becomes the whole story—but that's not the whole story.

The whole story is actually a CosmoErotic Universe that's filled with Eros, that's moving towards intimacy, with billions of acts of wild kindness and goodness and integrity and wonder and wholeness, which evoke radical amazement and unbearable beauty beyond measure, which suffuse all of Reality.

The Sound of Music got it right. The hills are alive with the sound of music. It's not in church; it's not in grandiose and empty cathedrals. That's not where She lives. She lives *everywhere*—She's in the brooks and the babbling waters, and in the rivers, and She's in the air that makes love with the thrust of birds that move through it. It's an entire Field of Radical Aliveness in which life itself is the value of Reality. It's a multidimensional Reality, which clearly doesn't exhaust itself in one world, which moves through cycles, moving through time, in which you don't have to search for meaning because everything is meaningful. The whole thing is meaningful on thousands of levels, self-evidently, but also philosophically. It's all meaning.

Postmodernity displaces all of that meaning and is therefore completely stuck in the void. Camus: *Mother died today or was it yesterday? And it doesn't matter.* But of course it matters!

308

In the end, the horror at suffering doesn't locate us in the void, because in the end, the horror itself is She. It's so deep.

Why am I horrified?

What's so horrible in a materialist, accidental, reductive, meaningless Cosmos, which is *a tale told by an idiot, full of sound and fury, signifying nothing, in which tomorrow and tomorrow creeps in its petty pace, day after day to the last syllable of recorded time?*

What's the problem?

Of course, you've got crazy, power-intoxicated Nazi commandants who walk behind people because they're intoxicated by their power and they shoot a bunch of people. Big deal. Genghis Khan did shit like that all the time. Why is anybody even moved by this?

Because as we deepen, and as we come into deeper and deeper senses of what it means to be *Homo amor*—a human being who incarnates the entire Field of Love, of Reality in me, as me, and through me—we are horrified by the violation. It's a violation of the Intimate Universe, because evil is a failure of intimacy. **You can only talk about evil as a failure of intimacy.** *Evil* is *live* backwards.

Eros is aliveness. Reality is radically alive. Reality moves towards aliveness. Evil is a violation of aliveness. It's a deadness. It's an ennui. That's why the orcs and the Eye of Sauron in Tolkien's vision of this are all about death.

Why are we yearning for life?

Because life is value itself and evil stands against aliveness.

Evil is a failure. Suffering is a failure. Suffering is a failure of intimacy.

If I didn't live in the Intimate Universe, and if the Intimate Universe didn't live in me, then the entire neoliberal order with its good ethics would make no sense. That sensibility is rooted in the sensuality of the lived experience of the Intimate Universe that allows me to do sensemaking.

HOW DO YOU WALK THROUGH THE VOID?

How do we walk through the void? What's the way through?

Nachman tells this story of Moses. Moses, a Solomon lineage mystic figure in the Book of Exodus, is the one who communicates with the Infinite and receives the way, receives what's called the *halacha*—the way, the law animated by love.

In this mystical story, Moses is on a very deep journey. He transcends the boundaries of time, and he finds his way into the first century, a couple of decades after Jesus has died, and he sees this great figure, Akiva. Akiva is a mad lover; the great master of his time. Akiva is the one who said that all the books are holy, but the Song of Solomon is the Holy of Holies—the Song of Songs, the story of Outrageous Love notes between a lover and the beloved, the great erotic love story is the most sacred text.

The Holy of Holies is the name of the inner sanctum of the Jerusalem temple, where two cherubs are erotically entwined with each other. Solomon says, there is a Holy of Holies in the temple, and he places in the Holy of Holies these erotically intertwisted cherubs above the Ark of the Covenant. And then, Akiva says, the temple has been destroyed, and we need a new temple. His new temple is the bed of Eros, the bed of the lovers, the bed of sexual communion—in whatever form. Sexual communion is not about just moving the energy up and down or yoga practices—as important as they are. **Sexual communion is the direct experience in the body that you are living in the Field of Outrageous Love.**

The Field of Outrageous Love is the prior condition. Outrageous Love is the love *before* creation. It's not the love that's responsive to a particular event. It's the love that's the heart of existence itself. It's the love of the prior condition. It's Outrageous Love. It's the love that everything arises within. It's the Eros Value that all of Reality arises within.

In the experience of erotic communion:

- I actually *am* Outrageous Love.
- I *am* the prior condition.
- I *am* the CosmoErotic Universe in person.

And that's actually the ultimate experience of this new Story of Value that we are telling and sharing together here in *One Mountain, Many Paths*—what we call *CosmoErotic Humanism*, the new Story of Value that can take us through the void. The core of this new Story of Value is that the human being becomes the CosmoErotic Universe in person:

- One of the ways to do that is through sexual communion, through the cherubs above the Ark.
- Another way to do that is through the creative act of Ark.
- And another way to do that is through the wild ecstasy of parenting.
- And another way to do that is through the depth of radical Outrageous Love friendship.

But I actually become it—I become Outrageous Love in person. It's deep, it's crazy, it's wild.

So, Moses traverses through time on his mystical journey, and he sees Akiva, who is the greatest sage that ever lived. And Moses says to the Divine,

> If you have a human being like this, who is so stunning, and so gorgeous, and so realized that he is the ultimate erotic mystic, why would you give the Torah—the way, the great revelation—through me? I'm nothing. I'm nothing.

And God says,

> Quiet, it's yours to receive the Torah on Sinai in the original story of the lineage, and it's Akiva's to live his life.

And Moses says,

> Well, what happens to him?

And then he sees, on his medicine journey, the scene in which Akiva—the chalice of love, the incarnation of Eros—is betrayed. He is betrayed, and his whole world is falling apart. He is being tortured by the Romans. And his students ask him, *Akiva, didn't you teach us V'Ahavta et Adonai Elohecha, love God madly? Can you love God madly in this?*

He says, *Yes, this is my ultimate moment to be a mad lover.*

And he cries out, *Adonai Echad, The Divinity of all Cosmos is one (Adonai, the Divinity of all Cosmos, echad, one).*

The word *one* is 13. There are three letters, and each letter has a numerical value. One is 13. And the word *ahava*, four letters, is also 13. They have the same numerical value. One and love are the same. When I explode in artistic ecstasy and I emerge, *basar echad, we become one flesh.* It's the movement of intimate communion where we don't disappear into fusion, but we disappear into this larger union of the One. *And you shall be one flesh*—erotic, intimate communion.

This is what Moses sees. As Akiva is taking his last breath, he cries out, *It's one. I am madly in love. I am madly in love.* Then the text says, *yatza nishmato b'echad*—as he said, *one love, it's one love, he breathed his last.* And Moses is devastated. And Moses says, *zu Torah v'zu schara? This is wisdom and this is its reward?* Moses says, *This is the void. There is no truth here. This is the void. It's all just a story. It's all just fiction. It's all just made up.*

And the Divine voice says, *Shtok. Kach alah b'machshava, be silent, so it was decreed before Me.*

In the simple reading, it would be a religious demand for faith. But that's not how the erotic mystics read it. They read it as the Infinite Intimate, God, turning to Moses and saying, *Shtok, Enter into the mad love that you experience in the depth of silence. And when you do that (kach, through that) alah b'machshava, you shall rise up. Machshava means mind.*

The Divine says, *Through silence, you will become one with the mind-heart of God.*

LOVE IS NOT HARD TO FIND—LOVE IS IMPOSSIBLE TO AVOID

There is a way through the void, and the way through the void is in the silence of presence, which is the song of the love story. You are sitting with someone you love madly. It could be a child. It could be yourself in the best moment. It could be a friend. It could be a partner. It could be someone you are creating with. And you've been deep inside. Then at some moment, the words fall away, and you are sitting together in silence, and words are unnecessary. You don't need them anymore.

Now, this is the story that happened to me. It was one of the most important moments in my life.

> *I am in Jerusalem, and I am walking late at night near the walls of the old city of Jerusalem. I am carrying a bunch of books, because I've just finished a talk; it's the dark side streets of a neighborhood called Yemin Moshe, this artistic colony right outside the walls of the old city of Jerusalem. And I feel this energy—it just blows me backwards. I look up, and I see this couple who were erotically engaged, and they didn't see me; I saw them. I should have looked away, but I didn't. I went into the corner.*
>
> *He must have been like 179 years old; the oldest person I've ever seen. She couldn't have been a day less than 176. And they walked so slow, they were walking backwards. And there were no words exchanged between them. They were just walking. And it was like I had met the king and queen. And then she trips a little bit. I look down. They don't see me. He looks down, she looks down, and they see that her shoelace is untied. And he slowly bends down. It was the archetype of arthritis at his hands. And it takes him three, four full minutes to finish tying her shoe—and she is standing, regally, a queen.*
>
> *Had I stepped out of the shadows to tie the shoe, they probably would have killed me with just a glance. I didn't have that right. He*

gets up and there is this moment when they are face-to-face, and they exchange a glance, no words, silence of presence.

All of the infinite love in the world was there, and all of the void, and all of the brokenness, and all of the broken vessels, and all of the broken hearts, and all of the betrayals, and all of the betrayals of the mother, and all of the fear, and all of the shattering. It was all in that look, and they stayed in, and they found each other again, and again, and again. And every holy and broken *Hallelujah* led to the next level of depth. And they stayed in, they stayed, they stayed.

And they stepped into this post-tragic truth:

- That it *all* matters, that you don't have to search for meaning—because it's all meaningful, that it's never *not*, that there's no place that it's not.
- And you don't have to search for love. Love's not hard to find. Love is impossible to avoid. Reality is shimmering and alive.
- And even my brokenness is a portal to the promise because I wouldn't be broken if it wasn't whole. And my heart wouldn't close if it didn't yearn to open. And I wouldn't be exhausted if I didn't know the sweet nectar of the energy and Eros of contact and aliveness.

It's all ever always already true. It's ever always already true. It's ever always already on the Inside of the Inside.

Eternity breathes Eros.

Eternity breathes meaning.

Eternity breathes goodness in every moment.

But I cannot find my way through a conceptual structure, although there is place for conceptual structures.

I cannot find my way only through distinctions, although we need distinctions.

And I cannot find my way through identifying the plotlines of Reality out there.

I need to go so deep inside, and to have direct access to taste the goodness, and the joy, and the insane crazy pleasure of just being here together, right now.

And in that look that they exchanged—that couple that were older than old, on that back road, that back alley of Jerusalem near midnight outside the walls, the lit-up walls of the old city of Jerusalem that survived for thousands of years, that itself is part of the holy and broken *Hallelujah*— She is always right there. It's always right there. There is no place to go.

IT'S A LOVE STORY, AND IT'S FILLED WITH MYSTERY

The jug breaks, the water trickles, and I'm awake. In every breaking, there is a breaking open.

There is no void unless there is a dance. I step into the void, and I dance, and I dance. That's the point. That's what dance means. The word for dance in Hebrew is *machol. Machol* means the empty space, the void. *Mechilot* is the empty space or a wind instrument, which is empty on the inside. It's called the *chalil.* The void space is the empty space. The word *mechilot* means void. And the way I move through the void is *machol,* dance.

- I dance through the void. I sit in the silence of presence through the void.
- I become the artist of dance.
- I become the artist of silence.
- I become the artist of song.

Why is the world filled with love songs? Crazy songs, crazy, silly love songs, off tune, on tune, all over the world, China, and South America, and Argentina, and Brazil, and Africa, all through the States, and Mexico, and Canada, and all through Russia. It's all love songs. And it's all about mother.

The one Russian song that I know goes like this:

Let there always be sun
Let there always be sky
Let there always be mama
Let there always be me

It's always mama. It's always blue skies. It's always sun. It's always you.

It's always right here. I walk through the void, not through conceptual structures. **I walk through the void by walking through the void,** and just looking in the eyes of my daughter, in the eyes of my beloved, whoever my beloved is, or I look in the mirror. I'm on a plane, and I look in the mirror, and the plane mirrors are great because they're not the ordinary mirrors of your house, where you can't see anything. You look in a plane mirror, you're surprised, there you are. And you look in the eyes of you, and *She* is always there.

How do I walk through the void?

- I walk through the void through song.
- I walk through the void through the silence of presence, which is the depth of love, mad love.
- I walk through the void through mad love.
- And I walk through the void through dance. I dance through the void.
- I walk through the void through art.

These are all part of the same realization. The realization is that it's a love story. And there's agony, and there's ecstasy.

Postmodernity was right. It said, **for it to be a love story, you've got to be willing to be in the mystery.** That's what postmodernity was reaching for. That's what it was right about.

We've got to throw out the old plotlines.

We got to throw out the dogmas.

We've got to throw out the old lies that lived in the story, the canards, the fictions. **Underneath all the fictions, underneath all the dogmas, is the *dharma*. And the *dharma* is simple: it's a love story.**

And how do I know it? Because it lives and breathes in me. When I love, I am home. When I love, I welcome the world home, and I am welcomed home. When I am in a love story, that love story becomes a *Welcome Home* sign, and I become a Welcome Home sign. That's *Homo amor*. That's the love story. That's the way through. It's the only way through the void.

The void is not an accident. The void is not a bug in Cosmos. I have no fucking idea why. And anyone who tells you they can tell you *why* there's a void is lying. Don't listen to a word they say.

We need to be heretics when it comes to that kind of faith. We need holy heresy, where we deny and reject the faith that's small. That's what postmodernity did.

The void is real—and it's not. And it's not. And it's more than one dimension. And we find our way through. In the end, it's all a love story. And then we fall back in the void. And then we get up and we realize it's all a love story.

If we dance around the void, we become fundamentalists. We get lost in dogmatic certainties, whether they are the dogmatic certainties of fundamentalism or not. If we're trying to dance around the void, or if we stay only in the void, we get lost in the dogmatic claims of certainty of scientism (not science, but scientism)—the dogmatic denial, which says there is *only* void.

Neither of those are true. It's a love story. And the love story is filled with mystery. It's filled with agony and ecstasy, but I know it's a love story.

- I breathe it.
- I live it.
- It sings me.
- It dances me.

317

INDEX

A

Abhinavagupta, 5
abyss, 44, 285
Adam, xv, 50, 184, 296
Adonai, 312
Akiva, 310, 311, 312
All-That-Is, xxix, 44, 108, 226, 227, 276
allurement, xix, xxxvi, xxxviii, 2, 4, 5, 27, 35, 129, 145, 152, 153, 154, 157, 165, 166, 171, 172, 173, 175, 178, 236, 237, 238, 239
aloneness, 29
Amorous Cosmos, 24, 50, 145
anthro-ontological, xxx
anti-erotic, 293
archetype, 313
Ark of the Covenant, 287, 310
arousal, 171, 223, 224, 225
Atar, 301
atoms, 31, 32, 33, 34, 36, 54, 66, 274
attraction, 145, 166, 173
Aurobindo, Sri, 301
autonomy, 8, 94, 98, 99, 145, 165, 173, 175, 182, 236, 272
Avinu Malkeinu, 86
avodah, 51
avra, 43
awaken, xxix, 14, 21, 30, 45

B

bara, 192
beauty, xxvi, xlii, 39, 43, 81, 85, 100, 117, 120, 121, 147, 155, 161, 165, 184, 196, 210, 229, 235, 259, 263, 269, 281, 299, 308
betray, 207, 248, 251, 295, 296, 298
Big Bang, 54, 145, 236
biosphere, 36, 61, 160, 193, 239
blood, 196, 295
Bohm, David, 223
Book of Exodus, 297, 310
brain, 57, 196, 206
breath, 21, 298, 312
Buddhism, xx, 5, 6, 59, 135, 307
bypass, 48, 79, 80, 217

C

calling, 11, 47, 73, 98, 246, 265, 282
Campbell, Joseph, 217
Camus, 185, 294, 308
catastrophic risk, 18, 40, 47, 75, 85, 123, 125, 140, 141, 258
Cathars, 5, 6
certainty, 33, 41, 61, 76, 95, 129, 152, 176, 216, 256, 274, 289, 291, 306, 307, 317
challenges, xxxii, xxxv, 47, 119
chant, 27

chaos theory, xx, 63

children, 44, 45, 71, 75, 87, 109, 127, 128, 149, 161, 163, 216, 277

choice, xxviii, xl, xlii, 21, 22, 94, 173, 301

Christ, 95, 136, 296

Christianity, 6, 87, 95, 136, 219, 307

clarity, xvi, 48

codependent, 272

collapse, xx, xxviii, xxix, xxxii, xxxiii, xxxiv, xxxv, xlii, 141, 210, 257, 267, 287, 288, 291

commit, 221, 251, 281

commitment, 8, 15, 47, 49, 72, 155, 169, 242, 248

common sense, 259

communion, xviii, xl, 5, 7, 94, 98, 100, 145, 173, 236, 243, 244, 266, 272, 273, 275, 276, 277, 310, 311, 312

communism, 100

community, xvi, 46, 48, 49, 88, 94, 133, 197, 239, 295

complexity, xx, 11, 63, 64, 65, 92, 167

configuration, xliii, 2, 14, 16, 24, 27, 35, 44, 55, 68, 238

conscious evolution, xv, 285

consciousness, xx, xxiii, xxiv, xxvi, xxx, 3, 14, 20, 24, 30, 31, 34, 44, 47, 58, 62, 75, 84, 86, 104, 105, 106, 107, 109, 110, 111, 114, 115, 119, 129, 135, 159, 166, 204, 212, 223, 232, 286

context for our diversity, xv, xviii, xxxii, xl, 143, 201, 268

continuity of consciousness, xxx, 24, 44, 204, 212

contraction, 19, 29, 50, 51, 110, 301

control, 36, 41, 291, 293

conversation, xxx, 42, 105, 112, 134, 144, 180, 187, 264, 266, 267, 292, 296, 299, 300, 306, 307

CosmoErotic Humanism, xv, xix, xx, xxiii, xxix, xxxvii, xl, 144, 188, 189, 200, 202, 215, 221, 238, 241, 311

CosmoErotic Universe, 50, 84, 145, 158, 308, 311

cosmology, 35

Cosmos, vi, viii, ix, xii, xvii, xviii, xx, xxiii, xxvii, xxix, xxxvii, 3, 5, 7, 21, 22, 23, 24, 25, 26, 28, 36, 37, 50, 52, 55, 65, 67, 80, 82, 84, 86, 87, 92, 94, 104, 107, 109, 120, 125, 126, 129, 130, 135, 143, 145, 150, 161, 171, 179, 182, 184, 187, 191, 210, 236, 237, 239, 240, 250, 257, 259, 261, 271, 272, 273, 277, 288, 292, 294, 304, 305, 309, 312, 317

covenant, xxiv, 129

creating, 7, 43, 46, 73, 83, 88, 89, 102, 175, 253, 313

creation, xx, xlii, 25, 149, 184, 192, 310

creative, xxxi, xxxix, 49, 151, 164, 170, 179, 274, 301, 306, 311

creativity, xxvi, 49, 81, 161, 220

Creator, vii, 192

crisis of intimacy, xxxvii, 123

crying, 89, 114, 147, 169

cultural, xvii, xxxiii, xxxviii, xl, 196, 291, 303, 304

culture, xvii, xx, xxiv, xxvi, xxxi, xxxii, xxxvii, xliii, 2, 10, 20, 40, 41, 47, 53, 61, 75, 84, 85, 86, 95, 104, 229, 235, 236, 248, 266, 276, 291, 294

culture of death, xxxvii, 248

culture of life, 229

D

daemon, 299

David Bohm, 223

death, 18, 39, 140, 179, 203, 210, 212, 213, 229, 230, 234, 248, 262, 277, 278, 285, 286, 287, 288, 306, 309

death of humanity, xxxii, 18, 39, 140, 179, 277, 285, 286, 288

death of our humanity, 140, 179, 262, 277, 286

deepest heart's desire, 25, 141, 170

delight, 7, 18, 45, 129

democracy, 248, 258, 278

denial, xx, xxxi, 178, 262, 289, 317

depression, 151, 167, 176, 293

desire, xxxiv, xl, xlii, xliii, 2, 9, 14, 21, 24, 25, 26, 27, 34, 35, 80, 106, 107, 109, 115, 116, 128, 130, 141, 142, 145, 148, 149, 151, 152, 154, 157, 160, 161, 162, 165, 166, 167, 168, 169, 170, 171, 172, 191, 192, 193, 224, 225, 227, 283, 300

dharma, xvi, xvii, xviii, xxi, xxii, xxiii, 15, 28, 88

dignity, 24, 25, 26, 27, 93, 94, 95, 96, 99, 100, 118, 126, 140, 148, 149, 150, 151, 153, 154, 161, 168, 169, 171, 184, 274, 275, 299

distinct, xxxvii, xxxviii, 60, 93, 108, 175

distinction, 28, 54, 60, 107, 216, 218

diversity, xv, xviii, xxxii, xl, 143, 201, 268, 273

divides, xviii, 201

Divine, ix, 27, 36, 73, 111, 118, 135, 136, 137, 172, 174, 183, 188, 230, 233, 255, 298, 300, 301, 302, 303, 306, 311, 312

divinity, 149, 150, 168, 169, 172, 176, 299, 312

dogma, xvi, xvii, 8, 179, 186

dominate, xxxi, 41

dreams, 84

E

Earth, xxviii, 40, 92, 161, 286, 305

Eastern, 95, 146, 232, 306

echad, 312

economics, xl, 175, 230, 231

ecstasy, 25, 128, 139, 311, 312, 316, 317

Eden, 145, 147, 237, 296

effective altruism, 123, 125, 127

ego, 29, 35, 49, 77, 96, 97, 166, 206, 273, 274

egocentric, 124, 128, 154, 155, 156, 158, 160, 244

ein, 178

El, 297

electromagnetic, 32, 36

electron, 238, 239

Elohim, 111, 192

embodied, iv, 100

embracing, 96, 100, 168, 176

emerge, 89, 104, 175, 185, 237, 288, 300, 301, 312

emptiness, xxxiv, 76, 151, 181, 225, 287, 303

enlightenment, xl, 48, 59, 63, 105, 106, 108, 110, 124, 136, 166, 184

Epic of Gilgamesh, 236

equation, xxix, 117, 134, 172, 191, 293

Eros, vi, x, xi, xix, xx, xxi, xxvii, xxviii, xxix, xxxiv, xxxvi, xxxviii, xlii, xliii, 1, 2, 3, 6, 9, 10, 11, 12, 13, 14, 15, 16, 35, 36, 44, 52, 55, 62, 63, 64, 66, 80, 81, 83, 84, 108, 120, 121, 126, 130, 135, 142, 143, 145, 146, 150, 151, 155, 157, 158, 164, 169, 170, 176, 179, 184, 186, 188, 189, 190, 191, 193, 203, 204, 210, 211, 216, 217, 223, 225, 230, 231, 237, 238, 239, 240, 257, 268, 269, 272, 276, 278, 281, 289, 292, 293, 294, 295, 299, 308, 309, 310, 312, 314

Eros Value, xvii, 130, 217, 235, 239, 268, 274, 310

erotic, xxxix, 3, 149, 161, 169, 174, 186, 189, 190, 238, 293, 299, 300, 302, 303, 307, 310, 311, 312

et, 312

ethnocentric, xvii, 3, 27, 155, 158, 160, 161, 259

ethos, xviii, xx, 41, 81, 263, 267, 292

evil, 11, 12, 75, 140, 198, 206, 207, 291, 305, 309

evolution, xvii, xviii, xx, xxv, xxvi, xxvii, xxxi, xxxvii, xxxix, xl, xlii, 1, 7, 8, 13, 20, 23, 24, 35, 36, 45, 47, 48, 52, 55, 72, 77, 97, 104, 116, 119, 129, 133, 135, 140, 142, 144, 153, 154, 155, 156, 160, 161, 162, 164, 170, 171, 173, 180, 193, 203, 206, 232, 240, 247, 274, 276, 286

of consciousness, xx, xxiii, xxiv, xxvi, xxx, 3, 14, 20, 24, 34, 44, 47, 58, 75, 84, 86, 104, 107, 110, 111, 115, 119, 129, 135, 204, 212, 223, 232

of Eros, vi, xi, xx, xxvii, xxviii, xxix, xxxvi, xlii, 1, 2, 3, 6, 9, 10, 11, 12, 13, 14, 15, 16, 36, 55, 64, 80, 84, 142, 143, 145, 158, 170, 188, 189, 190, 211, 216, 223, 237, 238, 239, 240, 268, 269, 276, 278, 292, 293, 310, 312

of intimacy, xxvii, xxix, xxxv, xxxvii, xxxviii, xxxix, xliii, 24, 25, 34, 52, 65, 68, 81, 82, 105, 108, 118, 119, 120, 123, 126, 142, 144, 145, 153, 154, 155, 162, 163, 173, 217, 237, 238, 301, 309

of love, xxv, xxvi, xxvii, xxviii, xxxix, xl, xlii, 1, 2, 3, 7, 8, 13, 17, 20, 24, 36, 43, 45, 47, 48, 53, 65, 80, 84, 104, 142, 144, 158, 166, 173, 232, 235, 237, 239, 240, 242, 278, 286, 309, 312, 316

of relationship, 123, 231

Evolutionary
chain, xxxvii, 60, 62, 173, 238,
239, 272, 306
family, 83, 154, 155, 156, 158,
199, 201, 205, 234, 244, 269,
270, 278, 282, 297
impulse, xxix, 7, 8, 9, 44, 116
Love, iii, vi, vii, viii, ix, x, xi, xii,
xiii, xvi, xxii, xxv, xxviii,
xxxiii, xxxvii, xl, xlii, 2, 4, 5,
8, 9, 13, 14, 15, 21, 22, 43,
44, 45, 48, 50, 52, 55, 59, 64,
65, 68, 69, 74, 77, 78, 80, 82,
84, 85, 86, 88, 90, 91, 116,
120, 121, 126, 127, 142, 143,
144, 157, 158, 159, 162, 164,
179, 180, 192, 193, 210, 221,
224, 229, 230, 232, 236, 251,
267, 268, 271, 276, 277, 281,
285, 289, 310, 311, 312, 314
Love Code, xxii, 74, 82, 91, 144,
289
sensemaking, 91, 309
Unique Self, vii, ix, xii, xvi, xix,
xx, xliii, 12, 13, 16, 21, 22,
28, 30, 31, 35, 36, 47, 48, 49,
51, 52, 79, 80, 81, 82, 83, 86,
88, 89, 102, 108, 109, 110,
111, 112, 113, 114, 115, 116,
117, 118, 119, 120, 121, 126,
143, 152, 171, 191, 205, 214,
218, 222, 270, 271, 274, 275,
276, 277, 279, 280, 281
Evolutionary Love Code, xxii, 74,
82, 91, 144, 289
exile, 137, 145, 147, 164, 198, 213,
241, 242, 244
existentialism, 263, 264

existential risk, xxvi, xxx, xxxi,
xxxiv, xxxv, xxxvi, xxxvii, xxxviii, xxxix, 18, 22, 29, 37, 39, 40,
41, 42, 48, 75, 125, 129, 140, 141,
261, 262, 277, 285, 286, 289
Exodus, 203, 297, 310
expand, xxvii, 14, 128, 162
exterior sciences, xvii, 4, 18, 30, 36,
145, 173, 232, 272
Eye, viii, 56, 57, 58, 59, 60, 61, 63,
64, 65, 66, 67, 68, 260, 265, 309
of Contemplation, 58, 59, 64, 65,
66, 67
of humanity, xxi, xxxi, xxxii, 18,
39, 40, 93, 128, 140, 149,
179, 239, 277, 285, 286, 288
of Spirit, 33, 60, 61
of the Heart, 58, 59, 64, 65, 66,
67, 68, 265
of the Mind, viii, 57, 58, 63, 64,
65, 67, 68
of the Senses, viii, 56, 57, 58, 63,
64, 66, 67, 68
of the Spirit, 58, 60, 64, 65, 66,
67, 265
of Value, viii, ix, xii, xv, xvi, xvii,
xviii, xix, xxii, xxiv, xxv,
xxvi, xxviii, xxxii, xxxiii,
xxxv, xxxviii, xxxix, xl, 43,
44, 58, 59, 60, 67, 75, 76, 80,
81, 82, 83, 84, 85, 87, 88, 89,
105, 106, 109, 115, 117, 125,
130, 134, 140, 141, 142, 143,
144, 172, 175, 178, 179, 188,
193, 196, 200, 201, 202, 204,
207, 215, 217, 218, 220, 221,
222, 260, 262, 265, 266, 267,
268, 269, 273, 276, 287, 308,
311

F

face, xxxv, 22, 28, 66, 73, 116, 156, 162, 170, 190, 287, 305, 314

fairness, 59, 126, 261

faith, 312, 317

false self, 29, 100, 101, 102, 104, 105, 110, 115

father, 71, 72, 73, 74, 76, 77, 78, 79, 80, 81, 83, 84, 85, 86, 87, 88, 89, 147, 148, 154, 199, 211, 278

features, xxii, 108

feelings, 14, 150

feminine, 13, 24

Ficino, Marsilio, 256

field, xxxvi, xxxviii, 4, 22, 23, 24, 25, 28, 29, 32, 33, 34, 35, 36, 51, 64, 67, 71, 82, 84, 87, 89, 103, 105, 111, 119, 128, 129, 155, 171, 221, 222, 223, 224, 225, 229, 251, 274, 276, 281, 292

Field
of Desire, x, 51, 105, 106, 109, 142, 143, 157, 224
of Eros, vi, xi, xx, xxvii, xxviii, xxix, xxxvi, xlii, 1, 2, 3, 6, 9, 10, 11, 12, 13, 14, 15, 16, 36, 55, 64, 80, 84, 142, 143, 145, 158, 170, 188, 189, 190, 211, 216, 223, 237, 238, 239, 240, 268, 269, 276, 278, 292, 293, 310, 312
of ErosValue, xvii, 217, 235, 268, 274
of Reality, vii, xi, xx, xxix, xxxviii, xl, xliii, 5, 6, 9, 14, 17, 21, 22, 23, 24, 28, 31, 34, 35, 37, 41, 42, 43, 53, 55, 57, 60, 62, 63, 65, 68, 84, 86, 89, 120, 125, 128, 130, 135, 140, 143, 145, 146, 149, 150, 159, 164, 165, 176, 183, 185, 186, 191, 193, 204, 208, 211, 217, 225, 227, 234, 241, 249, 250, 266, 273, 274, 275, 277, 291, 293, 302, 306, 308, 309, 310, 315
of Value, viii, ix, xii, xv, xvi, xvii, xviii, xix, xxii, xxiv, xxv, xxvi, xxviii, xxxii, xxxiii, xxxv, xxxviii, xxxix, xl, 43, 44, 58, 59, 60, 67, 75, 76, 80, 81, 82, 83, 84, 85, 87, 88, 89, 105, 106, 109, 115, 117, 125, 130, 134, 140, 141, 142, 143, 144, 172, 175, 178, 179, 188, 193, 196, 200, 201, 202, 204, 207, 215, 217, 218, 220, 221, 222, 260, 262, 265, 266, 267, 268, 269, 273, 276, 287, 308, 311

first person, xxiii, xxxi, 258

First Principles, xvii, xviii, xix, xxiii, xxv, xxvi, xxix, xxx, xxxii, xxxv, xxxix, xlii, 33, 39, 42, 46, 47, 48, 49, 58, 60, 75, 83, 89, 125, 130, 131, 185, 191, 200, 201, 225, 238, 239, 259, 271, 272, 292

first shock of existence, xxx, xxxi, 18

fMRI, 57

forgive, 251

fragile system, 124

freedom, 94, 202, 212

Frischmann, Brett, 181

Fuck, 169, 209, 264

fulfilment, 281

fundamentalism, 233, 317
fundamentalist, xxiii, 1, 46, 221, 259

G

Garden of Eden, 147, 296
gender, 87, 273
genetics, 33
gifts, xxi, xxiv, 14, 217
Global
  coherence, xxxv, xxxvi, xxxix, 119, 132, 257
  coordination, xxxvi, xxxix, 119
  intimacy, xx, xxvii, xxix, xxxiv, xxxv, xxxvi, xxxvii, xxxviii, xxxix, xlii, xliii, 2, 23, 24, 25, 30, 31, 32, 33, 34, 35, 52, 65, 68, 72, 81, 82, 105, 108, 118, 119, 120, 123, 126, 130, 132, 134, 135, 136, 142, 143, 144, 145, 153, 154, 155, 156, 160, 162, 163, 172, 173, 190, 211, 217, 237, 238, 250, 276, 300, 301, 305, 308, 309
  intimacy disorder, xx, xxxiv, xxxv, xxxvi, xxxvii, xxxviii, xxxix, xlii, 118, 119
  resonance, xxxv, 119, 132
Goddess, 24, 86, 87, 89, 135, 136, 137, 163, 164, 176
gorgeousness, 211, 296
grammar of value, xxxii, xxxv, xxxvi, xl, xlii, 143, 201
great chain of being, 60, 62
greatness, 50, 51, 84, 86, 213, 214
ground, xvi, xvii, xviii, xxx, xl, 48, 142, 143, 187, 233, 260, 303

H

Hafiz, 233, 253
ha-kelim, 145
hallel, 298
Hallelujah, xliii, 27, 87, 88, 174, 244, 297, 298, 314, 315
Hamas, 209, 233
Hasidic, 166, 167, 307
heart, xxviii, xl, xlii, 18, 20, 25, 37, 53, 55, 58, 62, 65, 66, 67, 68, 106, 107, 141, 143, 144, 145, 148, 151, 152, 154, 155, 156, 157, 158, 159, 163, 164, 165, 168, 169, 170, 174, 175, 176, 178, 189, 193, 195, 196, 197, 200, 220, 222, 236, 237, 240, 249, 250, 310, 312, 314
heartbreak, xlii, 140, 146, 148, 149, 150, 151, 152, 154, 155, 156, 159, 160, 162, 163, 164, 165, 167, 168, 169, 172, 173, 174, 175, 176, 229
heaven, 17, 62, 145, 183, 299
Hebrew, 43, 66, 77, 95, 96, 169, 174, 177, 189, 219, 232, 293, 298, 315
  wisdom, xvi, xviii, xx, 4, 20, 48, 51, 92, 95, 96, 139, 143, 208, 219, 231, 232, 287, 312
Hendrix, Jimi, 8
hero, iii, xlii, 195, 209, 210, 211, 215, 216, 217, 218, 219, 220, 221, 222, 223, 224, 225, 226, 227, 280
hevra kadisha, 275
hierarchy, 16
holelut, 298
holy and broken Hallelujah, xliii, 27, 314, 315
Holy of Holies, xx, 47, 287, 310

Holy Trinity, 109

Homo amor, xvi, xlii, xliii, 3, 9, 15, 20, 21, 22, 23, 25, 27, 42, 44, 46, 50, 52, 53, 59, 67, 68, 77, 116, 121, 124, 126, 127, 128, 130, 132, 137, 139, 144, 154, 156, 157, 158, 159, 210, 214, 217, 218, 219, 220, 221, 223, 241, 281, 282, 309, 317

Homo Deus, 291

Homo sapiens, xvi, 20, 21, 37, 42, 44, 52, 53, 116, 126, 154, 156, 281

Homo universalis, 22

honor, 8, 100, 222, 283, 290, 301

Hubbard, Barbara Marx, xv, 44, 88, 116, 123, 204

human, xx, xxviii, xxix, xxx, xxxi, xxxii, xxxiii, xxxiv, xxxvi, xxxviii, xl, xlii, 8, 14, 18, 19, 20, 22, 24, 39, 40, 42, 43, 44, 45, 46, 48, 51, 52, 55, 61, 73, 74, 76, 84, 85, 86, 87, 91, 93, 95, 96, 99, 107, 111, 116, 120, 121, 123, 124, 127, 128, 135, 140, 141, 143, 146, 148, 149, 150, 156, 159, 160, 161, 171, 172, 173, 174, 175, 183, 184, 187, 193, 200, 203, 206, 209, 210, 211, 217, 220, 230, 235, 236, 240, 241, 242, 251, 255, 257, 258, 263, 268, 274, 285, 286, 291, 292, 300, 304, 305, 307, 308, 309, 311

humanity, xvi, xix, xxi, xxxi, xxxii, 18, 19, 20, 22, 39, 40, 42, 45, 48, 52, 93, 99, 121, 128, 140, 149, 179, 209, 210, 211, 217, 239, 241, 256, 262, 264, 277, 285, 286, 288

humans, 242

I

identity, xviii, xxxiv, xxxvi, xxxvii, xxxviii, xl, xliii, 10, 18, 19, 20, 28, 31, 32, 33, 34, 35, 92, 94, 97, 99, 100, 101, 130, 132, 134, 172, 173, 198, 240, 249, 273, 274

illusion, 40, 107, 291

imagination, 89, 168, 196, 208, 253, 288

imagine, 164, 275

individual, xvii, xxviii, xxxviii, 8, 18, 22, 49, 61, 84, 87, 94, 95, 96, 100, 103, 104, 275

individuals, xxxii, 281

individuation, 28, 49, 51, 93, 100, 147, 236, 273, 274, 276

infinite, xxiii, 56, 81, 95, 117, 135, 136, 137, 140, 163, 191, 223, 300, 314

Infinite Intimate, ix, xxiii, 135, 136, 137, 149, 176, 188, 191, 301, 312

Infinity of Intimacy, xxiii, 24, 25, 26, 27, 68, 88, 149

Infinity of Power, xxiii, 24, 137

influence, xxvii, 52, 82, 108, 126, 162, 163, 242, 270

innocence, 165, 167, 168

integral, 206

integrate, 87, 92, 106, 112

integration, 1, 180, 225, 272, 273

integrity, xxii, 1, 88, 126, 206, 207, 248, 278, 279, 308

interior sciences, xvii, xxix, xxx, xxxix, xl, 18, 19, 30, 36, 66, 135, 145, 146, 148, 232, 233

internet, xxxii, 180, 181, 185, 186, 198, 207

intimacy, xx, xxvii, xxix, xxxiv, xxxv, xxxvi, xxxvii, xxxviii, xxxix, xlii, xliii, 2, 23, 24, 25, 30, 31, 32, 33, 34, 35, 52, 65, 68, 72, 81, 82, 105, 108, 118, 119, 120, 123, 126, 130, 132, 134, 135, 136, 142, 143, 144, 145, 153, 154, 155, 156, 160, 162, 163, 172, 173, 190, 211, 217, 237, 238, 250, 276, 300, 301, 305, 308, 309

Intimacy
  equation, xxix, 117, 134, 172, 191, 293
  intimate, xviii, xxiii, xxxvi, xxxvii, xl, xliii, 22, 23, 35, 94, 105, 111, 119, 135, 137, 141, 151, 161, 162, 172, 174, 243, 244, 250, 266, 272, 273, 275, 276, 277, 293, 300, 312

Intimate Universe, ix, x, xxxvii, 7, 20, 23, 65, 129, 139, 144, 145, 165, 172, 173, 202, 309

irreducible, 8, 28, 35, 51, 273

ISIS, 233

Israel, 21, 22, 209, 297

Izbica, 85

J

Jerusalem, 174, 287, 310, 313, 315

Jesus, 236, 251, 310

jihad, 200, 209

Jimi Hendrix, 8

Joseph Campbell, 217

joy, xvi, xxvi, 7, 18, 39, 44, 45, 48, 73, 121, 127, 139, 146, 148, 154, 155, 156, 159, 160, 164, 165, 175, 176, 201, 202, 203, 205, 221, 232, 244, 248, 293, 315

justice, 59, 248, 261, 287

K

Kabbalah, xx, 188, 270

Kant, 203, 208

Kant, Immanuel, 203

Kashmir Shaivism, xx, 5, 6, 87, 306

Kashmir Shaivites, 306

Kauffman, Stuart, 159

Kempton, Sally, xv

kindness, 261, 267, 308

king, 216, 244, 247, 248, 251, 252, 313

kiss, 78, 230

knowledge, xx, 50, 55, 56

Krishna, 66

Kuhn, Thomas, 56

L

Laing, R.D., 76, 247, 248

larger whole, 34, 104, 223, 274, 280

laughter, 48, 195, 197, 198, 199, 250, 269

Lifton, Robert Jay, 40

line, 54, 185, 216, 223, 224, 290, 301

lineage, xv, xvii, xx, 46, 47, 48, 49, 87, 137, 145, 174, 177, 223, 231, 247, 263, 278, 287, 288, 296, 297, 299, 300, 302, 310, 311

loneliness, 133

longing, 148, 150, 160, 163, 168, 169, 170, 172, 240

love, xviii, xxii, xxiv, xxv, xxvi, xx-vii, xxviii, xxxix, xl, xlii, xliii, 1, 2, 3, 4, 5, 6, 7, 8, 13, 14, 17, 20, 21, 22, 24, 26, 36, 37, 39, 43, 44, 45, 47, 48, 49, 50, 53, 55, 57, 59, 62, 63, 64, 65, 66, 67, 68, 69, 74, 75, 76, 77, 78, 80, 83, 84, 86, 88, 104, 107, 116, 120, 121, 125, 128, 132, 133, 135, 136, 139, 142, 143, 144, 146, 151, 155, 157, 158, 159, 160, 164, 166, 169, 171, 173, 175, 176, 187, 188, 190, 191, 192, 193, 196, 199, 200, 203, 204, 205, 207, 210, 217, 218, 219, 220, 222, 224, 225, 229, 230, 231, 232, 233, 234, 235, 236, 237, 238, 239, 240, 241, 242, 243, 244, 245, 246, 247, 248, 249, 251, 252, 253, 254, 255, 262, 271, 277, 278, 283, 287, 294, 301, 305, 308, 309, 310, 312, 313, 314, 315, 316, 317

Love

  desire, xxxiv, xl, xlii, xliii, 2, 9, 14, 21, 24, 25, 26, 27, 34, 35, 80, 106, 107, 109, 115, 116, 128, 130, 141, 142, 145, 148, 149, 151, 152, 154, 157, 160, 161, 162, 165, 166, 167, 168, 169, 170, 171, 172, 191, 192, 193, 224, 225, 227, 283, 300

  is real, xvii, xxxiii, xxxiv, 40, 55, 57, 63, 96, 97, 125, 142, 189, 204, 210, 263, 266, 271, 290, 292, 298, 304, 307, 317

  story, xviii, xxvi, xxxiii, xxxiv, xxxv, xxxvi, xxxviii, xxxix, xl, xlii, xliii, 3, 9, 11, 18, 19, 29, 39, 40, 41, 43, 45, 50, 51, 55, 62, 63, 64, 65, 68, 69,

74, 77, 80, 81, 93, 95, 96, 99, 100, 109, 110, 111, 112, 113, 116, 118, 123, 125, 126, 131, 141, 142, 155, 156, 165, 166, 167, 177, 178, 179, 184, 203, 234, 237, 251, 252, 256, 257, 258, 259, 261, 262, 266, 277, 279, 281, 296, 300, 301, 303, 305, 306, 307, 308, 310, 311, 312, 313, 315, 316, 317

LoveIntelligence, xxvii, 22, 28, 44, 108, 126

Lovejoy, Arthur, 60

Luria, Isaac, 188, 243

Lurianic Kabbalah, 270

M

Mahler, Margaret, 28, 93

Malchut, 216

manifestation, 155

Marsilio Ficino, 256, 270

masculine, 24

master, 47, 105, 136, 164, 231, 307, 310

materialism, xxx, 204, 303

mathematics, 53, 54, 57, 63, 64, 65, 66, 67, 300

matrix, xxxv, 287, 293

meditation, 27, 28, 29, 30, 59, 65

memory, xxxvii, xxxix, 7, 79, 85, 197, 203, 252, 256

memory of the future, xxxvii, 7, 85, 256

meta-crisis, iii, xv, xvi, xix, xxxiv, xxxix, xlii, 115, 118, 119, 120, 123, 127, 139, 143, 177, 178, 179,

209, 215, 217, 218, 230, 231, 232, 269, 287

metaphor, 19

Metatron, 36

mind, xxxi, 11, 15, 19, 20, 35, 57, 60, 61, 64, 96, 97, 99, 106, 107, 119, 126, 132, 156, 157, 183, 185, 199, 245, 292, 312

MIT Media Lab, 97, 98

model, 149, 166, 190

modern, xviii, xx, xxviii, xxxvi, xxxviii, xl, 10, 41, 56, 58, 80, 87, 92, 96, 105, 136, 183, 220, 257, 264

modernity, xii, xxxiii, xxxiv, 257, 258, 259

Moshe, 188, 313

mother, 28, 72, 73, 74, 76, 77, 78, 79, 80, 81, 83, 84, 85, 86, 87, 88, 89, 93, 94, 100, 101, 147, 148, 153, 154, 156, 158, 166, 167, 175, 278, 294, 295, 298, 306, 314, 315

Murder of Eros, vi, 1, 13

music, xxii, 12, 13, 45, 52, 53, 54, 55, 65, 66, 67, 68, 73, 120, 239, 257, 308

Myers-Briggs, 109, 143

mystery, xviii, 50, 68, 163, 174, 176, 187, 188, 243, 299, 315, 316, 317

Mystery School, 226

mystic, 169, 303, 310, 311

mysticism, 240

mythopoetic, 268

N

Nachman of Breslov, 307

neighbor, 304

New Age, 1, 6, 9, 24, 46, 89, 217, 268

new human, xlii, 19, 20, 22, 42, 43, 46, 48, 52, 116, 121, 124, 209, 210, 211, 217, 241, 285

new humanity, xvi, 19, 20, 22, 42, 48, 52, 121, 209, 210, 211, 217, 241, 285

new story, xv, xvi, xviii, xix, xx, xxii, xxiv, xxv, xxvi, xxxii, xxxiii, xxxix, xl, 42, 43, 44, 87, 89, 115, 117, 125, 126, 127, 141, 142, 143, 144, 175, 178, 188, 193, 215, 217, 218, 262, 287, 311

new Story of Value, xv, xvi, xviii, xix, xxii, xxiv, xxv, xxvi, xxxii, xxxiii, xxxix, 43, 44, 87, 89, 115, 117, 125, 141, 142, 143, 144, 175, 178, 188, 193, 215, 217, 218, 262, 287, 311

noosphere, 61, 239

Nussbaum, Martha, 147

O

obligation, xliii

ontogeny, 93

ontological, xxx, 302

otherness, xxxvi, xxxvii, 134

Outrageous Acts of Love, 45, 126, 162, 281

Outrageous Love, viii, x, xi, xvi, xxii, xxviii, xl, 13, 14, 48, 59, 65, 68, 69, 78, 86, 88, 90, 120, 143, 157, 158, 159, 164, 224, 230, 232, 251, 281, 310, 311

Outrageous Love Letters, 59, 65

Outrageous Love Story, xl, 68

P

Page, Larry, 98

panim, 156

pan-interiority, xxx, 60, 61, 62

paradox, 117, 140, 237, 278

partial, 60, 97, 99

particles, xxxviii, 5, 31, 33, 193, 239, 274

particular, xxix, 15, 27, 48, 60, 76, 86, 89, 96, 112, 115, 120, 149, 198, 204, 209, 223, 232, 236, 237, 238, 241, 242, 268, 271, 278, 290, 304, 307, 310

pathological, xxxvii, 71, 75, 76, 112, 148, 155, 158, 302

pathology, 93, 100, 151, 156, 272, 273

pathos, xxxvii, 31, 132, 134, 172, 245

pattern, 169, 279

peace, 211, 214, 287

Pentland, Alex, 98, 101

Peterson, Jordan, 303

phenomenology, 232

phylogeny, 93

physiosphere, 239

planetary awakening in love, 49, 121

pleasure, 26, 149, 150, 181, 234, 315

plotline, 126, 127, 178, 179, 184, 185, 193, 257, 258, 265, 273

Popper, Karl, 56

postmodern, xviii, xl, xlii, 43, 83, 87, 92, 105, 125, 143, 185, 196, 210, 262, 264, 266, 267, 286, 289, 290, 292, 305, 306

Postmodern, xii, 117

post-tragic, iii, xvi, xlii, 167, 207, 220, 221, 314

power, xxi, xxix, xxxiv, xl, xlii, 1, 2, 3, 4, 7, 8, 10, 25, 31, 78, 135, 136, 141, 175, 179, 184, 198, 205, 243, 244, 290, 291, 293, 305, 309

prayer, xxii, xxiii, xliii, 14, 24, 25, 27, 68, 69, 87, 92, 148, 149, 171, 303, 305

premodern, xviii, 27, 43, 87, 92, 183, 220, 221, 255, 256, 259, 280

pre-tragic, 147, 148, 153, 167, 220

pride, 72, 73

process, xvii, xxi, xxii, 20, 25, 35, 151, 153, 154, 237, 266, 289, 301

promise, 92, 177, 229, 288, 289, 314

prophet, 66, 67, 68, 233

proton, 32, 237

Psalms, 68, 127

pseudo-eros, xx, 81, 155, 190

pseudo-erotic, 186, 190

psychology, xxviii, 10, 80, 184, 185, 246

purpose, xxxvi, xxxvii, 31, 91, 130, 132, 134, 171, 172, 178, 182, 202, 263

Q

quantum, 5, 34, 36

R

radical, vi, xxix, 6, 18, 40, 49, 73, 128, 146, 180, 190, 226, 227, 237, 282, 293, 300, 306, 308, 311

Reality, vii, viii, x, xi, xvii, xx, xxiii, xxvi, xxix, xxxiv, xxxvi, xxxviii, xxxix, xl, xliii, 2, 5, 6, 9, 14, 17, 18, 19, 20, 21, 22, 23, 24, 26, 28, 31, 34, 35, 36, 37, 41, 42, 43, 44, 51, 53, 54, 55, 57, 59, 60, 61, 62, 63, 65, 67, 68, 71, 81, 82, 84, 85, 86, 87, 89, 90, 101, 102, 107, 115, 120, 125, 128, 130, 135, 140, 142, 143, 145, 146, 149, 150, 158, 159, 160, 164, 165, 176, 179, 183, 186, 191, 192, 193, 202, 204, 208, 211, 217, 218, 223, 224, 225, 227, 232, 234, 236, 241, 244, 245, 249, 250, 257, 259, 265, 266, 272, 273, 274, 275, 276, 277, 290, 291, 293, 295, 301, 302, 306, 307, 308, 309, 310, 314, 315

realization, xvii, xx, xxiii, xxix, xxx, xxxi, xxxix, xliii, 5, 30, 65, 79, 81, 85, 99, 100, 106, 108, 117, 135, 136, 143, 145, 147, 148, 165, 189, 200, 203, 242, 274, 276, 295, 299, 300, 301, 316

reclaiming, xxiii, 1, 169, 193

Reich, Wilhelm, 158

reincarnation, 6

relationship, 28, 33, 73, 77, 78, 123, 151, 165, 168, 173, 225, 230, 231, 241, 242, 245, 249, 257, 280, 292

religion, xxxiii, xl, 14, 41, 61, 86, 94, 143, 189, 231, 305

religiosus, 308

Renaissance, xxv, xxxii, 92, 95, 96, 188, 243, 255, 256, 261, 266, 270, 274, 275, 299

repulsion, 145, 173, 175

resonance, xxxv, 119, 132

revealed, 170

revelation, xxxiii, xxxiv, xlii, 84, 192, 196, 311

revolution of love, 48

role mate, 133

Rumi, xxvii, 143, 230, 231, 232, 233, 234, 235, 247

S

Sabbatean movement, 5

sacred, 7, 22, 50, 60, 65, 89, 116, 118, 140, 155, 165, 172, 183, 200, 234, 247, 259, 287, 297, 299, 300, 310

sacred autobiography, 89, 118

sacrifice, 149, 200

sapiens, xvi, 20, 21, 37, 42, 44, 52, 53, 116, 126, 154, 156, 281, 296

Schmachtenberger, Daniel, 129

scientism, 56, 317

scripts of desire, 152

second shock of existence, xxx, xxxi, xxxii, 18, 288

second simplicity, xvi, 92, 104, 167

security, 78

Self
  organizing, 2, 21, 33, 36, 52, 161, 212
  perception, 55, 56, 67, 192, 267

sensemaking, 91, 309

separate self, 22, 28, 29, 30, 34, 51, 95, 96, 97, 98, 99, 100, 101, 103, 105, 110, 111, 115, 118, 143, 223, 249, 250, 274, 275, 276, 280, 281

separation, 36, 93, 101, 107, 145, 173, 272

service, 51, 80, 205, 218, 226

sexing, 66

sexual, 3, 161, 174, 189, 190, 310, 311

sexuality, 113, 257

shadow, xlii, 28, 29, 93, 110, 111, 112, 113, 114, 115, 196, 231, 273, 275, 282

Shakti, 5, 126

shalem, 178

shalom, 214

shame, 109, 128, 167

Shekhinah, 137

shever, 177

shevirat, 145

Shoshana Zuboff, 181

Sinai, 311

social construction, 80, 84

Solomon, xx, 77, 78, 136, 137, 145, 148, 149, 174, 177, 231, 232, 237, 247, 287, 296, 299, 302, 310

Song of Songs, 78, 237, 310

soul, 6, 61, 62, 111, 133, 197, 200, 220, 222, 249, 295

soul mate, 133

Source, ix, 26

source code, xx, xxiv, xxvi, 20, 42, 47, 72, 75, 84, 86, 94, 104, 115, 121, 123, 125, 139, 140, 216, 247, 249, 250, 266

Spirit, 33, 58, 60, 61, 64, 65, 66, 67, 265

stealing, 182, 186, 187, 205

Stevenson, Ian, 5

story, xviii, xxvi, xxxiii, xxxiv, xxxv, xxxvi, xxxviii, xxxix, xl, xlii, xliii, 3, 9, 11, 18, 19, 29, 39, 40, 41, 43, 45, 50, 51, 55, 62, 63, 64, 65, 68, 69, 74, 77, 80, 81, 93, 95, 96, 99, 100, 109, 110, 111, 112, 113, 116, 118, 123, 125, 126, 131, 141, 142, 155, 156, 165, 166, 167, 177, 178, 179, 184, 203, 234, 237, 251, 252, 256, 257, 258, 259, 261, 262, 266, 277, 279, 281, 296, 300, 301, 303, 305, 306, 307, 308, 310, 311, 312, 313, 315, 316, 317

Story of Value, ix, xii, xv, xvi, xvii, xviii, xix, xxii, xxiv, xxv, xxvi, xxviii, xxxii, xxxiii, xxxv, xxxviii, xxxix, xl, 43, 44, 75, 80, 83, 84, 85, 87, 89, 115, 117, 125, 141, 142, 143, 144, 175, 178, 179, 188, 193, 196, 200, 201, 215, 217, 218, 222, 262, 267, 268, 287, 311

structure of Reality, 145, 208, 277

structures, 18, 175, 178, 180, 234, 239, 274, 287, 306, 314, 316

Sufism, xxvii, 87, 233, 307

suicide, 75, 220

synagogue, 15

synergy, xvi, 31

T

Talmud, 287

tantra, 232

Tao, the, 21

tech plex, 98, 99, 181, 182

telos, 178, 185, 188, 259, 261

temple, 169, 287, 310

Tenets of Intimacy, 129

the One, xvi, xxiii, xxvii, 69, 145, 157, 159, 312

the Universe, vii, viii, xi, xvii, 20, 22, 28, 34, 51, 64, 74, 77, 78, 80, 88, 108, 116, 136, 144, 159, 202, 213, 215, 216, 217, 218, 221, 225, 226, 227, 239, 276

The Universe
A Love Story, xxxvii, 64, 68, 78, 85, 116, 271, 277, 285

the whole, 225, 293, 308

third-person, xxiii, 23, 184, 257, 258

tikkun, 175

Toby Ord, 125

Torah, 311, 312

totalitarianism, 165, 180, 266, 267

traditions, xvi, xvii, xx, 4, 19, 20, 24, 25, 46, 87, 95, 105, 106, 107

tragic, iii, xvi, xlii, 94, 112, 147, 148, 150, 153, 155, 158, 167, 207, 220, 221, 225, 226, 229, 264, 272, 280, 314

transcend, 9, 51, 62, 99, 207, 280, 281, 282, 297

transfiguration, 25, 281

transformation, xviii, xix, xxix, 14, 19, 26, 29, 91, 171, 175, 227, 238, 245, 280, 281, 300

transmission, xix, xxi, xxii, xliii, 12, 47, 49, 85, 295

tribe, 155, 156, 158, 161

trinity, 234

True Self, vii, ix, 21, 22, 28, 30, 31, 34, 36, 51, 52, 60, 105, 106, 107, 108, 110, 111, 115, 118, 274, 275, 281

truth, xxvi, xxviii, xl, 4, 13, 14, 20, 22, 36, 39, 43, 53, 60, 97, 99, 100, 107, 117, 120, 124, 128, 170, 207, 209, 210, 249, 286, 312, 314

tshuka, 170

Tzaratam, 136

tzimtzum, 299, 301

tzorech, 51

U

unclench, 13

unconscious, 224, 274

understanding, xxi, 2, 24, 32, 37, 58, 60, 63, 67, 71, 84, 91, 92, 98, 100, 106, 131, 136, 249, 266, 269, 271, 286, 288, 293, 305

unique gift, xliii, 14, 82, 86, 108, 120, 143, 211, 227, 276, 282

unique intimacy, 143, 276

uniqueness, xviii, 8, 30, 35, 81, 107, 111, 119, 120, 126, 152, 169, 191, 238, 239, 271, 272, 273, 274, 275

unique risk, xliii, 211, 213, 214, 268, 269, 270, 271, 276, 277, 278, 279, 281, 282, 283

Unique Self, vii, ix, xii, xvi, xix, xx, xliii, 12, 13, 16, 21, 22, 28, 30, 31, 35, 36, 47, 48, 49, 51, 52, 79, 80, 81, 82, 83, 86, 88, 89, 102, 108, 109, 110, 111, 112, 113, 114, 115, 116, 117, 118, 119, 120, 121, 126, 143, 152, 171, 191, 205, 214, 218, 222, 270, 271, 274, 275, 276, 277, 279, 280, 281

Unique Self Symphony, ix, xii, xx, xliii, 16, 47, 49, 52, 89, 118, 119, 120, 126, 143, 205, 214, 218, 222, 270, 271, 277, 280, 281 universal grammar of value, xxxii, 143, 201

Universe, vii, viii, ix, x, xi, xvii, xviii, xxx, xxxiii, xxxiv, xxxvii, 7, 20, 21, 22, 23, 28, 32, 34, 36, 50, 51, 62, 64, 65, 68, 74, 77, 78, 80, 84, 85, 88, 108, 116, 126, 129, 136, 139, 144, 145, 158, 159, 161, 165, 172, 173, 186, 189, 190, 202, 213, 215, 216, 217, 218, 221, 225, 226, 227, 239, 271, 276, 277, 285, 308, 309, 311

utopia, xxxii, 1, 17, 18, 37, 39, 72, 85, 140, 209

V

Vajrayana, 5, 307

values, xvi, xvii, xxxiv, xxxv, xxxviii, xxxix, xlii, 125, 126, 130, 142, 184, 200, 201, 202, 292

vital, xix, xxi, xxii, 295

voice, xliii, 36, 126, 136, 183, 199, 302, 312

W

wake, xxxviii, xlii, 162, 230, 240

watch, 11, 73, 87, 264, 269

web-plex, 97, 98

Western, 51, 63, 158, 184

where we are, 21, 142

whole, the, xviii, xxiv, xxv, 5, 6, 7, 11, 14, 26, 30, 31, 32, 44, 51, 126, 128, 156, 159, 160, 221, 223, 224, 225, 233, 235, 241, 242, 243, 244, 245, 248, 249, 250, 253, 259, 262, 263, 268, 269, 270, 273, 275, 277,

279, 280, 281, 282, 283, 291, 304, 308

who we are, 42, 92, 99, 165, 227

Wilber, Ken, xv, xix, 206, 276

win/lose, xx, xxvi, xxvii, xxxi, xxxii, xxxiv, xxxvi, xxxviii, 29, 123, 141, 143, 178, 193, 232, 257, 280, 282

World War II, 199, 261, 263

X

xenophobic, 196, 202

Y

Yaakov, 297

Yah, 298

yearning, 24, 150, 160, 163, 169, 170, 172, 174, 223, 237, 240, 295, 309

Yichud, 243, 244, 249

yoga, 310

Z

zeitgeist, 289

Zion, 89

Zohar, 192, 231, 270

Zuboff, Shoshana, 181

Volume 36 — Awakening the New Human

LIST OF EPISODES

1. Episode 208 — October 4, 2020

2. Episode 236 — April 18, 2021

3. Episode 294—May 29, 2022

4. Episode 297 — June 19, 2022

5. Episode 317 — November 7, 2022

6. Episode 353 — July 16, 2023

7. Episode 354 — July 23, 2023

8. Episode 382 — February 4, 2024

9. Episode 384 — February 18, 2024

10. Episode 388 — March 17, 2024

11. Episode 413 — September 8, 2024

12. Episode 423 — November 17, 2024

13. Episode 427 — December 15, 2024

www.ingramcontent.com/pod-product-compliance
Lightning Source LLC
La Vergne TN
LVHW011319080426
835513LV00006B/129